How We Got Our Bible

# How We Got Our Bible

*Files from an Alttestamentler's Hard Drive*

JOHN D. W. WATTS

WIPF & STOCK · Eugene, Oregon

HOW WE GOT OUR BIBLE
Files from an Alttestamentler's Hard Drive

Copyright © 2011 John D. W. Watts. All rights reserved. Except for brief quotations in critical publications or reviews, no part of this book may be reproduced in any manner without prior written permission from the publisher. Write: Permissions, Wipf and Stock Publishers, 199 W. 8th Ave., Suite 3, Eugene, OR 97401.

Scripture quotations marked (NIV) are taken from the Holy Bible, New International Version®, NIV®. Copyright © 1973, 1978, 1984 by Biblica, Inc.™ Used by permission of Zondervan. All rights reserved worldwide. www.zondervan.com

Scripture quotations marked RSV are taken from the Revised Standard Version of the Bible, copyright 1952 [2nd edition, 1971] by the Division of Christian Education of the National Council of the Churches of Christ in the United States of America. Used by permission. All rights reserved.

Unmarked Scripture quotations are the author's own translations.

Wipf & Stock
An Imprint of Wipf and Stock Publishers
199 W. 8th Ave., Suite 3
Eugene, OR 97401

www.wipfandstock.com

ISBN 13: 978-1-60899-394-9

Manufactured in the U.S.A.

# Contents

*Introduction* / 1

## Part 1
## The Formation of Preliterary Traditions

1. Israel and Its Traditions / 13
2. Traditions in an Aural/Oral Age / 23
3. Patriarchs / 39
4. The Amphictyony: Ceremonies and Sanctuaries / 47
5. The Jerusalem Monarchy: David, Solomon's Temple / 63

## Part 2
## Jewish Literature from Josiah to the Late Persian Period

6. Beginnings / 81
7. Introduction to a New Paradigm / 90
8. The Beginning of Jewish Literature: End of the Assyrian Period / 106
9. Jewish Literature of the Babylonian Period / 120
10. Jewish Literature in the First Century of the Persian Period / 140
11. Jewish Literature in the Late Persian Period / 162

## Part 3
## Canons of Scripture

12. Turning Points for the Jew: Fourth Century BCE to First Century CE / 167
13. The Renaissance of Davidic Culture in Jerusalem / 172
14. Jewish Literature in the Hellenistic Period (332–164 BCE) / 190
15. The Roman Era Beginning in 67 BCE / 199
16. The Development of the Christian Canon / 203

*Appendix A: Words for "Writing" in the Hebrew Bible / 210*
*Appendix B: Canons of Scripture (Old Testament) / 215*
*Abbreviations / 221*
*Bibliography / 223*

# Introduction

ANCIENT ISRAEL, BEFORE AND during the monarchy, did not depend on a book. Archaeology and ancient historical study have established the existence of Israel in Canaan and the existence of an ancient Hebrew script. But archaeology is ill fitted to carry the story forward or to give a convincing account of how the contents of the Bible developed. The Old Testament tells about that period before the book and about the traditions that developed in it.

Otto Eissfeldt,[1] like most interpreters of the mid-twentieth century, understood that there was a "pre-literary" stage in the development of Old Testament literature followed by various stages of "literary prehistory" before the actual appearance of the book. Parallel to the appearance of Eissfeldt's work, a number of scholars used an approach called form criticism, which found that performances in early festivals and ceremonies had established the forms that later writings used.[2] More recent focus on the growth of Scripture has led to the neglect of work on these institutions and celebrations that preceded the written books. It would be good to keep the positive results of form criticism while building on the later studies of literary development.

More recent studies (Peckham, *History and Prophecy* [1993]; Akenson, *Surpassing Wonder* [2001]; Nigosian, *From Ancient Writings to Sacred Texts* [2004]; Schniedewind, *How the Bible Became a Book* [2004]; Carr, *Writing on the Tablet of the Heart* [2005]) have reached a consensus that the accounts of the Torah book found in the temple under Josiah (2 Kgs 22–23) and of Ezra reading Torah to gathered Jews at Jerusalem (Neh 8)

---

1. Eissfeldt, *Old Testament*.

2. Two prominent scholars who established this approach for Torah were Gerhard von Rad and Martin Noth. Others, including Herman Gunkel, used the method to study the Psalms.

are evidence of crucial turning points in the growth of a written Torah. The continuing discussion is illustrated and summarized in the papers of Rolf Rendtorff and David Clines at the 2006 international meeting of the SBL in Edinburgh published on the SBL Forum, August 7, 2006.

The growing consensus that one should look to the late Judean, early postexilic period for the time when the books of the Old Testament took on their present form has produced a number of attempts to assess what this does to Old Testament studies. The five books mentioned above bring together the results of the many articles and monographs on the subject. Peckham uses a kind of literary analysis that has characterized Old Testament studies for well over a century, but his strong unifying emphasis points to the prophetic character of the work. Akenson stresses the beauty and effectiveness of the finished products that together make up the Scriptures. The three other works stress the way that writing and composition made possible the literature and its effectiveness in creating the Jewish and Christian communities. Nigosian begins with a treatment of the forms of writing. He shows how the peoples of Canaan as well as the Greeks grew to use the alphabet to transcribe their languages and how both the Israelites and the Greeks were enabled to produce their extensive literature because of it.

Carr argues that the production of literature in Mesopotamia, Egypt, Greece, and Israel was intended to enculturate each new generation with knowledge of the ancient wisdom of each of these peoples. Writing serves the purpose of education of elites in each of these cultures. Like Nigosian, Carr shows the parallel development of literature in adjacent cultures and draws conclusions for the understanding of the motives and results of the process in Jewish literature. He stresses the role of oral presentation in this process, a role that preceded the written forms and continued alongside them.

Despite Carr's emphasis on oral reading and the importance of memorized material, he does not try to deal with the transmission of tradition prior to writing. Logically, his method, which stresses the unbroken line of oral presentation even after written texts are employed, should also have treated oral traditions before writing. Schniedewind traces the process by which oral memories and scattered written texts were shaped into the books and then "the book" that resulted. In this, his work parallels Akenson, but in considerably more detail.

All these draw heavily on the accounts in which extensive Scripture is read aloud to gatherings of the people: 2 Kgs 23, in which the scroll found in the temple is read to the gathered people (ca. 620 BCE), and Neh 8, in which the scroll of the law of Moses is produced by Ezra and read aloud to the assembled people (ca. 445 BCE).

The present book will cover much of the same ground but will begin with the use of oral traditions in festivals and sanctuaries before the accounts of reading the book of Torah in Josiah's day. The study of these oral traditions and festivals was very vital in the early twentieth century. Eissfeldt described them as where the small units in the literature had "their place in life." Von Rad and Noth showed the origins of the larger literary units in festivals and sanctuaries.

Judaism from the sixth century BCE onward is built upon the book (Torah, the Prophets, and, in time, the Writings). In the third century BCE the Torah was translated into Greek[3] in Alexandria. This came to be the Scripture for Hellenistic Judaism.

Christianity is built upon the Scriptures of Israel in Greek form, to which the Letters of Paul and other apostles, the Gospels, and the Apocalypse are added. So Christianity also became a religion of the book.

At each of these stages the truth about God and his people is inculcated in the gathered congregations through spoken words. Moses addresses the people on the plains of Moab. Joshua addresses the people repeatedly. Samuel addresses the people. In Judaism, readers take the place of these speakers, reading aloud from the Torah or the Prophets. Priestly scribes did it for Josiah. Ezra did it for the returned groups near Jerusalem. Synagogues set up Hebrew schools so that their sons could take turns reading aloud from Torah and the Prophets. Jesus read from the Prophets in synagogue service. Christians followed the reading of the old Scriptures with apostolic witness to the Christ, which became the Gospels, and the letters that exhorted them to faith.

The oral presentation of the message was and is always the direct means by which it is presented to the congregation. The earlier periods in Israel as well as early Christianity depended upon speakers of oral traditions. Later congregations heard readers who depended on written texts, as they do today.

---

3. Called the Septuagint for its supposed seventy translators.

This book will describe the growth of Scripture, beginning with the traditions that developed among Israelite tribes in Canaan and the Israelite and Judean monarchies that followed. Part 1 will treat the formation of oral rituals and traditions that came to be the contents of the written books. Part 2 will deal with the formation of the Hebrew Scriptures. Part 3 will deal with their growth and translation into Greek.

The story could be continued, dealing with the formation of the Aramaic (Syriac) Version, the Ethiopic Version, the Latin Bible, and so on. It could also be expanded to deal with the bodies of literature, including commentaries that grew up around each of the written versions.

Christianity comes into existence with roots in the Judaism of the Roman era. This Judaism was centered in the province of Judah from which Jesus and the apostles came. But it also had substantial communities in Egypt, in what is now Iraq, and in Asia Minor.

Jews are a people "of the book." This book existed in the first century in at least two forms. One, on leather scrolls, was written in Hebrew and was used for reading in the synagogues as a part of worship and in the synagogue schools for instruction of the boys. The Tanak, as it is called, consisted of three parts: the Torah (five scrolls), the Prophets (comprising four scrolls of history called the earlier prophets and four scrolls of Prophets [called the Latter Prophets]), and the Writings (which contained an alternate history [Chronicles and Ezra-Nehemiah], Psalms, books of wisdom [Proverbs, Job, the five small festival scrolls], and one book of later prophecy [Daniel]).

A second form of the Jewish Scriptures was a Greek translation, which was used in Hellenistic synagogues and came to be used in the earliest Christian churches, joined eventually by the books of the New Testament. This was written in a book on parchment, was arranged somewhat differently, and included a number of additions that we call Apocrypha. The translation of the Torah had apparently been made in Alexandria in the late fourth century BCE. The rest of the books were translated in the following century.

How did the Jews (Judeans) come to claim the book that tells of the origins of twelve tribes and of an Israel and a Davidic kingdom that no longer existed? The story that answers that question will show that the book is actually a Jewish book that collected and preserved the traditions of Israel and David's Jerusalem to claim them for its heritage. As Jews claimed to be heirs of Israel and David, so Christians also came to claim to be heirs of the heritage of that book through Jesus Christ, which the New Testament used to teach who he was and what his coming meant. The story will need to show how the tradition was formed, how it was preserved and transmitted, and how it came to be a book. This story must be extracted from the book itself, since no ancient independent account exists.

## FORMATION OF TRADITIONS

Judaism in the fifth to the first centuries BCE had several groups in Jerusalem that claimed ancestors who formed the major traditions on which Judaism rested:

- Levites and priests (particularly Aaronides), who were responsible for the temple and for the Torah that was taught there
- Prophetic groups, who made common cause with Levites to shape the Deuteronomistic History and the Latter Prophets
- Teachers of wisdom, who claimed a tradition begun by Solomon: Proverbs, Song of Solomon, and Ecclesiastes
- Temple singers, who claimed to have been founded by David: Psalms, Lamentations
- Monarchist groups, who claimed genealogical connections with the house of David (messianists)
- Samaritans at Shechem, whose priests claimed Levite and Aaronide ancestry and had a version of Torah

Each of these groups had scribes who kept their versions of the traditions up to date and provided copies for their constituencies.

These traditions had formed in relation to particular places like Bethel and Jerusalem; at special times, such as the annual festivals; and around special persons and groups. Patriarchal places kept the stories of the patriarchs alive. A major festival was held in the fall. At times it was simply an agricultural festival like our Thanksgiving. In other early times it was a celebration of the covenant that made Israel who she was. It was celebrated at Gilgal, at Shiloh, at Shechem, and at Hebron. Passover and the Feast of Weeks were celebrated in the home and in local places in the spring of the year. The Royal New Year was celebrated during the kingdoms in Jerusalem and in Bethel. The festivals served not only to shape the traditions preserved there but also to teach them to succeeding generations and to preserve them for the future.

## COMPOSITION OF THE SCROLLS

The use of writing had been in existence for some time. The army had its scribes to keep muster lists and records of provision. Merchants had scribes to make records of their stores and purchases. Kings had scribes to keep records of their laws and edicts and to write of their achievements.

In Hezekiah's reign (715–685 BCE), after the exile of large groups of people from the former kingdom of Israel, Judah experienced a substantial increase in population. Refugees from Israel, including many Levites, priests, scribes, and former government officials, fled to the south. Hezekiah probably welcomed them and put them to work. A major part of the work of scribes turned toward the preservation of traditions and records from Samaria and the various cult centers of the north. Hezekiah envisioned Judah to be the heir of all of Israel's religious traditions, in much the same way that David did.

Preserving this tradition was a massive project that extended well beyond Jerusalem. Hezekiah established many new villages (2 Chr 32:29), placing many of the refugees in them. Some of these were villages for priests and Levites (2 Chr 31:15–19), but some were probably also for scribes. Hezekiah may also have established schools for scribes. This massive bureaucracy set about the enormous task of transcribing the traditions (Prov 25:1) that had until this time been handed down orally in the various sanctuaries and holy places.

The scribes worked in the language that was current in Judah at this time and that we know as Classical Hebrew. The traditions had undoubtedly been transmitted orally in the various dialects and sub-dialects that the extended tribes had used since coming to Canaan half a millennium before. This gave their work a uniformity of language that could hardly have been imagined earlier.

By the time of Josiah a century later, the scribes' work had produced Deuteronomy (based on Gilgal traditions). They published it to Josiah and his assembled people (2 Kgs 22:8—23:3 / 2 Chr 34:14–32). The composition of the Deuteronomistic History (Former Prophets)—based on Gilgal and Shechem traditions (Samuel), tribal traditions (Judges), Shiloh traditions (Samuel), and Jerusalem/Samarian traditions and records (2 Samuel and Kings) followed soon after.

By the time of Jeremiah in the reigns of Jehoiakim, Jehoiachin, and Zedekiah in the last years of the kingdom of Judah, the composition and writing of his prophecies could be based on his own scribes' notes. This was done in Jerusalem. In the meantime, many of the best and most knowledgeable priests and scribes had been exiled to Babylon along with the royal house. They became the substantial core of the Jewish *Golah*, or Diaspora, which had much influence in emergent Judaism.

The composition of Ezekiel followed, apparently written by Ezekiel himself. This person who combined within his own person the skills of priest, prophet-visionary, and scribe is unique. He worked in Babylon.

The gathering and composition of many of the books of the Twelve Prophets (also known as the Minor Prophets because of their short length) by prophetic scribes in Jerusalem follow closely the blessings and curses in Deut 27–28, applying them to Yahweh's relation to Israel and Judah from the eighth to the late seventh centuries BCE.

The composition of Isaiah was done by another group of prophetic scribes in Jerusalem in the late sixth century, building on narratives about Isaiah, the prophet, which were found in 2 Kgs 18:17—20:19 = Isa 36–39 as well as others (Isa 7:1–17 and 20:1–6), which are not recorded elsewhere.

These works together formed a Deuteronomistic canon of Torah and Prophets for the exiles returning to Jerusalem in the late sixth century as they worked to restore the temple in Jerusalem (Deuteronomy, Joshua, Judges, 1 and 2 Kings, Jeremiah, Ezekiel, most of the Twelve, and Isaiah).

Scribes were among the notables of Judah who were sent with Jehoiachin to Babylon in 598 BCE. The move was one of the most fortuitous that anyone could imagine. The king's family was maintained in the royal buildings, while others were settled on land not far from the city. From them grew a Jewish presence that would continue for centuries. And among them developed important elements of what would be Hebrew Scriptures. The composition of an expanded Torah (Genesis through Numbers), the narrative frame plus inserts, probably took place there with priestly scribes being important contributors. This included the transcribing of the Jacob narrative (Gen 27–50) built on the collection originally told and retold around the sanctuary at Bethel.

The Abraham-Isaac narrative followed, based on stories gathered at Hebron and other southern sanctuaries. The Moses narrative took shape based on stories of the exodus gained from Passover stories, the wilderness tradition plus Sinai/Horeb inserts: Decalogue, Covenant Code

(Exod 21–23), tabernacle, and Holiness Code (Lev 17–26), taken from traditions preserved at amphictyonic sanctuaries like Hebron, Shiloh, and Shechem. The primeval narrative (Gen 1–9), the beginning to Noah, may be a rewrite of Babylonian traditions in a monotheistic setting.

Then these scrolls were sent to Judah and joined to the Deuteronomy–2 Kings corpus; the results were the Torah and the Prophets, which continued to be the Scriptures for Jews for centuries to come. This was pretty much the situation when Ezra, one of the Jewish scribes from the Babylonian/Persian court, appeared in Jerusalem to rally the people in a covenant ceremony related to the new temple. This Priestly edition, which inserted the account of the death of Moses, effected a division between Torah and Prophets, because it recognized only the Torah as authoritative Scripture.

The end of the Persian period and the beginning of the Greek period allowed a revival of Davidic traditions and interest in Jerusalem. Second Chronicles became the new history of the kingdom of Israel and Judah with a much more favorable view of the Davidic dynasty. This was preceded by 1 Chronicles, which allowed lists of genealogies to take the place of the earlier history. It was followed by the narratives of Ezra and Nehemiah.

The singers had regained a place in the temple's liturgies, and their scribes produced the collection of songs known as the Psalms. Royal wisdom was again in vogue, and its scribes textualized Job and Proverbs. The festival scrolls followed: Ruth, Ecclesiastes, Esther, Lamentations, and Song of Songs were each related to one of the five annual festivals of the Judaism of that period. And finally Daniel was written and joined the scrolls. (Note that Esther and Daniel are stories from the Babylonian dispersion.)

With this the collection that made up the Hebrew Bible was complete. It would take centuries to fully stabilize the text, but the Dead Sea Scrolls of the first century BCE demonstrate how similar the text of that time was to later forms. The final stabilization came through the work of the Masoretes in Tiberias in the ninth century CE.

# A SKETCH OF THE HISTORY OF ISRAEL AND OF THE JEWISH PEOPLE

*Prehistory: ca. 1600–1100 BCE*

- Exodus and Settlement
- Twelve Tribes in Canaan

*Prehistory: ca. 1000–586 BCE*

- The kingdom of Israel: Saul, David, and Solomon rule over twelve tribes; Solomon's temple in Jerusalem
- The divided kingdom: other sanctuaries in the kingdom of Israel
- Formation of religious traditions among syncretistic practices

*Babylonian Exile: (597) 587–ca. 535 BCE*

*The Persian Period in Canaan and the Diaspora (ca. 535–320)*

- Second Temple and Aaronide priesthood
- Torah and Prophets as Scripture
- First synagogues
- Strong communities in Judea, Babylon, and Egypt who keep Torah

*The Hellenistic Period in Canaan and Diaspora in Babylon and Egypt (320–66 BCE)*

- Oniad high priests displaced in second century by Hasmonean high priests and kings
- The Writings: Psalms, Wisdom, Chronicles
- Greek translation (Septuagint) of Tanak in Egypt
- Separation of Hebrew- and Greek-speaking synagogues begins
- Many Jews in Babylon

*The Roman Period in Judea; the Diaspora and the Christian Church throughout the Empire (ca. 66 BCE–300 CE)*

- Sadducees and Pharisees
- Desert covenanters (Dead Sea Scrolls)
- King Herod's new temple in Jerusalem
- Growth of Jewish Greek literature (Philo, Josephus)
- Jesus' ministry
- Zealot wars against Rome
- Destruction of Jerusalem and the temple
- Strengthening of rabbinic Judaism following destruction of Jerusalem
- Diminished role of priests
- Growth of messianic congregations following Jesus, especially in Greek-speaking synagogues
- Growing antipathy of Roman authority toward both Jews and Christians
- Growing distinction between Jews (using Hebrew Scriptures) and Christians (using Greek Scriptures)

Part 1

The Formation of Preliterary Traditions

1

# Israel and Its Traditions

### BEFORE THE BOOK

BEFORE JEWS HAD THE Bible from which to learn about their origins and their formative traditions, Israelites learned of them by going to sacred places, by participating in presentations, and by listening to lengthy speeches that shaped their understanding of the nature of the bonds that tied the tribes together and shaped their identity. At festivals they heard storytellers and singers rehearsing the stories and songs associated with persons for whom this place was famous. At festivals they saw dramatic presentations of their history.

Exod 24 tells of Moses receiving what came to be known as the book of the covenant from Yahweh and then of transmitting it to the people, first in spoken word (Exod 24:3), then in reading of a transcribed copy (Exod 24:4, 7) of those words.

Deuteronomy is a transcription of words that Moses spoke to the people. Israel first received the word from and about Yahweh as spoken words. Speech and speeches are prominent throughout the history.

Two words are used in Hebrew for oral speech: *'amar,* "say," and *diber,* "speak." The frequent use of the two words with the content of speeches shows the importance of the spoken word in the Hebrew Bible.

### ISRAEL'S STORYTELLERS

The narrative literature of the Old Testament is one of Israel's greatest achievements. Behind the narrative literature of the Old Testament lie the storytellers, who told what they knew of ancient people, places, and events long before they had anything to read. But storytelling did not cease when the stories were written down. On the contrary, it flourished in later years in the words of children at *seder* celebrations at Passover, of rabbis, of Sunday school teachers, and of preachers. It flowers in Heb 11.

At the sites associated with the patriarchs, they told the stories of the ancient fathers who had been there. At the great festivals related to the exodus and the covenant, they told the stories about Moses and the wilderness journey. The tribes had their storytellers who supported the book of Judges. The monarchies had their storytellers to tell of the exploits of their kings. The prophets and the priests had those who told their stories.

Even in oral form, these stories would have tended to be gathered around places and events. They would have developed a certain style that strongly influenced the narrative form of the literature while also keeping individuality and creative ways of speaking that continue to be represented in the written forms.[1]

David Carr has given us a word to define the purpose and function of Scripture in Judaism: *enculturation*. He combines it with "education" as "education and ongoing enculturation."[2] The texts of Scripture, says Carr, were composed deliberately to define how future teachers/leaders should educate children and adults in how to be Jews. The process parallels similar efforts in Greece, Mesopotamia, and Egypt, all of which produced written materials that were intended to be memorized in order to shape the personal and social participants in the culture and religion.

The idea "rings a bell" in our minds because that is precisely how Scripture has been used in modern instruction for Jews, Christians, and Muslims. Each of these communities has through the centuries struggled to define the essential character of their culture/religion and to present it in written form so that it could be used to shape the minds of its adherents. Carr's reminder that Scripture had this purpose is appropriate to this discussion. He concentrates on the Maccabean period and the efforts of Hasmonean rulers to resist the pressure of Hellenist culture and to preserve the distinct character of Jewish culture.

But Carr pays too little attention to the way that the Hebrew Scriptures have witnessed to the process of purely oral education/enculturation in Israel's history. He has dealt with the coming of Deuteronomy

---

1. Eissfeldt (*The Old Testament*, 12–128) summarized research into the earliest written sources for the small units of the literature.
2. Carr, *Writing on the Tablet*, 287.

in good fashion.³ It depicts Moses' efforts from Sinai onward as aiming to shape the former slaves into a people fit to be the people of Yahweh. Joshua's work and that of Samuel have the same purpose.

Worship around the ark and the temple pointed in the same direction. The proclamation of the book found in the temple by Josiah's priests is the first evidence of a written book read to the public for these purposes. Ezra continues the practice in trying to shape the people in Palestine after the exile.

Carr stresses the role of this enculturation process as "a means of resistance" to the prevailing culture of the time.⁴ This is true in Scripture throughout. The early forms of Judaism struggled to establish a distinct religious culture vis-à-vis Canaanite religion and culture.

In the exile, the Diaspora had to maintain itself over against Mesopotamian and Egyptian culture. In the Hellenistic era, it had to find its place in the dominant and pervasive Hellenistic culture. Judaism and Christianity (and then Islam) have done the same ever since. When medieval Christianity settled into maintaining the dominant religion through the mass, the cathedral, and the pope, Protestant reform returned to the use of the Scripture to "enculturate" its people through the use of Scripture.

Of course, the process in Israel used other means besides Scripture: festivals, temple, psalms, wisdom teaching, and others. It also used other personnel in addition to the priests. There were prophets and teachers, rabbis and preachers, singers and poets. These used the ancient traditions, reciting them at length, well before they were available in written forms. Whether depending upon the memory of the speaker or the writing being read by the reader, the goal was to "write them on the hearts" of the hearers (Jer 31:33; Heb 8:10). Oral presentation as the means of writing on the heart did not change.

Although Moses exemplified such enculturation in Deuteronomy and ordered that his words be written down and read to Israel again every seven years (Deut 31:9–13), the book of Judges shows little or no sign of such deliberate education. But Samuel with his circuit of major sanctuaries does seem to have worked within a system intended to accomplish this kind of education, but with no reference to written materials.

3. Ibid., 112–16.
4. Ibid., 9.

Josiah was presented with a book to be read to all the people. From that point on, the process of deliberate enculturation continued. It served the Diaspora in Babylonian exile and was brought back by Ezra to shape the newly reconstituted community in Judah. Through Genesis it taught a worldview that served the Jewish community well in its life among other cultures and religions. It shaped the religious life and thought of the people and gave them a positive self-image based on their retelling of the life and faith of their ancestors. It, along with the rebuilt temple, gave them a geographical sense of homeland, even when many of them lived far away. It provided them with a reasoned faith that stood up to the challenges of their times.

Carr has shown how it provided unity and formation to the people in Maccabean times, and in the Roman age that followed, to withstand the allure of Hellenism. Jews remained a distinctive and separate people who lived and believed according to the Torah. Christianity built on the foundation of the Tanak / Hebrew Bible, and Judaism.

Does the social background and economic position of the people in any given time play a role? The "elites" that Carr discusses[5] fit in a complex urban social structure such as the bureaucracy of the Mesopotamian or Egyptian court. They fit in the picture of Jerusalem's society in the united monarchy of Solomon's day with large commercial enterprises and a large temple, each with its own requirements for a trained bureaucracy and scribes. Solomon's love for proverbs would indicate the possibility of money and personnel for the arts (such as David's musicians, the special architects for the temple, etc.).

But the division of the kingdom reduced resources and needs sharply. The need for elites moved to the northern kingdom. Perhaps it reappeared in Jerusalem under Hezekiah.

But much of Israel's population and development through that period came in villages and small towns, in small sanctuaries, and without the "elites." Even the leaders hardly qualify as elite. What was enculturation like out there? The Old Testament story tells of that development. Even late books like Ruth, Song of Songs, and Ecclesiastes occur in village culture. Everything from Moses, Joshua, Samuel, the patriarchs, the sanctuaries, and the festivals fit in that more agricultural village culture. That is where Israel grew as a culture, not just in the capitals and the cities, not just around elites and kings. Even the scribes in Chronicles

---

5. Ibid., 13.

inhabit villages, as do the priestly families, and certainly the Levites. The roots of Israelite enculturation were here before they appeared in royal circles in Samaria, Jerusalem, Babylon, and Alexandria. And in many ways they were a counterforce to the ways of the courts and the elites, as Carr has noted for Deuteronomy. Wisdom is more at home in the palace. But Torah and Prophets are at least uncomfortable there, and also in the higher places of culture and education of later generations.

Look for the potential origin of Israelite enculturation in the villages and the provinces, not in the elites of cities and royal courts. This would be an enculturation that did not depend on writing or reading. Look for the ways that this other enculturation is introduced into a society that becomes more attuned to high cultures in the cities of the imperial ages of Babylonian, Persian, and Hellenistic times. And expect the role of the book, even in translation, to play a growing role there. And wonder at the capacity of the more simple forms to be adapted to the more complex societies and cultures.

Look at the role of the temple and its personnel (priests, singers, scribes). Note the counterattack of the "people of the land" through the public readings of Torah, the festivals (not necessarily in the temple), the prophets, the country Levites. Does the village economy regain its supremacy over that of the great cities at this time as well? Notice the way city and village relate to one another: priests, Levites, and scribes maintain ancestral homes in villages and go to work for short or long periods in the cities, which remain limited in terms of their economic viability and living space.

Differently from Carr, who looks for the origins of Mesopotamian and Egyptian culture in the royal courts and urban cultures, I suggest that Israel (and Greece) appears to draw its roots from non-urban societies. Israel has nothing to do with cities until the united monarchy. And even after that, Israel continues to have a vigorous religious and cultural life outside the cities. The Deuteronomistic traditions are rooted in sanctuaries and villages, also the Mosaic and patriarchal traditions, as well as the prophets. Even David starts outside the urban environment.

The tension continued between temple personnel and synagogue. Carr thinks the priests were the original teachers of Torah and the temple was its protector and house. But the synagogue eventually won that battle when the temple was destroyed. Torah's home became the synagogue and its teacher the rabbi. The scribal copyists of Torah found their customers in synagogues. The enculturating institution became the synagogue, whose personnel were the rabbinical teachers. Judaism lost both the temple and Jerusalem as great centers. But Judaism thrived, and Christianity thrived, without them, but with Scripture and local congregations, synagogues and churches. The role of weekly and annual celebrations continued to dominate their education/enculturation.

## FESTIVAL CELEBRATIONS AS ENCULTURATION

Carr makes the point that Scripture is intended for the education/enculturation of Israel. It is essentially for oral presentation. Even after it exists in writing, it is intended to be read aloud. He points to the temple and to priests as those most involved in its production and its presentation. Only later does it expand to education of all Jewish men through synagogue schools.

His presentation is compelling. But one thing is missing. His emphasis on the material presented leads him to neglect to show the times and places of its presentation, when the people were gathered, and who was gathered in addition to priests. Or was it only for priests to hear?

I propose that the occasions on which sizable portions of Torah and Prophets were read and heard were the annual festivals held at various sanctuaries through Israel's history and continuing into the Jewish period even after Sabbath readings became a prevalent time for reading Scripture. Personnel for these festivals and celebrations were much more diverse than priests. They included singers and storytellers, many of whom were Levites.

Three great festivals are prescribed in Torah:

- Passover/Unleavened Bread (redemption from Egypt)
- Weeks (entry into the promised land)
- Succoth or Feast of Tabernacles (Israel in the wilderness, Sinai/Horeb, covenant)

In time two other elements are added: New Year and Day of Atonement. All are harvest festivals tied to the Canaanite calendar and seasons. All are defined by the lunar calendar. But Hebrew forms tie them to events in Israel's history related by Torah.

Postexilic Judaism added two festivals:

- The Ninth of Ab (mourning for the destroyed city of Jerusalem)
- Purim (see the book of Esther)

Hasmonean Judaism added Hanukkah (celebration of the victory of Jews over the Seleucid armies).

The village culture used the festival scrolls to celebrate five festivals:

- Passover: Song of Songs
- Weeks: Ruth
- Succoth: *Koheleth* "the Preacher" (Ecclesiastes)
- The Ninth of Ab: Lamentations
- Purim: Esther

We learn in the book of 1 Samuel that Elkanah went up to the house of Yahweh at Shiloh "year after year." Eli and Samuel served there (1 Sam 1–3). The ark of Yahweh's covenant was there (1 Sam 4). Samuel also judged the people in an annual circuit, visiting Bethel, Gilgal, and Mizpah (1 Sam 7:16). At Gilgal he announced the anointing of a king for Israel, and there he gave his last speech (1 Sam 11–12).

Amos noted that people still worshipped (eighth century) at Bethel and at Gilgal (Amos 4:4; 5:5, 6; 7:10, 13), celebrating feasts and assemblies (Amos 5:21) as well as the Day of Yahweh (Amos 5:18–20). Hosea noted "celebrations, annual festivals, new moons, sabbath days, all her appointed feasts" (Hos 2:11) celebrated at Gilgal and Beth Aven (Hos 4:15).

David brought the ark to Jerusalem and held a single festival for the monarchy celebrating the kingdom of Yahweh, which has its seat in the temple in Jerusalem and the kingship of David, Yahweh's anointed. (See the royal psalms, such as Pss 2, 18, 20, 21, 72, 101, 110, 132, and 144:1–11.)

Earlier festivals were neglected in the monarchy but revived toward the end with the rise of Torah.

- All the appointed feasts (Hezekiah, 2 Chr 31:3)
- Passover (Hezekiah, 2 Chr 30) or Unleavened Bread (2 Chr 30:13, 21; 2 Chr 30:26: "not since Solomon"; 2 Kgs 23:22: "not since the days of the judges"
- Feast of Tabernacles (Ezra 3:4)

Observance of the seventh-day sabbath is commanded in all three legal collections (Exod 20:8–11; Lev 23:3; Deut 5:12–15) and is illustrated in Torah narrative. But it is missing in Joshua–1 Kings. The issue is complicated in that *sabbath* may also designate the day of a festival in which no work is to be done. "New moons and sabbaths," mentioned in

1 Samuel, Hosea, Amos, and elsewhere, may or may not be a reference to a seven-day week. References to sabbaths increase from the eighth century on, especially after the exile. It becomes the standard worship day for Judaism. New Moon observances are noted, but the content and description of the observance are not.

## PRELITERARY SOURCES AND TRADITIONS

The Old Testament gives evidence of drawing upon a vast reservoir of sources and traditions from the past to tell its story. It clearly contains some written sources that were forerunners of the current literature. There were ancient collections of songs: "the Book of the Wars of Yahweh" (Num 21:14) and "the Book of Jashar" (2 Sam 1:18). The book of Psalms probably drew upon similar sources for many of the psalms. The histories of the monarchy refer to sources: "the Book of the Acts of Solomon" (1 Kgs 11:41); "The Book of the Chronicles of the Kings of Israel" (1 Kgs 14:19; 16:27), or "the Kings of Judah" (1 Kgs 14:29 and parallel places in Chronicles). References to "the book of the law" (2 Kgs 14:6; 22:8, 10; and many others) seem to refer to an older form of the law available to the kings before the book mentioned in Neh 8:1, 2, 5, 6, 18, and following.

In addition, there are complexes of tradition that are apparently related to certain places and persons. These show inner consistency and independence in providing patterns of thought, worship, and behavior relating to the patriarchs, the tribal league, and Zion.[6] There are other traditions related to places, such as Bethel,[7] Shiloh, Gilgal, and others.

The canonical book of the Twelve Prophets contains books that were composed earlier and simply included within the growing composition. They are the Words of Amos and the two works without titles that we call Haggai and Zech 1–8.

How the composers of the biblical literature accessed these traditions is not clear. Nor do we have access to them except through their use in the literature. They are for the most part religious traditions growing out of Israel's religious practices.

---

6. See Watts, *Basic Patterns*, which is reproduced in an altered form here.
7. Blum, *Die Komposition*, 5–270.

*Religion* is used to describe the total experience that Israel had of God and with God. It has been said[8] that religion appears in three forms: as cult (worship), as myth (theology), and as ethic (morals). It is practically impossible to separate the three because they are closely interrelated.

One should beware of attempting to define any one of them exclusively by another. A single theology may be expressed in several worship forms. All three areas interact to form each other. This interaction is organic and reciprocal. Worship forms help to mold faith and ethics, while the content of faith sets limits for the choice of worship forms and creatively shapes an inherited ethic. No one of the three can be fully understood or described without reference to the other two.

Before describing or interpreting the early religious patterns that molded Israel's religious life and work, a brief look at the religious and social environment of early Israel is in order, as described in chapter 2. Then three chapters describe ways that her faith was nurtured and expressed, to which Jews consistently looked back as having been fundamental and formative for the faith that is expressed in their Scriptures. These forms were associated with the names of Abraham, Moses, and David.[9] I present these patterns in the conviction that they represent three distinct and fruitful religious forms of Israel's early faith experience and the way that they were taught and transmitted before the Jewish Scriptures used them for instruction and worship.

*Pattern* is used here to describe the form that grew in the interrelation of worship, theology, and morals, which became distinguishable and transmittable to influence later generations.[10] Each pattern was shaped in a period of historical reality. With the passing of that period, the actual pattern disintegrated or degenerated. Parts of it were preserved, as its influence on the following period shows. Finally, the content of the pattern found its way into literature as it influenced the shaping of theology. Sometimes this use in literature is explicit in quoting or retelling the

---

8. Mowinckel, *Religion und Kultus*, 7.

9. Modern study is accustomed to delineating various types of influence according to the role leaders played (as sheik, prophet, priest, judge, king, or wise man), the type of thinking reflected (legal, historical, cultic, prophetic or didactic; cf. Smend, *Elemente alttestamentlichen*, 4), or the forms of literature (e.g., narrative, law, instruction, prayer). The forms presented here are much broader, more elemental, and basic.

10. My use of *pattern* does not imply support for the so-called theory of patternism in the Near East, although I have learned from its advocates to appreciate the interaction of various parts of life within a form.

traditions of the pattern. Sometimes it is only implicit in the ideas and forms the writer uses.

The patriarchal period ceased before the twelfth century BCE. The original form disintegrated and no longer existed. But a pattern emerged that shaped the faith traditions and worship of sanctuaries in Shechem, Bethel, Hebron, and others. These holy places continued to be active and popular, giving succeeding generations fresh access to patriarchal traditions. At the same time, the traditions were absorbed into amphictyonic traditions and creatively influenced them at decisive points.

The confederation of twelve tribes that occupied Canaan before the monarchy has been called an amphictyony by some modern scholars because of similarities to groups in Greece that were united by their worship at a common shrine. This association apparently existed at least from the conquest under Joshua until the death of Saul in the tenth century BCE. The disintegration of the amphictyony was survived by a pattern preserved in festival celebrations and traditions at amphictyonic shrines like Shechem and Gilgal and in its influence on the shape of things in David's city.

The Davidic monarchy had historical limits (930–586 BCE). With its disappearance, only a pattern was left. But that pattern lived on in the psalms and in messianic hope, as well as in certain festival occasions.

The religious patterns of Judaism were different and diverse. The synagogue and the temple, the Zealots, the wise, and the Pharisees had their places. The mystic and the scribe vied for an audience.

The theological literature of Judaism (the Hebrew Bible) grew out of the patterns of worship and religion of ancient Israel.[11] I will treat that growth of the canon of Old Testament Scriptures in part 2 and in part 3.

---

11. A bibliography on the religion of Israel would need to include Renckens, *Religion of Israel*; Ringgren, *Israelite Religion*; and Fohrer, *Geschichte der israelitischen Religion*. Books on worship in Israel include Vriezen, *De Godsdienst van Israel*; Rowley, *Worship in Ancient Israel*; and Harrelson, *From Fertility Cult to Worship*.

2

# Traditions in an Aural/Oral Age

ISRAEL DID NOT ALWAYS have a written book from which to learn its most treasured traditions. But learning those traditions made possible the communal life of the people.

The traditions were communicated by storytellers, prophets (preachers), Levites, priests, and politicians at gatherings, formal and informal, at various shrines scattered through the land. These were places where some unusual event had occurred or where a major figure in the tradition had had a vision or experienced the presence of God in a particular way. Some of them were gravesites of the ancients.[1]

## SANCTUARIES

Certain prophets were related to particular sanctuaries: Amos at Bethel (Amos 7:10–17); Isaiah (Isa 1:1; 6:1), Jeremiah (Jer 1:1), and Ezekiel (8:3) to Jerusalem, as well as Shemaiah (1 Kgs 12:22; 2 Chr 11:2; 12:7), Nathan (2 Chr 9:29), and Ahijah (1 Kgs 12:15; 2 Chr 9:29). The use of *devarim,* "words, speeches, sayings," in the title of scrolls is appropriate where the written scroll is a transcription of things that had been transmitted and presented orally (of Moses in Deut 1:1, of Jeremiah in Jer 1:1, and of Amos in Amos 1:1).

At these places, the people assembled for religious festivals that celebrated and inculcated the unity and meaning of the whole people. They were the places to which the people rallied in times of threat or war. They were the places where leaders were installed or in which they

---

1. Knight (*Rediscovering the Traditions of Israel*) has surveyed thoroughly the research during the twentieth and twenty-first centuries on oral traditions in Israel.

retired. They appear in the written narrative and prophecies. But they existed and performed their functions long before those were available in Israel in written forms. They have continued to perform their service of education even until today when guides repeat the stories for tourists and pilgrims as they make their way to the shrines.

These places are Bethel and Gilgal, Jerusalem and Samaria, and many others. Each is responsible for a particular part of the tradition. Patriarchal traditions of Abraham, Isaac, and Jacob are associated with special places. Amphictyonic traditions of the twelve tribes who came up out of Egypt are related to others. Traditions of the kingdoms are based in others. Some places are related to more than one of these layers of history and tradition.

Equally important, these places commemorate God's history in dealing with Israel. It will be this feature that ties the stories together when they are written. Yahweh's name related to the patriarchs, Moses, and the kings gives them a mutual identity and provides the religious identification between them and the pilgrims that hear the stories in visits to these places. Yahweh's name is related not so much to the places as to the persons who experienced his presence at these places. Though Yahweh can be known because of a place, as the name El-Bethel shows, the normal epithets are "the God of Abraham, Isaac, and Jacob" or "the God of Moses," or "the God of David."

### Bethel

Bethel was one of the most enduring sanctuaries. It was located near the center of the land. Bethel was traditionally the place where Jacob had his vision of the ladder into heaven with angels ascending and descending; in this vision the word of God promised Jacob's return to the land and his inheritance of the blessing of Abraham (Gen 28:10–22). Both Abraham (Gen 13:3) and Jacob (Gen 35:10) were said to have built altars to Yahweh in that sanctuary. Yahweh was called *El Bethel*, "God of Bethel," there (Gen 35:7). Jacob received his new name, Israel, there (Gen 35:9).

Bethel was a custodian of amphictyonic tradition that was important before the beginning of the kingdom. Samuel included Bethel in the cycle of places to which he went annually in reviving the vision of Israel as a nation of twelve tribes. The others were Gilgal and Mizpah (1 Sam 7:16).

Jeroboam (1 Kgs 12:29-33) made Bethel one of two (the other is Dan in the north) national sanctuaries for the northern kingdom, installed two golden bulls as icons, and invoked the dissident tradition of the exodus in saying "these are the gods that brought you out of Egypt." (Cf. the story of Aaron's golden calf at Horeb [Sinai] in Exod 32:4.) Amos recognized this connection (Amos 7:10-17) when he was confronted by Amaziah the priest of Bethel with the words "this is the king's sanctuary."

Amos and Hosea understood the sanctuaries, including Bethel, to have been corrupted by the worship of other Gods. Josiah saw this in Bethel and had it destroyed because of this desecration (2 Kgs 23:15).

Bethel appears again after the exile, but now in the hands of the mixed population of Samaria (Zech 7:2). When Jesus sits at Jacob's well at Sycar near Bethel (John 4:6), the place is clearly in Samaritan territory and supports the self-understanding of the Samaritans, as when the woman speaks of "our father, Jacob."

## Gilgal

Gilgal, in the plain of Jericho near the Jordan river, was a much more specialized place. It was related exclusively to the traditions of the occupation and was associated with the covenant that Moses made. It held special importance in the association of tribes that we call the amphictyony.

The traditions that lie behind Deuteronomy came from here. This is the first place that Israel gathered after crossing the Jordan into the land proper. The people were reminded of what Moses had said and made a firm covenant to abide by the law he had given. They made a monument there of twelve stones from the bed of the Jordan (Sam 4:3, 20). The men were circumcised (Sam 5:2), and they celebrated Passover (Sam 5:10).

Deut 31:10 stipulates that all Israel is to gather every seven years at the Feast of Tabernacles to listen to a reading or recitation of the law of Moses (covenant law). If this covenant law is the substance of the book of Deuteronomy, the requirement of its reading would imply the need for a period of covenant renewal. It is clearly a means of communicating orally the heart of Israel's faith to all the people, a means of teaching it to each new generation.

This is what Samuel did (1 Sam 7:16) when he rallied the tribes to a new sense of unity and purpose. His final speech was at Gilgal (1 Sam 11:14—12:25). Joshua's final speech, which does the same thing, was at Shechem (Josh 24). When the book of the law was presented to the priests in Jerusalem in Josiah's day (2 Kgs 22), this function passed over to Jerusalem.

When these stories were repeated at these places, they shaped the consciousness of Israel as the people of Yahweh in the land. They also strengthened Yahweh's and Israel's claim to the land. They formed the basis for the written documents that tell the broader story.

### Burial Sites

Other places that helped to form the traditions of the amphictyony include the following burial sites:

- Bethlehem/Ephratha: Rachel (Gen 35:20)
- Macpelah, near Mamre: Sarah (Gen 23:7, 17; 25:9); Abraham (Gen 25:9)
- Mamre (Hebron): Isaac (Gen 35:27); Jacob (Gen 50:7, 17); Abraham (Gen 50:13); Sarah (Gen 23:19); Rebecca (Gen 35:8; Gen 49:30–31); and Leah (Gen 49:30–31)
- Shechem: Joseph (Josh 24:32)

### Patriarchal Sites

The following is a list of other patriarchal sites and their significance:

- Beer Lahai Roi: location of a well where Hagar rested (Gen 16:14); where Isaac lived (Gen 24:62)
- Beersheba: location of the well where Abimelek swore to respect Abraham (Gen 21:11); the location of Isaac's vision and commemorative altar (Gen 26:23–25, 32–33); the place where Jacob's family offered sacrifices on the way to Egypt (Gen 46:1)
- Bethel: the location of an altar Abraham built on the way to the Negev (Gen 12:8); the location of the altar El-Bethel, which Jacob built (Gen 35:1, 7); the place of Jacob's encounter with God where he was renamed Israel (Gen 35:9)
- Hebron: Abraham's encounter with God near the great tree at Mamre, where he built an altar (Gen 13:18; 18:1); Israel's location when he sent Joseph to look for his brothers (Gen 37:14)

- Mizpah: the altar where Laban departed from Jacob (Gen 31:49)
- Moriah: the land where Abraham attempted to offer Isaac as sacrifice (Gen 22)
- Salem/Jerusalem: kingdom where Abraham encountered Melchizedek (Gen 14:18).
- Shechem: land offered to Abraham by God (Gen 12:6); where Jacob bought land and built an altar called El-Elohe-Israel (Gen 33:18); where Dinah was defiled by Shechem (Gen 34); the place where Joseph's brothers herded their flocks and abandoned him (Gen 37)

*Amphictyonic Sites*

The following are important amphictyonic sites:

- Gilgal: first camp and sanctuary in the land (Josh 4:19–24; 9:6; 10:6, 15; 14:6); place where twelve stones marked the dry crossing of the Jordan (Josh 4:15–18); place of the new circumcision (Josh 5); place of the first Passover in the new land (Josh 5:10)
- Mount Ebal: location of an altar and copies of the laws of Moses in the new land (Deut 27:4–8; Josh 8:32–33)
- Mount Gerezim: place of blessing in the new land (Deut 27:11–13; Josh 8:32–33)
- Shiloh: place where the tribes receive the assignments of their lands (Josh 21:2)
- Shechem: location of Joshua's last speech (Josh 24:1)

The book of Judges speaks of incidents that had mainly tribal or regional significance. However, the major places appear occasionally throughout the literature:

- Bethel: Judg 1:23; 1 Sam 7:16 (Samuel's visits to Bethel, Gilgal, and Mizpah)
- Bethlehem: Judg 12:8; 1 Sam 16:1, 18; 17:58
- Gilgal: Judg 2:1–4
- Hebron: Judg 1; 1 Sam 39:27

- Jerusalem: Judg 1:4, 8; 19:10, 11; 1 Sam 17:54
- Mizpah: Judg 10:17; 20:1; 21:1, 5; 1 Sam 7:5
- Nob: 1 Sam 22:11 (the priests at Nob)
- Ramah: 1 Sam 7:17 (an altar to Yahweh); 8:4; 15:15
- Ramoth: 1 Sam 30:27
- Shechem: Judg 9:6; 21:19
- Shiloh: Judg 21:12, 19; 1 Sam 1:3 (annual festival); 3:21; 4:1–9 (the ark of the covenant)
- Saul's journey:
  - Bethel: 1 Sam 10:3 ("going up to God")
  - Gibeah: 1 Sam 10:5, 10 (see also 1 Sam 11:4; 14:3; 15:35; 26:1)
  - Gilgal: 1 Sam 11:4, 14–15 (see also 1 Sam 15:12)
  - Mizpah: 1 Sam 7:5 ("gather all Israel")
  - Zelzah: 1 Sam 10:2 (Rachel's tomb)

### David's Story

The following place names are important to David's story:

- Hebron: 2 Sam 2:33; 3:19, 20; 4:12; 5:1, 3, 13
- Jerusalem: 2 Sam 5:6–10; 6:1–21 (city of David, location of the ark); 7; 8:15 (David king over all Israel). Jerusalem becomes the symbolic center for all Israel. Solomon's temple becomes the center for celebrations and festivals.
- Gibeon: 1 Kgs 3:4 (Solomon's dream)

### The Divided Kingdoms

The following places are landmarks in the divided kingdoms:

- Beersheba: 1 Kgs 19:3
- Bethel and Dan: 1 Kgs 12:29 (sanctuaries for the kingdom of Israel with golden calves "who brought you out of Egypt"); 1 Kgs 13:1, 4, 10, 11

- Geba and Mizpah: 1 Kgs 15:22 (see also Gibea in Hos 5:8; 9:9; 10:9)
- Horeb: 1 Kgs 19:8 (mount of God)
- Jezreel: 1 Kgs 18:45; 21:1, 23
- Mount Carmel: 1 Kgs 18:19 (Elijah)
- Ramah: 1 Kgs 15:17, 22
- Samaria: 1 Kgs 16:24, 28; 29, 32 (altar to Baal); 20:1, 10; 21:18
- Shechem: 1 Kgs 12:1 (Rehoboam); 1 Kgs 12:25 (Jeroboam; Sycar near there; Jacob's well in John 4:6)
- Shiloh: 1 Kgs 14:2
- Tirzah: 1 Kgs 14:17; 15:33; 16:6, 8, 9, 15, 17, 23

*Elijah's Last Journey*

These landmarks are significant to Elijah's last journey:

- Bethel: 2 Kgs 2:2, 3, 23 (continued as seen in Amos 7:10 [the king's sanctuary] and in Zech 7–8, where it is used by the mixed congregation; cf. 2 Kgs 17:28). This is the only shrine related to the patriarchs (Jacob), to the exodus (Jeroboam's "these are the gods that brought you out of Egypt"), to the kingdoms (Jeroboam's sanctuary; Amos 7), and to postexilic worship (Zech 7–8).
- Gilgal: 2 Kgs 2:1; 4:38 (bridges the exodus and the amphictyony; see also Hos 9:15; 12:11)
- Jericho: 2 Kgs 2:4, 5, 15, 18
- Mount Carmel: 2 Kgs 2:25
- Samaria: 2 Kgs 2:25; 3:1, 6 et passim

## SPEAKERS AND HEARERS

The basic elements of communication for the shaping and transmission of tradition that defines and guides a people are two, oral and written, and both depended on aural reception.[2]

---

2. Graham, *Beyond the Written Word*.

In early society the speakers enunciated words that had been passed on to them orally and that had to be remembered, only to be passed on again (performed), generation after generation. The tradition depended on maintaining an unbroken line of those entrusted with it. In Israel these were the priests or Levites, although speakers were often prophets and other kinds of leaders instead. Traditions were maintained in particular places and rehearsed (performed) during specific festivals or other occasions. This was possible so long as a people remained in traditional locations, maintained traditional calendars, and had traditional tradents, or bearers, of the stories, songs, and laws.

Later speakers read from documents that contained the written tradition. They were not necessarily those who memorized the words (although many did and do, using the writing to aid memory, not replace it). Scribes and readers had to be trained to read and to enunciate what was read. Writing stabilized the transmission and gave more structure and uniformity to the tradition. Written Scriptures could be transported to other places to be read. They were not dependent upon specific localities, or even specific persons or families. They could be used and developed in places far away from traditional lands.

Both systems of transmission were vulnerable. The line of oral speakers could die out or be destroyed. But the written record could also be destroyed. In either case, reconstruction of the tradition(s) would be difficult or impossible after a period of time. The change from oral transmission to written had to occur while there were still those alive who knew and could recite the old traditions so that they could be recorded or shaped into the writings.

The change from oral transmission to written was not simply a recording of the oral forms, although they were influential in shaping the written forms. The writing moved toward literary forms and fulfilled literary requirements that were unknown to the oral speakers. They reshaped the traditions in ways that conformed with the needs of the age.

## TRADITIONS

The cultivation, repetition, and learning of traditions helped a society define itself and maintain its structure and identity.[3] Traditions were essential to maintaining order and unity. In a society without writing,

---

3. Carr (*Writing on the Tablet*) has called this process "enculturation."

traditions were maintained and transmitted at specific places and community events, like festivals. They were related to the maintenance of specific institutions.

In Israel, some of the traditions related to the meaning of Israel and the relation of the tribes to the larger entity of Israel. These traditions have been passed down in the stories of the patriarchs in Genesis and in the stories of the judges.

A specific institution of "all Israel" and the twelve tribes designates that association we call the amphictyony (Deuteronomy and Joshua). It is related to Moses and Joshua and was likely celebrated on three- or seven-year intervals at Gilgal.

Another institution was the monarchy. It was carried on by the kings from Saul, David, and Solomon, to Jeroboam and their successors in both Jerusalem and Samaria. Annual royal festivals were celebrated: the new year festival in Jerusalem's temple and the annual royal festival in Bethel. The temples and the high places were religious institutions in their own rights and had their own festivals.

## THE TWELVE TRIBES OF ISRAEL

That Israel was composed of twelve tribes, descendants of the twelve sons of Jacob, is a fixed notion in the Deuteronomistic and prophetic literature. The documentation is more varied as you can see in the table.

| Twelve Tribes | Fewer Than Twelve Tribes |
|---|---|
| Gen 49:28 | |
| Exod 1:1–5; 15:27; 24:4; 28:21; 39:14 | Exod 6:14–27 (Reuben, Simeon, Levi) |
| Num 1:5–15, 20–43, 44; 2:3–34 (cf. Ezek 48:1–7, 23–28); 17:6; 31:5 | Num 32 (Reuben, Gad, half-Manasseh) |
| Deut 1:23; 33:6–24 | Deut 34:1–3 (all the land: Gilead to Dan; Naphtali, Ephraim, Manasseh; Judah to the western sea, the Negev) |
| Josh 3:12; 4:2–20 | |
| Judg 19:29 | Judg 1:2 (Judah: Simeon, Caleb, Kenites), 21 (Benjamin), 22 (house of Joseph), 27 (Manasseh), 29 (Ephraim), 30 (Zebulun), 31 (Asher), 33 (Naphtali), 34 (Dan) Judg 2:8 (Joshua of Nun) Judg 3:9 (Othniel, nephew of Caleb) Judg 3:15 (Ehud of Benjamin [Ephraim]) Judg 4–5 (Deborah or Ephraim, Barak of Naphtali, Zebulun); 5:14 (Ephraim, Benjamin, Issachar); 5:15b–17 (did not join Barak: Reuben, Gilead, Gilead, Dan, Asher) Judg 6–9 (Gideon from Manasseh); 6:35 (Asher, Sebulun, Naphtali); 8:1 (Ephraimites) Judg 10:1 (Abimelech of Issachir); 10:3 (Jair of Gilead); 10:9–12 (from Gilead: Judah, Benjamin, and Ephraim) |
| 1 Chr 2:1–6:81 | |
| Ezek 47:13 | |

Most of the narrative of the wilderness journey speaks only of Moses and Aaron (Levites) and thus fits the description of the Israelites coming out of Egypt, comprising Levites, Simeonites, and Reubenites. But in Exod

32:17 and 33:11, Joshua (Ephraimite) appears. In Exod 35:30, Bezalel (Judah) is mentioned and in Exod 35:34 and 38:23 Oholiab (Dan).

Sampson is from Dan (Judg 13-16), but no other tribes are mentioned in his story. Judg 17-18 speaks of Ephraim, Levi, and Dan. Note that Judg 19-21 speaks of Israel without using the word *twelve*, although the narrative is much concerned about missing one tribe from the whole of Israel. Benjamin and Judah are called by name.

There is no question that the picture of Israel is deliberately that of twelve tribes descended from Jacob. However, were all these tribes in Egypt? Did all of them move with Moses through the wilderness? Did they face God at Sinai? Did they all enter the land from east Jordan?

The biblical books tell of at least three entrances into a new land. One is the trip of Abraham that brought his family and his descendants into Canaan (Gen 12-50). A second is the story in Exodus through Joshua describing the departure from Egypt. This narrative speaks of two entries: one from Kadesh Barnea up into Judah, which was rebuffed by the city rulers, and a second move up around Edom and Moab to enter over Jordan with "all Israel" in one united army under Joshua.

The third, described in the book of Joshua, is a united entry into Canaan west of Jordan. Judges (after chapter 1) never pictures "all Israel," unless the united group against Benjamin included all the tribes (Judg 20).

If one tried to reconstruct a combination of these accounts, it would look something like this: Some of the tribes owe their presence in Palestine to descent from Abraham's family. If they were in Egypt at all, they did not stay in Egypt long. This might even apply to the "house of Joseph." Their relation to each other was an implied relationship of kin.

If Exod 6:14-27 is to be followed, Reuben, Simeon, and Levi make up the "Israel" that was brought out of Egypt. Moses and Aaron are both Levites. Reuben and Simeon both settled in the south of Palestine. Simeon was never strong and soon became assimilated into Judah. Reuben settled in east Jordan. These, especially Levi, would then be the tribes that were at Sinai, making them the bearers of the tradition, the original participants in covenant. Levites received special inheritances among the other tribes in order to carry out their priestly duties.

Deuteronomy's picture of a great gathering east of Jordan for Yahweh to renew his covenant with "all Israel" could show the way that tribes already in the land were recruited to join with the new entrants to identify themselves with the experience of coming out of Egypt, of meeting Yahweh at Sinai, of being offered covenant—including the tablets of stone, the ark, and the larger law—and of being invited to participate in a move to unify themselves as a force to occupy the land. (However, such a unity is not attested before the time of David. And even that does not last long. The monarchy is divided into two [or three] parts with no further claim to be of twelve tribes.)

But Hezekiah, Josiah, and Ezra all claim in their own ways to be representing the "Israel" of twelve tribes, as Judaism will continue to do. Even the Christian book of Revelation envisions twelve gates of the new Jerusalem named for the twelve tribes (Rev 21:12) and 144,000 people representing the twelve tribes (Rev 7:4).

## THE HEBREW LANGUAGE

Israelites are presumed to have spoken Hebrew, a Canaanite dialect. The early tribes in Canaan probably had several different dialects. The use of the shibboleth formula in Judg 12:6 illustrates one such dialect difference. There may well have been significant differences to be heard in the various sanctuaries of ancient Israel, at least as different as those preserved in the Samaritan Pentateuch.

The language was stabilized in the Judean dialect of Hezekiah's time before the writing of the first portions of the Hebrew Bible, which continued to follow that standard. This form of Hebrew is usually called Biblical Hebrew. Later Hebrew carried other names. The written scrolls preserve only the consonantal text. There may well have been considerable fluctuation in the pronunciation of the read texts. Finally by the tenth century CE the Masoretes of Tiberius, who were the actual scribes copying the texts in that period, devised ways of indicating the proper pronunciation of the text, although various branches of Judaism still had some different ways of pronouncing the Hebrew. The Mishnah was written in Hebrew, and its language is called Mishnaic Hebrew. The documents of the Dead Sea Scrolls were written for the most part in Hebrew. Modern Israeli Hebrew, while based on Biblical Hebrew, has developed its own vocabulary and style.[4]

---

4. Kutscher, *History of the Hebrew Language*; Weitzman, "Why Did the Qumran Community Write in Hebrew?" 35–45. See Driver, *Semitic Writing*; Moscati, *Ancient Semitic Civilizations*.

As Aramaic became the universal language of great empires, Hebrew remained the liturgical language of the Jerusalem temple and the synagogue. Synagogues made sure succeeding generations of Hebrew men were able to read the Scripture in Hebrew by providing Hebrew classes for boys, as they still do today (now for girls as well).

## BACKGROUNDS

Before studying Israel herself, a sketch of the life and worship of her forebears and neighbors will prepare for a better understanding of her distinctive practices as well as those that she held in common with her neighbors and cousins. Three concrete circles of identification, from broader genealogical and social categories to her nearest neighbors and kin, describe her setting in Near Eastern life and history. Israel was Semitic, was once seminomadic, and finally settled down to agriculture and commerce in Canaan.

In the Near East, the culture that in historical times became dominant is called by the general term *Semitic*.[5] Israel was one of the Semitic peoples.[6] The term is drawn from the table of the nations in Gen 10. The peoples known to that writer were grouped under the three sons of Noah. The sons of Shem (Semites) included Aram, Ashur, and Eber, meaning the Arameans, Assyrians, and the Hebrews.[7] Thus the term *Semite* has come to be used for these peoples and others closely related to them.[8]

Common linguistic characteristics indicate a clear demarcation between the languages of these peoples and other linguistic groups like the Indo-Germanic. These similarities are so marked that they can only be accounted for by supposing a common origin. Scholars have even composed a hypothetical "original Semitic" language by pooling their common elements.

---

5. Wolf, "Semite," 269; Moscati, *Ancient Semitic Civilizations*; Soden, "Semiten," 1690–93; Hammersgaimb, "Semiten," 1694–96.

6. Note the distinction between "Semites" (desert bedouin) and "Semitic peoples" (settled and mixed populations) made by Moscati, *Semites in Ancient History*, 31–32.

7. Moscati, *Ancient Semitic Civilizations*, 23.

8. Moscati, *Semites in Ancient History*, 42: "we may define the Semites as that people which, at the beginning of the historical era, is found dwelling in the Arabian desert, in homogeneous linguistic, social, and racial conditions. They were pastoral nomads, sheep herders, whose natural trend was to occupy the more fertile neighboring lands, which offered the possibility of agriculture and of a settled mode of life."

Known Semitic languages are usually classified in three[9] or five groups.[10] Northeast Semitic or Akkadian includes the languages of Assyria and Babylon. Northwest (or West) Semitic is subdivided into the Canaanite, a group of diverse languages and dialects spoken in the area of Canaan (including Hebrew, Moabite, Ammonite, Edomite, Ugaritic, Phoenician, and Punic), and Aramaic, a set of dialects first found in upper Syria. South Semitic may also be subdivided into North Arabic (including the classical language of the Qur'an and Nabataean) and South Arabic (including Ethiopic, Minaean, and Sabaean).

If there are distinctive common characteristics for the Semites in their languages and cultures, there are also many differences that distinguish them from one another. What Semites have in common may be best explained by the hypothesis of a common origin.[11] The most likely place of origin seems to have been the Arabian peninsula.[12] The desert left its stamp on these peoples.[13]

The great differences that appear among them may be traced to cultural mixture with settled non-Semitic cultures whom they conquered or absorbed. At every stage in which ancient Semitic cultures are known, they were already thoroughly mixed with other peoples who had settled in the more fertile areas long before them.[14] At whatever point one meets these ancient Semites, their cultures represented some stage in the movement from nomadic to settled life.[15] Although many elements, especially in the latter, may have been of non-Semitic origin, it is not possible to separate and identify them accurately. This is particularly true of Semitic

---

9. Diringer, "Semitic Languages," 1014–15.

10. Moscati, *Ancient Semitic Civilizations*, 29–30; idem, *Introduction to the Comparative Grammar*.

11. Henninger, *Über Lebensraum*, 35; Moscati, *Ancient Semitic Civilizations*, 11.

12. Henninger, *Über Lebensraum*, 35; Moscati, *Semites in Ancient History*, 31–32.

13. Smith, *Early Poetry of Israel*, 33.

14. Hooke, "Early Background," 273. The evidence suggests that "as far back as the historian can go the 'Semitic' area was a meeting place for many different and conflicting elements, and that 'Semitic culture' is sometimes specifically the new formation that arose, perhaps as a compromise between the desert and the more exposed surrounding lands" (Cook, "Semites," 237).

15. This may be "the distinctive" in their religion as well. Eissfeldt ("Gottesnamen und Gottesvorstellungen," 35 [204]) suggests that all Semitic religions show a tendency to move from nature deities to those pictured as leaders (lords) of human societies or groups. In this he does not adequately distinguish the interrelation of nomadic and sedentary elements, but the basic observation can stand.

religion.[16] The result is that scholars are much more reserved than W. Robertson Smith[17] was in the late nineteenth century in talking about Semitic religion.

Israel's self-identification took full cognizance of her ethnic Semitic heritage. Small though she was, Semitic culture bloomed in her history in a unique way. Throughout her history Semitic characteristics of language, temperament, and outlook found expression in every area of her life.

Israel came from seminomadic stock. She was fully aware of this and recorded it in the stories about the patriarchs and the judges. Her psychology owed much to this heritage. Many points of view belonging to this background were never relinquished.

Israel finally settled in Canaan. Her sedentary life was influenced at every level by the older and more advanced Canaanite civilization. Partially through assimilation and partially by resistance, she made use of this environment.

These three circles of identification—Semitic, seminomadic, and agricultural—mark many stimuli, many limits, and many directions that affected Israel's growth in her understanding of God and of herself as his people. The student will be aware of them on every page of the Old Testament.

## FAMILY PIETY AND WORSHIP

A substantial place for oral enculturation of Israelite religious knowledge was in the family and its worship.[18] The recognition of patriarchal sites belonged to family piety that sought to emulate the piety of Abraham. Family prayer and faith were paramount here, recognizing the God of the fathers who had led Abraham from Ur of the Chaldees and promised him and his descendants this land.

---

16. Eissfeldt, "Gottesnamen und Gottesvorstellungen," 169: "Für den Semiten ist die Welt, in der er lebt, voll von übermenschlichen, dämonischen, göttlichen Gewalten, gesättigt mit potentieller göttlicher Dynamik, die sich bei den allerverschiedensten Anlässen in aktuelle Göttlichkeit umsetzen kann."

17. *Religion of the Semites.*

18. Albertz has written on the role of the family in ancient Israel: "Religious Elements of Early Family Groups," 25–39; "Family Piety in the Later Pre-state Period," 94–104; "Family Piety in the Late Monarchy," 186–94, all in *From the Beginnings.* Also see Carr, *Writing on the Tablet,* 12–13, 20–21, 65–67, 129–30, 143–44, 203, 205–6, 208, 277, 284.

The Feast of Firstfruits as described in Deut 26 was a family festival for an agricultural economy. The Feast of Weeks could be as well.

The biblical narratives tell of strong family worship and piety from the patriarchs onward. Judaism treated Passover as a family celebration. But 2 Kgs 23:21–22 says that Josiah's command to celebrate Passover came from reading the Torah found in the temple (Deut 16:1–6) and that it had not been celebrated in that way since the days of the judges. (Perhaps the writer is aware of Josh 5:10–11.) The command to observe Passover is firmly rooted in the Torah (Exod 12:11–48; 34:25; Lev 23:5; Num 9:2–14; 28:16).

Second Chronicles 30 tells of a celebration in Hezekiah's time "according to what is written" (2 Chr 30:5) as a part of the Feast of Unleavened Bread. The chapter also notes that nothing like this had happened in Jerusalem since the days of David and Solomon (2 Chr 30:26). Second Chronicles 35 also tells of the celebration in Josiah's time, including the note that it had not been celebrated like this since the days of Samuel and that no king of Israel or Judah had ever celebrated Passover in this fashion (2 Chr 35:18), apparently unaware of the narrative in chapter 30 about Hezekiah. In neither Josiah's celebration nor that of Hezekiah is it a family festival. The parallel festival of Unleavened Bread was an agricultural festival in which families surely participated. Families traveled to the sanctuary for the celebration, as Samuel's family traveled to Shiloh for the annual festival (1 Sam 1:3).

Deuteronomy prescribes things to be done in the home to educate the children in the way of Yahweh (Deut 6). Ezra and Nehemiah are sensitive to the negative potential for miseducation by the presence of foreign wives in the families. Stories of early life in Canaan tell of family shrines and even family priests (Judg 17:5, 10–13; cf. Judg 6:24, 25; 8:27 [Gideon]).

The next chapters in part 1 will picture the patterns that revelation assumed in the worship and faith of Israel prior to the writings stating her faith in theological terms. The patterns broke the almost universal hold that superstition and unworthy worship had on the people. They laid foundations for the faith proclaimed in the Old Testament and in the New Testament.

3

# Patriarchs

A GREAT DEAL OF tradition dealt with the patriarchs, the earliest progenitors in the genealogies of the tribes. Israel was the alternate name for Jacob, the father of twelve sons, who produced the twelve tribes.[1]

Although the tribes were spread out around Canaan, it was their recognition of common ancestry in Jacob, Isaac, and Abraham that gave them a sense of culture, religion, and history to write about, or to provide perspective and content. Until the time when Genesis was written, the stories had been transmitted orally by storytellers, singers, and judges to pilgrims at sanctuaries associated with the patriarchs.

## PLACES

The patriarchs were associated with particular places in Canaan. Later generations continued to hear about them in sanctuaries related to those places and with the names of the patriarchs.

Hebron, also identified as Mamre, with specific reference to the cave of Macpelah where the grave of the patriarchs was located, is mentioned as the burial site for Sarah (Gen 23:17–19), Abraham (Gen 25:8–10), Isaac (Gen 35:27–29), and Jacob (Gen 49:28–33 (also Rebecca and Leah). This site would have been the most influential in teaching generations of Israelites about all the patriarchs.

Bethel is the location of an altar that Abraham built and where he worshipped (Gen 12:8; 13:3); Jacob had his vision of God at the head of a staircase to heaven and anointed a pillar there (Gen 28:10–22; 31:13;

---

1. This chapter is adapted from Watts, *Basic Patterns*, 39–63.

35:1–16). It continued to be a favorite place of worship until after the exile (Amos 3:14; 4:4; 7:10; Josh 16:2; Judg 1:22; 4:5; 21:2; 1 Sam 7:15–16; 10:3; 13:2; 30:27; also several mentions in Kings, Ezra, and Nehemiah; Hos 10:15; 12:4; Zech 7:2).

Beersheba is associated with stories of Abraham (Gen 21:14, 33; 22:19), Isaac (Gen 26:33), and Jacob (Gen 28:10; 46:1, 5; Josh 19:2; 1 Kgs 19:3; Amos 5:5; 8:14).

Mizpah is important to the understanding of Jacob's story (Gen 31:49; Judg 10:17; 11:11; 20:1; 21:5; 1 Sam 7:5, 6, 16; 10:17; 22:3; Jer 40:10–15; 41:3, 14; Hos 5:1).

Shechem appears in the stories of Jacob (Gen 33:18; 35:4) and his sons (Gen 37:12–14; Josh 24:1). It is the burial place for Joseph (Josh 24:32), who had died in Egypt (Gen 50–26) and was brought back by Moses (Exod 13:19). In Jesus' day the well at Shechem was still thought of as having been given by Jacob (John 4:12).

Jerusalem gained prominence as the location of Solomon's temple on Mount Moriah (2 Chr 3:1), but the mountain was first significant because Abraham brought his son Isaac here to sacrifice (Gen 22:2). Abraham was blessed by Melchizedek of Salem (Gen 14:18), another name for Jerusalem.

Note the speeches of Moses (Deuteronomy) spoken beyond the river but repeated at gatherings in Gilgal and written in a book to be kept with the ark (Deut 31:22, 24–26), and the speeches of Joshua (Josh 24) spoken in Shechem, and Samuel (1 Sam 11:14—12:24) spoken at Gilgal. At Gilgal, Samuel declaimed the regulations of kingship, wrote them on a scroll, and deposited them before the Lord (1 Sam 10:25). Gilgal continued to be a significant location to the people throughout their history (1 Sam 7:15; 13:7–15; 15:12, 33; Joshua, Judges, Hos 4:15; 9:15; 12:11; Amos 4:4; 5:5; Mic 6:5).

Shiloh was an important location for worship and assembly during the time of Joshua and Judges (Josh 18:1, 8, 10; 21:1–3; 22:9; Judg 18:31; 21:12–21). See these and additional patriarchal sites enumerated in chapter 2.

The recognition of places where one or another of them had lived or died defined their relationship and unity. It gave the Israelites evidence for their claim to the land. "Abraham slept here, and he was my ancestor" was the motto. Each of the tribes had its own points of recognition and history, but the recognition of Abraham, Isaac, and Jacob belonged to all of the tribes. It marked them off from their neighbors.

## THE PATRIARCHAL PATTERN

The Hebrew Bible does not recognize festivals related to the patriarchs. The festivals served other purposes and other traditions.

When the time came to write and publish Torah, stories about the patriarchs, Abraham, Isaac, and Jacob were assembled and organized into a continuing narrative that provided the setting and background for the story of the exodus. They picture Abraham's entry into Canaan from Mesopotamia assured by God that this land was to belong to the generations that followed him. They show the patriarchs living in tents and moving around the land with stays at important cult centers that later came to be known and used by Israelites. The stories did much more. They accounted for much in Israel's life, faith, and culture that they valued.

Studies of the patriarchal stories in Genesis have emphasized the essential accuracy with which they portray the conditions and customs of the Near East in the first half of the second millennium BCE.[2] Archaeology, anthropology, and history have contributed to this judgment, especially in noting the accurate transmission of names, social customs, laws, racial distribution, and political conditions that can now be checked through archaeological finds.[3]

If this essential accuracy in regard to details of history and society can be confirmed, what of the faith, worship, and piety that are attributed to the patriarchs? Can these also be traced to those early beginnings?[4] Or must these be viewed as projections into the past of views held by much later writers?[5]

---

2. See de Vaux, "Les patriarches hébreux," 321-48, 321-47, 5-36; idem, *Die Patriarchenerzählungen*; Rowley, "Recent Discoveries," 44-79; Albright, "The Biblical Period"; idem, *Yahweh and the Gods of Canaan*, 47-50; Gordon, "The Patriarchal Narratives," 56-59; Kapelrud, *Israel*, 14; Van Seters, "Problem of Childlessness," 401-8.

3. Especially those at Nari, Nuzu, Ras Shamra, and more recently in the Negev. Cf. Gibson, "Light from Mari," 44-62. Note the more skeptical tone of archaeologists in the meantime.

4. Some rather negative answers: Gottwald, *Light to the Nations*, 100-1; Wright, "Present State of Biblical Archaeology," 91; Rost, "Die Gottesverehrung," 346-59. But see the excellent little volume by Pfeiffer, *Patriarchal Age*.

5. Thus the older criticism. See the comments of von Rad, *Old Testament Theology*, 1:165; Eichrodt, "Religionsgeschichte Israels," 377.

All that we know of the patriarchs is contained in writings whose present form dates from much later in Israel's history than the times they describe. They are built on traditions and stories that were told in Israel for a long time before they achieved written form. Numerous items in the Genesis accounts parallel Canaanite worship and may well owe their presence in these stories to influences that affected the stories in their transmission. This is particularly true of the names of God formed with *El* and some relations to Palestinian sanctuaries.[6]

What language did Abraham and his family speak? Their origins in Mesopotamia and Syria suggest Akkadian or, possibly, Aramaic. Did he and his family live in Canaan long enough to have changed his mother tongue for a form of Canaanite? When Joseph went to Egypt, he would have had to use Egyptian in his work. But his extended family apparently kept their own dialect through the years as Moses' story of meeting an Israelite shows (Exod 2:11–14). Is this grounds enough to suggest that Moses was at least bilingual with a Semitic dialect and Egyptian at his disposal? His stay with Jethro might have helped prepare him for going to Canaan later. But even when Israel settled in Canaan, the tribes were separate and seem to have developed tribal dialects.

Only when David and Solomon united the tribes into a kingdom around 1000 BCE was there pressure to form and cultivate a single language. It has been suggested that the Hebrew of our Bible reflects the Judean dialect of Hezekiah's time around 700 BCE.

The stories of the patriarchs make clear that Israel's ancestors had not always worshipped Yahweh (or even Elohim) as later Israel knew him.[7] They recognize a heathen background, which may have been that of moon worship in Haran,[8] other types of Aramaean idolatry (*teraphim*),[9] or some form of polydemonism,[10] without hesitating to contrast it with what the reader recognized as a legitimate forerunner of his/her own faith. The stories show that this older pattern of heathen worship was broken in the experience of Abraham and the patriarchs. A new pat-

---

6. Baudissin, *Kyrios*, 3:124–64; Albright, *From the Stone Age*, 184.

7. Josh 24:2; Hooke, "Early Background," 135; Bright, *History of Israel*, 91.

8. Rowley, "Recent Discoveries," 279, 299; Liagre Böhl, "Die Zeitalter Abrahams," 37.

9. Gen 31:19. Cf. Greenberg, "Another Look," 239–48; Jirku, "Die Mimation," 78–80; Labuschagne, "Teraphim," 115–17.

10. Whatever may be the background of Gen 32:24–32.

tern of faith, worship, and piety was established for their descendants.[11] The old paganism was ultimately broken in the telling of these stories in Jewish settings after the exile (fifth century BCE).

Research in this field has outlined those elements of patriarchal faith, worship, and piety that did not come from the purposes of the pentateuchal authors or from Canaanite influence.[12] This research uses the method of form criticism and comparative religion to make and bolster its case. It studies the patriarchal stories as traditions that have been handed down for centuries before being reduced to writing. It analyzes reasons for telling the stories in their final forms and in their earlier forms.

In 1929 Albrecht Alt published *Der Gott der Väter*,[13] which presented the results of studies carried out along these lines.[14] He found a type of religion that is distinct from others known in the Near East. It is characterized by a personal revelation to an individual, which leads to a cult of the God of this person. This God is only known by association with the founder of the cult, as in "the God (or Shield) of Abraham,"[15] "the God (or the Fear) of Isaac,"[16] and "the Mighty One of Jacob (or Israel)."[17] Here God is not bound to a place but is united to a person. God had by free choice sought this relation to the founder of the cult and others that participated in it.

Alt's work became the starting point for other treatments of patriarchal religion.[18] Perhaps the treatment that went creatively beyond Alt

---

11. Gen 12:1–3. Note the emphasis on Abraham as the original father of Israel.

12. Convenient summaries may be found in Leslie, *Old Testament Religion*, 69-70; Albright, *From the Stone Age*, 236-49; Eichrodt, "Religionsgeschichte Israels," 377-80; von Rad, *Old Testament Theology*, 177; Hyatt, "Yahweh," 130-35; Bright, *History of Israel*, 87; Andersen, "Der Gott," 170-88.

13. Alt, "God of the Fathers," 1–77.

14. For further studies using form criticism see Noth, *Überlieferungsgeschichte des Pentateuch*, esp. 58-62; von Rad, *Problem of the Hexateuch*, esp. 62. Both these men were students of Alt and carried his method a step further. Their main concern in these works was with the relation of the various elements to the Pentateuch as a whole.

15. Gen 15:1; 24:12, 27, 42, 48; 31:42, 53; 32:9.

16. Gen 31:42; 32:9.

17. Gen 49:24; Ps 132:2, 5; Isa 1:24; 49:26; 60:16.

18. May, "Patriarchal Idea of God," 113-128; idem, "God of My Father," 158; Hyatt, "Yahweh," 130-35, contains references to other literature: Cross, "Jahweh," 225-59, and the works of Leslie, Liagre Böhl, Hooke, Albright, Eichrodt, von Rad, and Bright. Opposition to the idea has not been lacking: Steuernagel, *Jahwe und der Vätergötter*; Hoftijzer, *Verheissungen*; Ringgren, *Israelite Religion*, 17-26; Harrelson, "Religion of Israel," 335-38.

was Victor Maag's "Der Hirte Israels" ("The Shepherd of Israel") and his added comments in the paper "Malkût JHWH." These emphasized the nomadic (or seminomadic) situation of the patriarchs and the very fitting way in which their faith belonged to this way of life. God was experienced as a Divine Shepherd. He was the leader of the clan and accompanied them on their migration, protecting them and caring for their needs. He appeared in visions and voices to give instructions about their movements. His revelations contained commands and promises. The piety, so inspired, included trust, obedience, and solidarity with the tribe. Such religion tended toward the worship of one God.

This picture of patriarchal religion fits the Israelites' way of life. They are consistently pictured as seminomadic sheep herders and traders, moving from place to place on the fringe of settlements, in search of pasture.[19] A locally bound cult with complicated service and personnel would have been impossible for them.

In addition, the biblical account pictures Abraham breaking his relation with his family (Gen 12:1) and his former home in founding a group that moved at God's command and in search of fulfillment of his promise.[20] The break with family and subsequent transmigration is pictured as religiously motivated.[21] The work of Alt and Maag make it possible to describe the type of religion practiced and founded by the patriarchs.

Alt refers to the "gods of the Patriarchs." He believed that this type of religion led to separate cults of Abraham, Isaac, Jacob, and perhaps others, which Israel then identified with Yahweh.[22] They identified other El gods worshipped by their neighbors with their own God and made little effort to distinguish between them. The religious conflict seen from

---

19. Note the frequent moves from Shechem to Bethel to Hebron and even further, plus the fact that they are pictured as living in tents. Cf. Albright's thesis in *Yahweh and the God's of Canaan*, 56, that they were primarily traders using donkey caravans. He may well be right. This would explain their peaceful and friendly relation to the inhabitants of the land.

20. The theme of the Abraham cycle is this tension between the promise and the faith needed to respond.

21. Liagre Böhl, "Die Zeitalter Abrahams," 37–39; Eichrodt ("Religionsgeschichte Israels") calls the journey a *hejira;* see also Bright, *History of Israel,* 91; Alt, "God of the Fathers," 48. Maag's discussion ("Malkût JHWH," 134) in terms of parallel transmigrations occasioned by economic pressures may apply to the migration to and from Egypt, but there is no indication of decisive similar pressure to the case of Abraham.

22. But see Rowley, *Biblical Doctrine,* 29.

Exodus onward is not found in Genesis.[23] The evidence of the type "God of the Fathers" would tend toward a monolatrous practice, i.e., the worship of only one god even if others are recognized.[24] They worshipped one God who called them, went with them, cared for them. When they encountered other worshippers, they tended to accept their high gods (as distinct from demons and spirits) as other manifestations of their own true God.[25]

## THEOLOGICAL IMPLICATIONS OF THE PATRIARCHAL PATTERN

The Genesis accounts leave no doubt that this religious pattern was the result of the religious experience of the patriarchs. The knowledge of God that they transmitted to their children and through them to all posterity was the result of personal contacts with God. Through these they learned to say "the Lord is my shepherd" (Ps 23).

Understanding God as the divine Shepherd[26] was a natural way for wandering shepherds[27] to think of God. In this form God met their most pressing needs, inspired their grandest hopes, and led in their greatest deeds. It was also a powerful element in the faith that sustained the people in Babylonian captivity.

The stories about Abraham insist that in him God began a new chapter in the history of humankind. The relation to God on which Israel built began with Abraham. God's call to him cut all ties to previous family or land. God had both the power and the right to make that choice.

The figure of the divine Shepherd left an abiding impression on Israel. Among this people, a part of which maintained a living contact with a shepherd's life for a millennium, this form of faith must have first been transmitted through the stories told about the patriarchs at the various places related to them that were later documented in literature

---

23. See the revealing study of Gemser, "God in Genesis," 1–21.

24. Maag, "Der Hirte Israels," 14. This seems to be the general conclusion of Alt, "God of the Fathers," 26; Bright, *History of Israel*, 92; and others. Gordon ("Patriarchal Narratives," 58) speaks of a "monotheistic development."

25. Gemser, "God in Genesis," 1–21; Gordon, "Patriarchal Narratives," 58. Cf. Kilian, *Die Vorpriesterlichen Abrahamsüberlieferungen*; Schmidt, *Alttestamentlicher Glaube*.

26. Maag, "Der Hirte Israels," 14.

27. "Der Wegegott der wandernden Viehzüchter" (Eichrodt, "Religionsgeschichte Israels").

of abiding worth and inspiration.[28] Israel was proud to draw a high proportion of her leaders from shepherd families—Abraham, Jacob, Joseph, Moses, Elijah, David, Amos, and others.

When Israelites later went into exile, they took with them the lessons that patriarchal faith had taught. They continued to see themselves as a people especially chosen[29] and led. They kept their eyes on the homeland that God had chosen for Abraham and his descendants. They learned to live quietly amid potentially hostile neighbors. They expected the "blessing" of God and prayed for its effects on their neighbors (Gen 12:2–3).

The God of their fathers continued as their God, revealed through the patriarchs as personal and superior to all other powers. He had been revealed to be closely attached to their tribe, moving with them wherever they went. He was exalted in sovereign authority, yet was always near. He had chosen them, and they in obedience chose him. He cared for his people according to his promise. Yet his authority and his concern were for the whole world. His purpose for the faithful group, children of Abraham, extended finally to the whole world.

---

28. Ps 23; Ezek 34; Isa 40:11; 44:28; Zech 11. In the New Testament, Matt 15 and 25; John 21.

29. Rowley, *Biblical Doctrine*; see other literature on p. 61, notes 43–46.

## 4

## The Amphictyony: Ceremonies and Sanctuaries

THE TRADITIONS THAT LIE behind the twelve-tribe confederation of Israel[1] are based on stories of patriarchal origins (Jacob's twelve sons) and on stories of Israel's rescue from Egypt by Moses. All claim Abramic origins, but some point to the growth of the tribes in Canaan while others emphasize their approach to Canaan through the wilderness after a stay in Egypt.

Exod 6:13–27 says that Reuben, Simeon, and Levi were in Egypt with Moses and Aaron. Moses and Aaron are both Levites. Simeon settled in the south of Canaan near Beer Sheba. Reuben settled east of the Dead Sea close to Gad. The center for Aaronic priests was in Hebron (1 Chr 6:54–60). Moses is pictured in Deuteronomy as the leader of covenant renewal ceremonies east of Jordan in country that would become Reubenite.

Note that Joshua is an Ephraimite. If, as many scholars now think, many of the tribes as they are pictured in Judges did not participate in events in Egypt or Sinai but thought of themselves as descendants of Abraham (i.e., kinsmen of the "out of Egypt" group), they would have been prime candidates for an appeal to join together to achieve unity in face of the many challenges they faced (such as the pressures from the Philistine cities). If they came out to join the incoming tribes under Moses and agreed to make covenant to be one people in terms of the Mosaic covenants from Sinai and now renewed, they would be in position under their own leader (Joshua) to work toward power and unity in Canaan. The book of Joshua tells of Joshua leading a united group of twelve tribes across the Jordan. He prepares for a ceremony of covenant

---

1. Albertz, *From the Beginnings*, 70–71.

between all twelve tribes and Yahweh by being sure that everyone has been circumcised, thus affirming their adherence to Abramic origins and covenant. He then makes covenant again with the twelve tribes of Israel, and prepares for the conquest of the land.

According to the book of Judges, a political and military unity among the tribes hardly precedes the stories of Samuel and was not achieved before David. First Chronicles 27:16–22 tells of David's officers over the tribes of Israel: Reuben, Simeon, Levi, Aaron, Judah, Issachar, Zebulun, Naphtali, Ephraim, half-tribe Manasseh, half-tribe Manasseh in Gilead, Benjamin, and Dan (thirteen; Gad is missing). David and Solomon used other means of defining administrative districts, but they also dealt with the tribes. This unity did not outlive David and Solomon. The number twelve is meaningless for the years of the divided monarchy. Only as hopes for reuniting the land and the people resurface under Hezekiah and Josiah do they return. This is the period in which the traditions behind the written Torah take shape.

The amphictyony, that association of Israelite tribes devoted to the preservation of their God and locations of worship, functioned in the centuries before the monarchy. The descriptions in Deuteronomy and Joshua fit ceremonies held at Shechem, then at Shiloh and Gilgal, in which the original covenant was solemnized and in which succeeding renewals were celebrated.

Samuel's efforts to renew the sense of unity and purpose in the tribes included annual visits to Gilgal. The amphictyony was the model he followed before the people asked for a king. His speech to "all Israel" (1 Sam 12:1) before announcing Saul as king cites the names of Moses, Aaron, and Jacob (1 Sam 12:6–8) as well as Yahweh's action to bring Israel out of Egypt and into "this place" (1 Sam 12:8). His speech is cut from the same cloth as Deuteronomy, requiring the people to serve Yahweh (1 Sam 12:20) and calling on them to repent and return to Yahweh when they do evil (1 Sam 12:20–25). Parallel to these, Hebron was a gathering place for southern tribes and subtribes (1 Sam 30:30; 2 Sam 1–5).

In 1971 I wrote a detailed summary of research on the subject with an emphasis on worship forms and theological significance.[2] Now I want to extract something from that understanding of oral and written traditions that grew out of amphictyonic worship and that became the

---

2. Watts, *Basic Patterns*, 64–118.

books of Exodus, Leviticus, Numbers, Deuteronomy, and Samuel in the Hebrew Scriptures.

Three fundamental traditions support amphictyonic worship and faith. The first is the tradition celebrated in the Festival of Unleavened Bread, the story of the journey from Egypt to Canaan and of the conquest of the land. This festival, held annually at Gilgal, celebrated Israel's election as the people of Yahweh.

A second tradition centered on celebration of "the land" and included the ceremonies dividing the land between the tribes. It was celebrated at the Festival of Weeks at Gilgal and later at Shiloh. The ceremony recorded in Deut 26:5b–9 and the liturgical traditions behind Josh 9–23 fit here.

A third tradition is of covenant renewal celebrated in relation to the ark of the covenant (and/or the tent of meeting) in Hebron and Shechem at the Festival of Booths. They lay the foundations of the Sinai/Horeb traditions of Exodus and Deuteronomy.

## THE AMPHICTYONY

The Israelite amphictyony was called "the people of Yahweh," *'am yhwh*. This must be carefully distinguished from the term for nation: *goy*. A people is not necessarily a political entity expressing itself in terms of territory and effective authority. "The people" were "the assembly," *'edah* and *qahal*, of men capable of full participation in cultic ritual, in the execution of justice, and in war.[3] It was an assembled able-bodied male constituency.

The name of the amphictyonic people of Yahweh was Israel. The constituents of this assembly lived in Canaan, although there were large portions of the land that they did not control. They gathered as representatives of twelve tribes. The biblical accounts are interested almost exclusively in the larger whole of Israel's life and activity. These expressed a common faith and were bound up in a common worship. These factors gave Israel her distinctive character and claim to a particular contribution to humankind.

The amphictyony did not represent all the life of this people. The tribes continued their separate existence and regulated their own affairs in areas not touched by amphictyonic injunction.

---

3. Köhler, "Die Hebräische Rechtsgemeinde."

The variety of happenings in the book of Judges serves as a warning against trying to systematize and unify the picture of Israel's life in this period. Israel is pictured as a very loose confederation of tribes throughout the period of the judges. Most of her life was controlled by local customs and practices that varied greatly from tribe to tribe. The practice of justice was done by elders "in the gate" or local judges.[4] Tribes or groups of tribes were capable of engaging in war without reference to the federation as a whole (Josh 13:13–19).

Local sanctuaries continued to be the focus of most worship. There the "new moons and sabbaths" (Exod 12:2; Num 10:10; 28:11; Hos 2:11; Amos 8:5) were celebrated as well as other occasions. Local priests sacrificed (1 Sam 20:5–6) and conducted old and established rituals that may have varied greatly from place to place. The process of assimilation and identification threatened the purity and the power of Yahwistic faith. At the local shrines God might be worshipped as El of the fathers or as Baal or in other ways identified with deities that had been worshipped at that spot as long as one could remember.[5]

The unifying force in most amphictyonies lay in the maintenance of a common sanctuary.[6] Such a common sanctuary played a role in Israel as well. Her nomadic background is reflected in the moveable nature of its distinctive amphictyonic sanctuaries. Two of them served as symbols of the confederacy.

The most important was the ark of the covenant.[7] It was a box-like portable object that, more than any place or person, symbolized the gathered people of God. It was known to have existed through the history of the amphictyony in Canaan. The closest association of the ark was to covenant, as the name implies, but it was also a symbol of the theophany and everything that pertained to the amphictyony. Wherever the ark rested was the official meeting place of the people.

---

4. De Vaux, *Ancient Israel*, 152.

5. The place-of-sanctuary legends played a great role. See Keller, "Über einige alttestamentliche Heiligtumslegenden."

6. Noth, *History of Israel*, 91.

7. See the bibliography appended to Davies, "Ark of the Covenant," 1:226. In addition, see Nielsen, "Some Reflections," 61–74; Eissfeldt, "Lade und Gesetztafeln," 281–84; Dus, "Der Brauch," 1–16.

A second portable sanctuary is identified as the tent of meeting.[8] It origins are as obscure as its history. Although it figures prominently in the traditions, its place in the history of Israel in Canaan is difficult to trace; scholars have connected it with the ceremonies in Hebron.

A number of places are identified with amphictyonic meetings. These include Shechem,[9] Gilgal,[10] and Shiloh.[11] At these places the ark is reported to have stayed or covenant ceremonies had taken place. In certain periods of its history Israel gathered at these places for distinctive celebrations or deliberations. See a more detailed list of amphictyonic sites in chapter 2.

The amphictyony acted as a unit in three ways: in regular meetings at great festivals, in called gatherings for war, and to settle differences between the confederation and one or more tribes. In each of these functions Yahweh was understood to be present and involved. The amphictyonic leader or mediator represented him.[12] His right to lead was established by charismatic gifts that showed that God was working and speaking through him.

Moses was the archetype of such leadership.[13] Joshua[14] and the judges of Israel filled the role throughout a long period.[15] They combined military, judicial, and ritual functions and served the amphictyony in each of them. Priests also served the amphictyony.[16] Levitical priests were the recognized clan. Aaronide priests were dominant in Hebron.

---

8. Cf. the summary by Kutsch, "Zelt," 6:1893-94, and the bibliography cited there.

9. Harrelson, "City of Shechem"; Nielsen, *Shechem;* Anderson, "Place of Shechem," 10-19.

10. 1 Sam 7:16; 11:14—12:24; 13:7-15; 15:12, 33; Joshua, Judges, Hos 4:15; 9:15; 12:11; Amos 4:4; 5:5; Mic 6:5. Alt, "Josua," 13-29; Kraus, "Gilgal," 181-91; Muilenburg, "Site of Ancient Gilgal," 11-27.

11. Josh 18:1, 8, 10; 21:1-2; 22:9; Judg 18:31; 1 Sam 1:3, 9, 24; 2:14; 3:21; 4:4, 12. Kjaer, "Shiloh," 71-88.

12. The idea of Covenant Mediator has been presented in the work of Martin Noth and Gerhard von Rad. See also Kraus, *Worship in Israel,* passim.

13. Von Rad, *Old Testament Theology* 1:289-90.

14. Josh 24. Alt, "Josua," 13-29.

15. M. Noth, "Das Amt des Richters Israels," 404-17.

16. The clearest example comes from the family of Eli, which was well established at Shiloh, as the stories in 1 Sam 1-4 indicate.

The subject of holy war has received considerable attention[17] and has contributed to the understanding of many texts in the Old Testament. On such occasions the ʻam, "people" (male of course), were summoned in the name of Yahweh to fight against an enemy.[18] It was understood that they fought only for the cause of Yahweh[19] or that Yahweh himself fought with them[20] or on their behalf.[21] The soldiers prepared themselves by purification rites like those for worship.[22] The goal of the action was *herem*, "ban," in which the enemy, his cities, and all booty were to be destroyed.[23] They belonged to Yahweh and could not be appropriated to private use. Crimes against these rules of holy war were treated as crimes against holiness, not against morals. On these occasions Yahweh summoned the ʻam yhwh, "people of Yahweh,"[24] to war to maintain the integrity of the people of God from external threat.

On other occasions they could be summoned to meet a threat involving injustice between tribes in the confederation. They were forced to act against a member of the amphictyony to maintain the integrity of the group within itself. The case of Benjamin's failure to secure justice for a traveling Levite provides the classic example of such procedure (Judg 19–20).

The battles described in the book of Judges were defensive in character. With the possible exception of Gideon's battle, none gained new territory for Israel. It is a tribute to the power of amphictyonic faith that Israel survived at all. That Canaan lay in the backwash of a great political vacuum following the disintegration of Egyptian control of the area explains the historical possibility for this phenomenon. The period was brought to a close by the Philistine invasions.

Of more interest to us than the scattered reports of history that are impossible to piece together in a connected narrative are the traditions

---

17. Von Rad, *Holy War*; Fredriksson, *Jahwe als Krieger*; Tombs, "Ideas of War," 797–98; Christensen, *Transformation*; Lind, *Yahweh Is a Warrior*; Longman and Reid, *God Is a Warrior*.

18. As in Judg 4:6.

19. Judg 4:6–7.

20. Exod 14:14; Deut 9:3; 20:4; Judg 4:14.

21. Josh 10:10; Judg 4:15; 2 Sam 5:24.

22. 1 Sam 21:26.

23. Deut 7:4–6; Josh 6:17; 1 Sam 15:3.

24. Exod 17:16; Num 31:3.

## The Amphictyony: Ceremonies and Sanctuaries 53

that are constitutive of the amphictyony itself.[25] They contain the deposit of faith that, more than anything else, explains and expounds the meaning of the amphictyony.

The core of this material lies in two great complexes of tradition. The one most central to the very existence of the amphictyony is the covenant tradition.[26] Because the amphictyony was a covenant league, this material was indicative and constitutive of its very being. The basic material is recorded in the Sinai section of the Pentateuch (Exod 19–Num 10), to which the book of Deuteronomy and Josh 24 must be added. This tradition is composed of a variety of materials that have been transmitted through oral and written traditions, through different places and interpreters over a long period of time, before taking the literary forms that we now read.[27] Yet the fundamental unity with which the basic convictions of covenant relation to Yahweh are presented is both striking and significant.

The second great complex of tradition deals with the conquest of Canaan.[28] It includes the accounts of the deliverance from Egypt, the wilderness sojourn, and the actual conquest.[29] Traditions concerning the patriarchs are integrated into it.[30]

Moses figures in both traditions.[31] He and the ark along with the references by name to the twelve tribes constitute the motifs that bind the two traditions together and show them both to be essentially amphictyonic.

A particular feature of amphictyonic worship and faith was the place the people gave to historical events.[32] They understood revelation as something anchored in history. This is in contrast with worship patterns among their neighbors. Early Israel found meaning for life in his-

---

25. Noth, *History of Israel*, 109.
26. Ibid., 126.
27. Newman, "Sinai Covenant Traditions"; idem, *People of the Covenant*.
28. Von Rad, *Problem des Hexateuch*, 48.
29. Exodus through Joshua without the Sinai section and Deuteronomy.
30. Von Rad, *Problem des Hexateuch*, 62–63.
31. Von Rad, *Moses*, 9.
32. Weiser, *Glaube und Geschichte*, 35; Wright, *God Who Acts*; von Rad, *Old Testament Theology* 2:103; Noth, *Überlieferungsgeschichte des Pentateuch*, 45.

tory rather than in nature. Its festivals and their interpretations of faith kept alive the memory of those great events.[33]

The people understood that meaning lay not in any or all history but in particular events that reflected the "mighty acts" of God, events such as the exodus or the conquest of Canaan. This linear view of history had its roots in their nomadic heritage when they were constantly traveling toward some goal. The beginning of their history as a people was stamped by the memory of a divine oath made to their forefathers (Exod 3:6). In the amphictyonic celebrations, the content of this revelation and its implications were worked out and presented.

The content of historical revelation in the amphictyony consisted primarily of a series of events in which the name and person of Moses were prominent.[34] The amphictyonic account is a prehistory for the story of Israel, transmitted and interpreted in terms of faith and in forms of ritual for the edification of the believing community. The amphictyony was a believing and worshipping community. They were "the people of Yahweh." All amphictyonic life, practice, and meaning are wrapped into that phrase.

## AMPHICTYONIC WORSHIP

Two old sources in the Old Testament record a command to appear "before Yahweh" three times annually. Both the Covenant Code (Exod 23:14–17) and the so-called Yahwistic Decalogue (Exod 34:18–28) name these occasions as the Festivals of Unleavened Bread *(Mazzoth)*, Weeks, and Tabernacles *(Succoth)*.

The festal seasons were based on the calendar of harvest festivals determined by the agricultural year in Canaan.[35] They coincided with the beginning of the barley harvest (later fixed as the vernal equinox); the end of the wheat harvest (later fixed as seven weeks later);[36] and the end of the fall harvest (later fixed as the autumnal equinox),[37] also called

---

33. This process is often called "historicizing." Kraus, *Worship in Israel*, 45.

34. This is true in each of the documentary divisions as well as in the two complexes of tradition. Cf. Johnson, "Moses," 441.

35. Kraus, *Worship in Israel*, 26–92; de Vaux, *Ancient Israel*, 468–73.

36. Lev 23:15; Deut 16:9.

37. Exod 23:16; 34:22; Deut 16:13.

"the turn of the year,"[38] the last celebration before the beginning of the rains would inaugurate a new agricultural cycle.

At the three festivals, the Israelites gathered to renew their faith through dramatic ritual and reenactment of the basic events of their faith. They renewed their covenant with Yahweh. The Israelites had taken over the festival calendar of their new home, but the very nature of amphictyonic worship decisively changed the nature of the festivals and their interpretation. They became "festivals to Yahweh."[39] Their content turned on history, not nature with its seasons.

The fundamental statements of amphictyonic faith were rehearsed,[40] dramatized (as in Passover),[41] and preached[42] until they were absorbed by the people. The content of these ritual dramas and sermons provided Israel's confession of faith, composed of the salvation story and the law of God, which were eventually recorded to become the Pentateuch.

### The Feast of Unleavened Bread

*Mazzoth* was the first of the prescribed pilgrimage festivals. By using the early chapters of Joshua[43] and Exod 19:3b-8,[44] the outline of a festival of Israel's election held at Gilgal to celebrate both the exodus and the occupation of Canaan can be sketched.

1. The program of ritual events included a procession across the Jordan east to west to Gilgal in accordance with that described in Josh 3. The crossing symbolized simultaneously the Red Sea crossing (cf. Josh 4:23-24) and the crossing under Joshua at this same place. The celebrants took part in the appropriation of the land of promise. The procession ended at the sanctuary at Gilgal marked by the twelve stones taken from the bed of the Jordan (Josh 4).

2. As a part of the ritual, the assembly was reminded of the tenets of her "salvation history." Yahweh defeated Egypt to obtain the release

---

38. Exod 34:22 NIV.
39. Kraus, *Worship in Israel*, 48.
40. Deut 26:5-10.
41. Exod 12:14-20.
42. Deut 1:12.
43. Kraus, "Gilgal," 181-91; von Rad, *Das Formgeschichtliche Problem des Hexateuchs*, 53.
44. Wildberger, *Jahwes Eigentumsvolk*.

of Israel's slave forefathers, he protected them through the long wilderness journey, and he brought them to himself at Sinai and in Canaan. In the ritual he challenges them to heed his voice and keep covenant. He climaxes the occasion with the announcement of their election to be his own special possession, a kingdom of priests, a holy nation. The people respond with an oath of acceptance and fealty (Exod 19:8).[45]

3. A series of lesser motifs is mentioned in Josh 5.

a. The first motif is circumcision (Josh 5:2–5). The celebrants are exclusively male. No uncircumcised male could take part in Passover (Exod 12:48). Provision had to be made for persons that had not been circumcised before. The remark in Josh 5:9 that relates circumcision to "the reproach of Egypt" connects it with the themes of Passover and Unleavened Bread.

b. The second motif is a Passover celebration (Josh 5:2). Passover was intended for celebration in family groups, and even at such a great festival the celebratory meal was probably eaten in smaller groups at their tents. The date of the Passover was fixed by the full moon, whereas Unleavened Bread was determined by the week. This means they were not correlated with one another. But Passover's basic theme of preparation for the flight from Egypt as well as Yahweh's preservation of Israel's firstborn on Egypt's night of terror fit it nicely to the themes of *Mazzoth* just mentioned.

c. The third motif speaks of eating unleavened bread and parched grain taken from fields in Canaan for the first time (Josh 5:11–12). The manna that had been the means of survival in the wilderness had ceased. By eating this first meal of Canaanite flour, the worshipper testified to the faithfulness of God in bringing them to the promised land.

4. Every day of the seven days of the festival played a part in the last and climactic rite. The fall of Jericho reads like a ritual—a procession repeated daily for seven days, led by priests and instruments, and climaxed with a great shout (Josh 6).[46] Interspersed between the daily processions, the tales of conquest were rehearsed for each new generation

---

45. Ibid., 14–15.

46. Kraus, *Worship in Israel*, 164, recognizes this as a cultic demonstration of holy war, which was also related to the ark.

(Josh 7–12). Warnings of dire consequences for those who disobeyed Yahweh's orders or who covetously misused his gift of the land were repeated in stories like that of Achan's sin (Josh 7).

Gilgal was an important amphictyonic center from the conquest until the days of Saul. It was still active in the days of Hosea and Amos (eighth century BCE). With such important monuments to Israel's history as the stones at Gilgal, the ford of Jordan, and the ruins of Jericho, it could not be easily forgotten. What gave it abiding significance for all Israel was the festival of election celebrated there, a festival that preserved and repeated the traditions of the rescue from Egypt at the Red Sea, the providentially led wilderness journey, and the divine victory granted to them over their enemies in the land.

### The Festival of Weeks

The second festival was called Weeks, a shortened form of "seven weeks after unleavened bread."[47] It was less important than the other two and was celebrated for only one day.[48] There is little direct information about it in preexilic times, but the very fact that it regularly appears in the ritual calendars indicates that it filled a greater role than most studies have given it.

Von Rad connected Deut 26:5b–9, which was spoken as an Israelite brought the gift of firstfruits to the temple, with the Festival of Weeks.[49] This suggestion fits the emphasis on the grain harvest that is noted for it (Exod 23:16).

Von Rad then suggested that the entire occupation tradition belonged there with the Festival of Weeks and was celebrated at Gilgal. Both Kraus and Wildberger[50] have shown that the festival in which the occupation tradition fits is Unleavened Bread. But von Rad is correct in relating firstfruits to the Feast of Weeks and with it the credo of Deut 26. Every description of Weeks links it to Unleavened Bread through its place in the calendar and its name. It is unlikely that the two marked the beginning and the end of the grain harvest, but the relation remains.

---

47. Rylaarsdam, "Weeks, Fest of," 827–28; Kraus, *Worship in Israel*, 55–61.

48. Although Num 28:24 says that it too lasted seven days.

49. Von Rad, *Das Formgeschichtliche Problem des Hexateuchs*. For a different view, see Rost, *Das kleine Credo*.

50. Kraus, "Zur Geschichte des Passah-Massoth-Festes," 47–67; idem, *Worship in Israel*, 152; Wildberger, *Jahwes Eigentumsvolk*.

The theme of Weeks is "the land." Not the occupation, but the division and possession of the land are the central subject (Deut 26). Another block of Scripture with evidence of liturgical formulation, Josh 9–23, fits this description.

These chapters are only loosely linked to others of the Gilgal cycle. They hark back to the division that Moses had made for the two and a half tribes on the east side of Jordan (Num 32–36; Josh 13). They describe Joshua's allotment to Caleb, Judah, and Joseph at Gilgal (Josh 14–17) before depicting the general division to the other seven tribes at Shiloh (Josh 18–21).

Shiloh was one of the important amphictyonic sanctuaries from earliest times.[51] It would be a likely place for such gatherings. In repeated celebrations of the Feast of Weeks, the people emphasized thanksgiving for the land that belonged to Yahweh that he had allotted to Israel by tribes and by fathers' houses. The Israelites recognized their obligation to him through the bringing of the sacrifice of firstfruits.

### The Festival of Ingathering

The third pilgrimage festival was called the Festival of Ingatherings in the earliest reference (Exod 23:16; 34:22) but later bore the name Festival of Tabernacles (Deut 16:13, 16; Lev 23:34). Its history reflects changes that have left the final Jewish celebration complex.[52] Theories concerning its origin and history vary.

Murray Newman has suggested that there are traditions here from two amphictyonies.[53] A twelve-tribe amphictyony was centered in the ark of the covenant and had its seat at Shechem. The six-tribe amphictyony

---

51. The tent of meeting was there (Josh 18:1). Cf. Josh 22:9, 29. Judg 18:31 indicates its continued importance. Judg 21:19 refers to "the annual feast of Yahweh at Shiloh." This might be the Feast of Weeks or of Tabernacles (as Kutsch, "Erwägungen zur Gerschichte," 1–35, and others have assumed). The reference to the vineyards indicates a place, not a season, for the dances. The same may apply to the "feast of Yahweh" held annually at Shiloh mentioned in 1 Sam 1:3. The references to Samuel presuppose the presence of the ark (1 Sam 3:3; 4:3). Kraus, *Worship in Israel*, 125–26, has noted the possibility that more than one sanctuary could serve as amphictyonic centers simultaneously. The three festivals may have been celebrated in different centers with the ark present in each of them in turn.

52. See de Vaux, *Ancient Israel*, 495–506; Rylaarsdam, "Booths, Feast of," 455–58.

53. Newman, *People of the Covenant*. Von Rad, Kuschke, and Noth had already recognized the likelihood of two amphictyonies, one with the twelve tribes of Israel and the other with Judah and the southern clans.

centered in the tent of meeting and had its seat in Hebron. The first was custodian of the traditions recorded in the so-called E and D sources of the Pentateuch, while the second lies behind the J and P sources, as proponents of the source criticism teach.[54] Both amphictyonies claimed Mosaic authority and Mosaic traditions.

Newman suggests that the festivals were both concerned with covenant renewal.[55] Josh 24 portrays Shechem as the place where covenant ceremonies were regularly repeated. These ceremonies of covenant renewal were the place and time where and when the distinctive apodictic laws of the Decalogue—those laws that are stated as direct commandments—were pronounced. The festival may be understood as the *Sitz im Leben*, the cultural context, of the Sinai section of the Pentateuch and of Deuteronomy. This observation may now be refined by recognizing the parallel covenant ceremonies, both claiming Mosaic origin with portions of the Sinai sections assigned to each.

An outline of the covenant renewal ceremony at Shechem can be based on Deuteronomy, Josh 24, and the E source.

1. The pilgrims of the twelve tribes of "all Israel" appeared before the ark of the covenant. The ark was the focal point for a dramatic reproduction of theophany, an appearance of God. As thunder had stressed the presence of Yahweh at Sinai, so now the ceremonies surrounding the ark proclaimed the enthroned presence of Yahweh over the ark. The sound of the shofar, "ram's horn," symbolized his voice (Exod 19:16, 19; 20:18).

2. The proclamation of the name Yahweh formed a second climactic moment in the ceremony (Exod 20:2; Josh 24:2). God's name is intimately associated with his being.[56] Yahweh is God's covenant name, and in the proclamation he revealed himself and gave himself to Israel. In 2 Sam 6:2 this proclamation of the name is related to the ark.

3. A reminder of the mighty acts of Yahweh followed (Exod 20:2; Josh 24:2b–13). The name is given positive content through the deeds related to it. These deeds reveal him to be gracious to Israel, extending salvation in acts of power and in judgment against her enemies. The key event is the exodus, but elements from the stories of the patriarchs and

---

54. See further discussion of Wellhausen's concept of JEDP sources in chapter 7.

55. Kraus, *Worship in Israel*, 61, had already held this.

56. Von Rad (*Studies in Deuteronomy*, 38) has traced the distinctive "name theology" of Deuteronomy to this ceremony.

of the conquest of Canaan may be added (Josh 24:2b-13). The recital identifies Yahweh, but it also identifies the Israel of "today" with that of "yesterday," emphasizing the "you" and "we" as participants in the drama (Josh 24:5-7, 16-17).[57]

4. The proclamation of Yahweh's law was next (Exod 20-23; Deut 12:1—26:15; Josh 24:25). Most important are the distinctive apodictic statements (commands) of Yahweh's will that form the core and outline of covenant law (Exod 20:2-17; Deut 5:6-21; Lev 19:1-37). Around these are gathered the casuistic (conditional) regulations that govern all life for Israel, for Yahweh is recognized as the source of all law and order.

5. The ritual of the renunciation of foreign gods was an important element of early ceremonies (Josh 24:14-18; Gen 35:2-4).[58] It is a logical application of the first commandment for newcomers joining the confederation and for Israelites who fall back into idolatry. It is the negative side of the positive oath that follows.

6. The oath of obedience by which Israel accepted covenant conditions and by which the covenant became operative again formed the climax of the celebration (Exod 24:3, 7; Josh 24:24). The high and holy moment of rededication to Yahweh and to his covenant was surely one of the most significant and fruitful in Israel's experience. Israel belonged to God and he to them.

7. The serious and solemn meaning of covenant was emphasized by a repetition of apodictic requirements by alternating choirs in terms of blessings and curses on the mountains of Ebal and Gerezim near Shechem (Deut 27:11-26; Exod 23:20-33).

8. The covenant renewal was sealed by appropriate sacrifices and rites. Burnt offerings and peace offerings were prescribed, the latter being a communion meal, most fitting for the occasion (Exod 24:5; Deut 27:5-7). Blood was sprinkled on the altar and on the people (Exod 24:6-8). The provisions of the covenant were recorded for future reference (Exod 24:7; Deut 27:8; Josh 24:26). Perhaps the reference in Exod 24:5 to "young men of Israel" tells of a custom in which each year those coming of age to enter covenant serve at the altar.

57. Noth, "Die Vergegenwärtigung des Alten Testaments," 54-55.
58. Newman, *People of the Covenant*, 117; Muilenburg, "Form and Structure," 358-59; Alt, "Die Wallfahrt," 79-88; Kraus, *Worship in Israel*, 139-40; Nielsen, *Shechem*, 234-39; idem, "Burial of the Foreign Gods," 103-22.

It is possible that a parallel form of covenant renewal was practiced elsewhere and was later incorporated into the worship in Jerusalem.[59] The southern alternate does not enter into the discussion in this chapter because its influence on "all Israel" did not come until the time of the monarchy.

Covenant ceremonies of the type pictured were conducted by a covenant mediator. Moses was the original mediator (Exod 19–24; Deuteronomy). Afterward Joshua (Josh 24) and Samuel (1 Sam 3–12) served in this capacity. Samuel displayed the essential understanding of the amphictyony in his closing speech (1 Sam 12:1–17), an understanding he had gained from his training at the hand of Eli, priest at Shiloh (1 Sam 1:25–28; 2:26). The role of judge may have included this role. Such charismatic leaders tended to be replaced by Levitical priests whose regular duty was to care for the ark. By the time Deuteronomy is written, one of them portrays Moses *redivivus*, who speaks the "words of Moses," shaping Deuteronomy into a series of speeches of Moses.[60]

The ark was the cult symbol of the covenant. It was the presence of the ark that made covenant ritual legitimate. In this sense, Israel had a "central sanctuary" from the beginning. The people of Yahweh gathered wherever Yahweh chose for the ark to rest.

From the Shechem ark-covenant ceremonies came two bodies of covenant "tradition" that have found literary expression in the E source of the Tetrateuch (Genesis–Numbers) and in Deuteronomy. This traditional material was in the custody of the same Levitical circles that cared for the ark until its loss to the Philistines (1 Sam 4).

This worship was by "all Israel." The presence of the twelve tribes is presupposed. It was worship directed "to Yahweh." This was the distinctive covenant name. The historical content of the worship traditions, centering in the covenant at Sinai and the exodus-occupation accounts, sets them apart from all others. In them myth, as such, is eliminated. Revelation is

---

59. Newman (*People of the Covenant*, 140–48) has drawn upon the Yahwist account to suggest an outline for the gathering of the six-tribe amphictyony around the tent of meeting in Hebron one month earlier than that in Shechem: (a) gathering before the tent of meeting with the pilgrims probably living in tents (Exod 33:7–11); (b) the ritual theophany (Exod 19:9a, 11b–13; 34:1–4; 33:18–23; 34:5); (c) the announcement of Yahweh's name and nature (Exod 34:6); (d) proclamation of Yahweh's law (Exod 34:10–26); (e) the oath by the people or their representative (Exod 24:7); (f) the covenant meal (Exod 24:1–2, 9–11).

60. Von Rad, *Deuteronomium-Studien*, 8–9; Wright, "Book of Deuteronomy," 315–16.

understood in terms of historical events and Yahweh's "mighty acts" in history. The central purpose of worship was renewal of personal bonds with Yahweh, their God. The means used were personal confrontation, rehearsal of the traditions, and the renewal of vows of loyalty and faithfulness.[61] Ancient Near Eastern treaties show parallel outlines.

---

61. Documents of ancient Hittite and Assyrian treaties display a form similar to these. See McCarthy, *Treaty and Covenant*; idem, *Old Testament Covenant*. Weeks (*Admonition and Curse*, 174) says, "The best explanation of the . . . form is that those who compose the texts have a concept of relationships, especially of the loyalty due a suzerain and the beneficence he bestows."

5

## The Jerusalem Monarchy: David, Solomon's Temple

THE PEOPLE WHO FACED Samuel apparently felt that the institutions of amphictyony were insufficient for the needs of their day. They wanted more direct political and military leadership. They wanted a political structure to compete with their neighbors. They asked for a king. Samuel gave them Saul, who won some initial military success but who was not up to the other demands of kingship.[1]

David united the tribes and conquered the neighboring peoples. He chose Jerusalem as his capital and moved the ark there to give it religious relevance. This united monarchy lasted through the reign of Solomon. Solomon built a temple to Yahweh. He instituted a great annual festival of the reign of Yahweh in that temple. He brought prosperity and security through his foreign relations.

Solomon's son, Rehoboam, was not able to hold the kingdom together. Ten of the tribes became independent under Jeroboam and took the designation "kingdom of Israel" with them. Eventually Ahab would build Samaria as its capital. This northern kingdom came to an end under the Assyrian invasions of the late eighth century. Rehoboam and his successors governed the kingdom of Judah, with the tribe of Benjamin remaining loyal to him; his capital was Jerusalem. This southern kingdom survived the Assyrian invasions but was destroyed by the Babylonian king Nebuchadnezzar in 587 BCE.

The traditions of the monarchy are most clearly represented in the book of Psalms. They reflect ritual worship in a festival celebrating Yahweh's kingship, David's election and succession, and Yahweh's

---

1. This chapter is adapted from Watts, *Basic Patterns*, 119–58.

patronage of the temple in Jerusalem. The festival was celebrated annually in Jerusalem.[2]

The traditions of Jerusalem and its temple have informed the books of the Bible. The psalms sung in the temple under the monarchy and afterwards continue many traditions about David and Solomon. The records of the monarchy have structured the books of Kings and Chronicles.

## THE MONARCHICAL PATTERN

The introduction of the monarchy in Israel was an innovation so distinctive that it was bound to bring with it many changes in life and worship.[3] The conviction that the monarchy was a foreign institution containing many elements detrimental to Israel's faith may be detected in the account of its institution (1 Sam 8).[4] However, Saul's rule brought few major changes in Israel's life.

David's reign was quite another matter. The concept of kingship pictured in 2 Sam 7 with its dynastic election was very different from the amphictyonic doctrine of election of all Israel.[5] David's moves to consolidate his kingdom included shrewd use of Israel's ancient religious traditions as well as bold adaptation of ideals of Canaanite kingship to produce something new on the face of the land.

Parallel to the understanding of David's election as "the anointed of Yahweh" was the portrait of Jerusalem's choice to become the residence of Yahweh. Jerusalem as David's city became representative of the new institution of monarchy, its ideology and its cultus.

Typical of the Davidic blending of ancient Israelite faith with its new adaptations was the relation of the temple and the ark.[6] David brought the ark to Jerusalem, symbolizing his adherence to the old amphictyonic

---

2. Ibid., 129–37.

3. Bright, *History of Israel*, 163; Noth, *History of Israel*, 164; Rowley, "Israel, the History of," 754–57; Alt, "Königtum in Israel," 1709–12; Galling, "Das Königtum," 133–34; Soggin, *Das Königtum in Israel*; Wallis, *Geschichte and Überlieferung*; Seebass, "DieVorgeschichte," 155–71.

4. Irwin, "Samuel," 113–34; Mendelsohn, "Samuel's Denunciation," 17–22.

5. Rost, *Die Überlieferung*, helps to clarify a number of things in this connection. Newman, *People of the Covenant*, traces the view of a dynastic covenant back through the "J source," the Aaronide priests at Hebron, to the Kenites. He thinks David adopted a doctrine of a priestly dynasty to fit a royal dynasty.

6. Kraus, *Worship in Israel*, 207; Wright, *Biblical Archaeology*, 140–41.

faith of Israel.⁷ When Solomon placed the ark in the holy of holies in the temple, he was reaffirming his adherence to the old amphictyonic faith.

Jerusalem and the temple reflected a different turn. The temple was the seat of the official royal cult. It was, first of all, a royal chapel that served as a national shrine.⁸ Its ritual reflected Israel's changed status. Israel was now a nation among the nations. She maintained diplomatic missions in other countries and entertained such missions in Jerusalem. Her ritual reflected this relation to the nations and their cults. Solomon established private chapels for his wives and diplomatic representatives in Jerusalem.⁹ The temple cult spoke an important word on the issue. That Israel was even open to discuss or tolerate the worship of other gods on its soil showed what great changes had occurred. The architecture of the temple reflected the important contribution of Canaanite cult to its worship.¹⁰

The same blending of Israelite with Jerusalemite elements can be seen in the designation of priests. David brought Abiathar from the traditional Israelite amphictyonic worship at Shiloh to serve the ark in Jerusalem.¹¹ He also appointed Zadok to serve with him.¹² Zadok's background is obscure,¹³ but the suggestion that he is a representative of older Jerusalem worship is credible.¹⁴

Worship in Jerusalem during the kingdom turned on Zion's as well as David's election,¹⁵ the place of the temple as an official royal cult, and a combination of cult features from Salem and Israel.

---

7. Davies, "Ark of the Covenant," 1:254, with relevant literature.

8. Stinespring, "Temple, Jerusalem," 534-60.

9. 1 Kgs 9:24; 11:7-8.

10. K. Möhlenbrink, *Der Tempel Salomos*; Wright, *Biblical Archaeology*, 140-41; Ouellette, "Le Vestibule du temple," 365-78; Busink, *Der Tempel Salomos*.

11. 2 Sam 8:17; 15:24-29, 35; 19:11.

12. 2 Sam 15:24-37.

13. Rowley, "Zadok and Nehushtan," 113-41; idem, "Melchizedek and Zadok," 461-72.

14. Corney, "Zadok the Priest," 928-29; Judge, "Aaron, Zadok, and Abiathar," 70-74; Gunneweg, *Leviten und Priester*; Cody, *History of the Old Testament Priesthood*.

15. Kraus, *Worship in Israel*, 210-15.

The Old Testament is remarkably silent on the details of the Jerusalem cult.[16] The best sources for historical studies are the psalms,[17] especially those ascribed to David, and some of the early stories of the period, especially the biography of David in the books of Samuel. Later, Deuteronomic opposition seems to have silenced other witnesses.

## THE FESTIVAL

The three festivals of the amphictyony were apparently reduced to one in the latter days of the judges or in the early kingdom. It was called "the festival."[18] A clear description of the celebration of the festival in Jerusalem is needed for a proper interpretation of the psalms and of the religion of the era.

Sigmund Mowinckel[19] has sketched a celebration of Yahweh's enthronement, which climaxed a festival of several days. This fall festival included what in later Judaism came to be celebrated separately as the Day of Atonement, New Year's Day, and the Festival of Tabernacles.

The enthronement festival featured two high moments: (1) the re-creation of world order and life and (2) Yahweh's mounting the throne to "become"[20] king again. Cultic rites at this time included thanksgiving acts of bringing tithes and firstfruits; the sacramental meal of sacrifice, light, and fire ceremonies; water-pouring rites at the altar; dances around the altar with green twigs in hand; and a grand march around the walls of the temple. Yahweh's entrance was a cultic expression of his reign. According to Mowinckel, the festival was a repetition of the first enthronement and royal procession that sacramentally realized Yahweh's victory and its results in the present.[21]

---

16. Except for the dedication of the temple in 1 Kgs 8 and Chronicles' description of the choirs.

17. Especially Mowinckel, *Psalmenstudien*, vol. 2; idem, *Psalms in Israel's Worship*; A. R. Johnson, *Sacral Kingship*; Saur, *Die Königspsalmen*.

18. Judg 21:19; 1 Kgs 8:2; 12:32; see also John 7:2; A. R. Johnson, *Sacral Kingship*, 48. Note 1 Kgs 9:25 to the contrary, but see Kraus, *Worship in Israel*, 242.

19. *Psalmenstudien* 2:44–145. See also Tate, "Yahweh Reigns as King," 504–31; Watts, "Yahweh Malak Psalms," 341–48.

20. S. Mowinckel, *Psalmenstudien*. Cf. his defense of this interpretation in *Psalms in Israel's Worship* 1:115, and see Kapelrud, "Nochmals Jahwä Mālāk," 229–31.

21. Mowinckel, *Religion und Kultus*: "Das Kultdrama ist eine dramatische darstellung und ein Wiedererleben der 'Heilsgeschichte,' eine neue Verwirklichung von ihr" (p. 76). "Im Kultfest wird die Vergangenheit wiederholt und die Zukunft geschaffen" (p. 79).

The cult myths included those of creation and victory over the dragon, the victory over the gods, the exodus, the battle with the nations, judgment and determination of fate, and deliverance from great need.

In *He That Cometh*,[22] Mowinckel summarized the outline of the festival against the background of withered vegetation from summer's heat. It included two main sections: (1) Yahweh's epiphany in which he was revealed to the gathered people by recital of his mighty acts of combat and victory against chaos and death, resulting in the re-creation of the world, and (2) the restoration of his kingdom in which he "became" king, was enthroned, and then sat in judgment over his enemies, thereby assuring the well-being of his worshippers for the coming year. Mowinckel stresses the forward look of the festival long before these ideas were formulated into an eschatology, i.e., a belief regarding the end times.

The studies listed all acknowledge the existence of a royal or covenant festival.[23] There is also general agreement that it was a kind of new year festival. But there the agreement vanishes. It must have been a grand occasion with all the pomp and splendor the monarchy could afford, combining the themes of a Jerusalem royal new year with those of Israelite covenant renewal. David and Zion under Yahweh dominated and unified the themes.

The festival can best be described in terms of preparation, four main divisions, and a farewell ceremony. The first division celebrated the election of Zion as Yahweh's dwelling; the second his presence as king over heaven and earth; the third, his coming to judge; the last, his righteousness and *hesed*, "covenant love," to Israel, David, and Zion.[24]

Worship at a central sanctuary had always meant pilgrimage and was the high point of the year of religious life for the Israelites. With deep longing the pilgrims looked forward to their goal: the place of Yahweh's dwelling, the very presence of God.[25] The joy with which they

---

22. Other studies relevant to this topic are Mowinckel, *Zum Israelitischen Neujahr*; Oesterley, "Early Hebrew Festival Rituals," 122–46; Snaith, *Jewish New Year Festival*; Aalen, *Begriffe 'Licht' und 'Finsternis'*; Weiser, *Psalms*, 23–35; Kraus, *Die Königsherrschaft Gottes*; idem, *Psalmen* 1:xliii, 204; idem, *Worship in Israel*, 242.

23. Ringgren, "Enthronement Festival," 45–48.

24. The principal source of information for all of this comes from the psalms. Particularly important are the psalms that contain the cry "Yahweh reigns" (Pss 47, 93, 96, 97, 99). Watts, "Yahweh Malak Psalms," 341–48.

25. Ps 42:1–2; 84:3.

heard the call to pilgrimage is reflected in several psalms.[26] Not only faithful Israelites but representatives of "the nations" and the peoples were called.[27] Whether in reality this included only vassal nations is not clear. That they symbolized "the kings of the earth" is clear from the royal psalms that follow. Pilgrimage brought many hardships of travel[28] as well as the difficulties of transporting gifts and sacrifices.[29] But the expectant joy of the pilgrims put aside all other thoughts as they pressed toward the holy city.[30] As they traveled, they sang. Some of these songs have already been noted. In addition, the songs of Zion (Ps 137:3),[31] such as Pss 46, 48, 76, 84, 87, and 122, must have filled the valleys with melody as the columns of pilgrims moved through them. As they approached the city, praise was followed by prayers and wishes for Zion.[32]

Preparations in the temple were made at a fever pitch. The merchant and the innkeeper were busy with preparation for the "rush season," while temporary facilities for sacrificial animals and camps for the visitors were built. The ritual preparation of the temple, its personnel, and its holy things moved apace. The forerunner of the postexilic Day of Atonement belonged here.[33] The king, also, was prepared for his part in the ceremonies by appropriate rituals.

### Day One: Celebration of Zion as Yahweh's Dwelling

The festival began outside the city. It celebrated Yahweh's election of Zion and used the story of David's bringing the ark to Jerusalem (2 Sam 6).[34] The central ritual act was a processional that reenacted the story.

Ps 132 combines the themes of 2 Sam 6 and 7. It provides the best means for reconstructing this part of the festival.[35] The sacred ark was

---

26. Ps 122:1; perhaps also in 2:3.
27. Pss 47:1, 9; 69:2–5.
28. Ps 84:7.
29. Jer 41:5.
30. Pss 84:8; 122:2.
31. Gunkel, *Psalmen*, 309; Kraus, *Psalmen* 1:liii–liv.
32. Pss 122:6; 84:7–10.
33. Pedersen, *Israel III–IV*, 447.
34. Kraus, *Worship in Israel*, 196; Bentzen, "Cultic Use of the Story," 37–53; Porter, "Interpretation of 2 Samuel VI," 161–73; Mowinckel, *Psalms in Israel's Worship* 1:174–76.
35. Crim, *Royal Psalms*, 46–50.

hidden outside the city. Then the king with an escort of priests and companions looked for it. The gathering pilgrims looked on and waited. When it was found, a shout went up. "We heard of it in Ephrathah; we found it in the fields of Jaar" (Ps 132:6 RSV).

A bow or genuflection toward the holy mountain of God's presence would have been appropriate at this point. Hymns calling for ascending the holy mountain and entering the sanctuary started the procession.[36]

At the head of the procession moved the ark, whether carried by Levites, as in Priestly accounts,[37] or on a cart, as in the Samuel story,[38] cannot be determined. Officials of Jerusalem, including members of the royal court and priests, followed. Perhaps kings (or their representatives) from neighboring peoples were included.[39] Symbols of heavenly powers in the procession paid tribute to Yahweh, King over Israel, over Heaven and the Land, in Zion. The bulk of the procession was made up of pilgrims, joined by local worshippers.

The procession moved slowly with plenty of time for singing. Cult prophets[40] (and priest teachers) repeated ancient stories about the election of Zion to be Yahweh's dwelling, the first bringing of the ark,[41] and oracles concerning the election of the Davidic dynasty.[42] The procession was acting out dramatically the ancient story. Every worshipper was a part of the sacred drama, appropriating the meaning for himself in the present.[43] It was a kind of ritual dance.[44]

As the ark moved up the mountain, the assembly broke out into the ancient battle shout that traditionally greeted its appearance in battle.[45] The thunderous acclaim mixed with blasts from rams' horns. Ps 132 suggests that the election of the Davidic dynasty as well as of Zion was the theme of the celebrations in which Yahweh's covenant was acclaimed.

36. Pss 95:1-6; 99:9; 132:7-18. Mowinckel, *Psalms in Israel's Worship* 1:170-73.

37. Exod 25:14; 40:20-21; cf. Num 3:31; 4:5-15; Josh 3.

38. 2 Sam 6:3-5.

39. Cf. Psalm references addressed to the kings: Pss 2:10; 48:4; 68:29; 72:11; 139:4; 148:11.

40. A. R. Johnson, *Cultic Prophet*; Haldar, *Associations of Cult Prophets*.

41. 2 Sam 6.

42. 2 Sam 7.

43. Mowinckel, *Religion und Kultus*, 74; A. R. Johnson, *Sacral Kingship*, 65.

44. Cf. Sam 6:5; Ps. 42:5; 87:7; 150:4. Mowinckel, *Psalmenstudien* 2:112.

45. In Hebrew, *teru'a*. Kraus, *Psalmen* 1:146; Humbert, *La "teroua."*

Before the gates of the temple, the procession paused as priests intoned the "Torah of Entrance" still preserved in Pss 15:2 and 24:4.[46] The association of worship and ethics appears in them. Reminding the people of these requirements elicited repentance and a change of heart before entering the presence of Yahweh. Prophetic calls for repentance may also have been heard in the gate.[47] The preparations for entrance for a large group required much time. Rituals of purification were performed for pilgrims and the worshippers.

*Day Two: Yahweh Recognized as King over Heaven and Earth*

With all required rites of purification cared for and the pilgrims settled for their weeklong stay, the worshippers gathered inside the temple court to celebrate Yahweh's presence in Zion as the king over heaven and earth. The celebration emphasized three elements of the theme. First came Yahweh's appearance. This essential element of the older Israelite covenant ceremony was now observed in Zion's temple.[48] The ark, as the symbol of Yahweh's presence, made its ceremonial entrance to the words of Ps 24:7–10. The divine appearance (theophany) was very realistic and brought reminders of theophanies that had occurred at decisive points in Israel's history.[49]

The theophany reached its peak in the proclamation of the name: "Yahweh Zebaoth (of Hosts), King of Glory."[50] In this form God was introduced in Zion. This same formula had been used in traditions and rituals related to the ark in old Israel at Shiloh. The entrance of the ark had been greeted in similar fashion on great covenant-renewal occasions.

The great moment was greeted with praise and prostration.[51] The threefold sanctus of Isa 6:3 and psalms like Ps 150 were appropriate

---

46. Kraus, *Psalmen* 1:110–11, 193; Mowinckel, *Psalms in Israel's Worship*, 177; Koch, "Tempeleinlassliturgien und Dekaloge," 45–60.

47. Ps 95:8–11; Jer 2.

48. Weiser, *Psalms*, 29.

49. Weiser, "Die Darstellung der Theophanie," 513–31. Westermann *(Loben Gottes)* distinguishes between "theophany" and "epiphany."

50. On the meaning of the name, see Wambacq, *L'épethète divine*; Eissfeldt, "Jahwe Zebaoth," 128–50; Maag, "Jahwäs Heerscharen," 27–51; von Rad, *Old Testament Theology* 1:18; Crenshaw, "YHW$^e$ba'ōt Š$^e$mô," 156–75.

51. Ps 132:7.

songs. Instrumental music was played before the Divine King. Gifts and sacrifices were brought in abundance.

Around this feature of the worship clustered teachings concerning God's dwelling in his holy sanctuary.[52] Being related to the ark did not mean he was bound to it in any magic sense. He was understood to "come" to the temple, and they prayed for him to appear.[53] Jerusalem's worship owed much to old Sinai tradition, which made so much of "glory" theology,[54] as expressed in Exod 16:1—20:6 and Isaiah.

The ceremonies moved without a break from theophany to proclaim that Yahweh, who now appeared, was king forever.[55] The group of psalms that contain the shout, *Yahweh malakh*, "Yahweh is king,"[56] reflect the heart of meaning in this liturgy. Yahweh's rule over heaven and earth in might, righteousness, and justice is secure. This reign was witnessed in Zion by Israel, the peoples, and the nations.[57] They shouted "Yahweh is great and to be feared above all gods."[58]

Yahweh's rule over nature and the chaos powers was proclaimed[59] and perhaps dramatically represented.[60] This rule had been established in the primeval past through acts that made possible the creation of world order.[61] It continued undiminished in the present, guaranteeing cosmic natural order and stability.[62] The practical application of this teaching promised nature's blessings (especially rain) for the new year. Yahweh was celebrated as king because he is responsible for nature's order and

---

52. 1 Kgs 8:12–13; Ps 132:13–14.

53. Num 10:35; Pss 50:2; 80:2.

54. Von Rad, *Das Formgeschichtliche*, 18; idem, *Deuteronomium-Studien*, 28.

55. Kraus (*Worship in Israel*, 215) is correct in placing the Yahweh-king psalms here. But he does not imagine an important enough place to explain their rich content and weighty subject matter. Cf. Watts, "Yahweh Malak Psalms," 341–48.

56. Pss 93, 97, 99. See also Pss 47, 96. Other psalms echo the same themes and should be considered part of the group.

57. Pss 96:3; 97:6. The group also includes Pss 24:1–2, 7–9; 29:1–10; 33:2–12; 46:1–11; 48:1–10; 74:12–17; 86:8–10; 89:5–14; 93; 95:1–5; 103:19–22; 135:5–7; 145:3–13; 146:6–7; 148:1–13.

58. Pss 95:3; 96:4; 97:9; 135:5.

59. Pss 24:1–2, 7–9; 29:1–10; 33:2–12; 46:1–11; 48:1–10; 74:12–17; 86:8–10; 89:5–14; 93; 95:1–5; 96; 97:1–7; 103:19–22; 135:5–7; 145:3–13; 146:6–7; 148:1–13.

60. As A. R. Johnson (*Sacral Kingship*, 53) suggested.

61. Pss 24:2; 93:2; and others.

62. Pss 96:10; 97:11–12.

blessing. Nature testified to his power, faithfulness, and righteousness. All expressions of nature's bounty belonged to him. He made, established, and judged them. Key words are "established"[63] and "forever."[64]

The rule of Yahweh over the cosmos was characterized by might, righteousness, and justice.[65] He was faithful and true in all his acts. His rule was witnessed by creation and nature.[66] It had been established in the past and continued in the present. Because of it, the future was secure. It had been established over opposition and continued despite threats. As a result, the stability and permanence of nature's order were guaranteed by Yahweh's rule and power.

The second element spoke of his rule over the heavens and the gods.[67] The emphasis was upon present rule. No hint is given as to how this ascendancy had been achieved, and nothing is mentioned about any sort of opposition. Yahweh's rule is absolute. He allows no competition from other powers. Therefore, the future poses no threat to those who believe in him and worship him.[68]

The third element proclaimed his rule over the land, for all the land belongs to him.[69] The time viewpoint is again present, but it looks to the future. The mood is one of trembling joy at his present reign and hope for his righteous judgment in the future. He is coming to judge the land.[70] He is exercising his reign over the nations and over Israel.[71] All of this is revealed in Zion.[72]

Having established Yahweh's reign over cosmos, heavens, and the land, the ceremonies moved to the relation of the mighty king to the gathered congregation: to Israel and the symbolic representatives of the land's rulers. A second group of psalms dealing with Yahweh's kingship pro-

---

63. Pss 24:2; 89:37; 93:1–2; 96:10; 119:90.

64. Pss 10:16; 45:6; 48:8; 89:37; 93:2. The word is *'olam,* "an age or era," i.e., "from the age" or "to the age." The idea of an infinite "forever" without any end is not known in Hebrew.

65. Ps 97:2, 6.

66. Ps 89:1–2.

67. Pss 96:3; 97:4–5; 98:7–9; 29:1; 135:5–7.

68. Ps 96:10–13.

69. Ps 95:4–5.

70. Pss 96:13; 98:9.

71. Ps 96:3, 10.

72. Pss 48:2; 97:8.

claimed the basis of his rule in terms of his historical relation to Israel.[73] They signaled a development in the ritual as well as in psalmnody.

Yahweh is king over Israel and the nations. His rule is proved by the justice he had established in Israel and his faithfulness on her behalf. He had given her Canaan.[74] He had exercised covenant love and faithfulness toward her.[75] He had established justice in Jacob.[76] These testified to his rule established in the past and continued in the present. The worshipping community was called upon to praise him and to tremble before him.[77]

The theme of expectancy that Yahweh is coming to judge the land, including Israel and the nations, ran throughout this part of the festival.[78] Yahweh's epiphany preceded the judgment scene.[79]

The joyous mood of these festal themes may have continued for two or three days. The climax of the festival occurred during the last two days.

### Day Six: Yahweh's Coming as Judge

A group of psalms portrayed Yahweh enthroned for judgment.[80] Yahweh represents justice for the widow, the orphan, and all that are oppressed. He is called upon to correct injustice and to establish righteous judgment in the land. Once he acts as judge among the gods,[81] they are reproved for failure to bring justice for individuals in the land. These psalms served as a bridge between the themes of divine reign and judgment.

The climactic latter half of the festival featured Yahweh-King coming to judge. Heavens and Earth are his witnesses.[82] Israel is summoned before Yahweh in covenant judgment.[83] This element of old amphic-

---

73. Ps 47.
74. Ps 47:4.
75. Ps 98:3.
76. Ps 99:4.
77. Pss 98:4–6; 99:3.
78. Ps 98:9.
79. Not the reverse. Mowinckel and others thought that the coronation as king was the end and climax of the festival, but this is wrong. The festival begins with celebration of his rule.
80. Pss 9:7–12; 10:16; in Ps 33 the element of wisdom is particularly strong.
81. Ps 82.
82. Ps 50:1–6; Deut 32:1; Isa 1:2.
83. Ps 50:7–23.

tyonic worship lived on in Jerusalem, although it faded in significance behind themes related to the Davidic house. Ps 50 presents a scene of judgment that has several parallels in Old Testament literature.[84] The frequency with which the motif occurs in the classic prophets is witness to the continuation of the practice during the monarchy.

Israel was called to give evidence of her loyalty and obedience in the covenant[85] while cult prophets and priests recited the evidence of Yahweh's faithfulness and righteous acts on her behalf.[86] Israel stood condemned by her failure to keep covenant.

In Jerusalem the climax of judgment centered in that over the Davidic house.[87] This was also covenant judgment. At the same time and through the same cult drama, Yahweh's judgment of the nations was portrayed.[88]

In elaborate preparation for the judgment drama, the covenant basis of the Davidic king's relation to Yahweh was recited.[89] Prophetic speeches against the "nations" were included. This is the *Sitz im Leben* (place in life) of "foreign prophecies."[90] The combination of "foreign prophecies" with judgment on Israel in Amos[91] demonstrates how closely the two were linked in ritual.

The issue was critical: nothing less than the continued existence of Davidic reign in Zion.[92] The form that the drama assumed was ritual combat. Enemy forces representing darkness, evil, and the nations gathered against the king and against Zion in the gathering dusk.[93] The king had to stand against them to demonstrate his own righteousness and justice, the virtue of his elect status and blameless rule. Yahweh allowed the combat as a test by ordeal of his obedience and faithful fulfillment of covenant stipulations.[94]

---

84. Deut 32:1–43; Isa 1:2–3; Jer 2:4–13; Mic 6:1–8.
85. Deut 32:5, 15–33; Mic 6:1–8.
86. Deut 32:4, 6, 14; Mic 6:3–8.
87. A. R. Johnson, *Sacral Kingship*, 94; Engnell, *Studies in Divine Kingship*.
88. Widengren, *Sakrales Königtum*, 65.
89. 2 Sam 7; Ps 89:4–5, 19–37.
90. Isa 13–23; Jer 46–51; Ezek 25–32; Obadiah, Nahum, and others.
91. Amos 1–2.
92. Ps 89:35–45 and parallels.
93. A. R. Johnson, *Sacral Kingship*, 103.
94. Ibid.

Through the night the mock battle raged.⁹⁵ The king and his forces were pressed back and out of the city. He was defeated and humiliated to the point of death.⁹⁶ His cause was apparently hopeless as he pleaded for aid from on high, for the vindication of his righteous cause, for salvation from the very jaws of death.⁹⁷ His pleas of innocence and righteousness underline the vicarious nature of his trial.⁹⁸

The drama portrayed a bitter and critical moment in which the fate of the nation hung in the balance. The course of the battle had convincingly demonstrated the king's inability to perform his office in his own strength. His helpless plight showed his utter dependence on Yahweh.⁹⁹ Without Yahweh's help he could maintain neither life nor realm. Yahweh's proclamation that the hope of salvation, light, and blessing for the nations depended on David's reign stressed the ironic point that they could actually lose that hope of life by winning their battle against him.

In the deep darkness before dawn, the judgment by ordeal in combat reached its climax. It showed, through the rebellion of the nations against Yahweh and his anointed, Israel's lack of "wholeness" and spiritual vitality, which, represented in the king, made him too weak to withstand the assaults of the nations. The king was helpless to master the situation in his own strength. The hour was dark, bitter, humiliating, and apparently hopeless.

### Day Seven: Yahweh's Righteousness and Covenant Loyalty

At dawn everything changed. When the king appeared to be on the verge of death, Yahweh intervened, granted him a reprieve from certain destruction, and routed the enemies that threatened him, giving him new life and strength.

The sign that revealed this joyful turn of events was a cloudless sunrise: a "day of light."¹⁰⁰ On the equinox, the rays of the rising sun could shine through the great east door of the temple, opened only for this occasion, and fall in full glory on the brass altar before the holy place.¹⁰¹

95. Ps 134; Isa 30:29 for references to night rituals.
96. Pss 89:38–45; 18:4–5.
97. Ps 18:6.
98. Pss 18:20–29; 89:38; 101.
99. A. R. Johnson, *Sacral Kingship*, 108.
100. Amos 5:18.
101. Morgenstern, "Amos Studies I," 19–40.

The "new day" began with a ceremony by Gihon's pool.[102] The king had been driven out of the city into the Kidron valley during the night of terror and humiliation. At Gihon's pool a ceremony took place that symbolized God's gracious and saving act on his behalf. The waters symbolized restoration to life and vigor.[103]

A joyful and victorious procession then mounted the hill of Zion for the second time that week.[104] The king led the way. God's gracious act had rehabilitated him. Yahweh's ancient promises to David his forefather had been kept.

The king rode his royal mule or horse while the crowd outdid themselves in adulation and jubilation. They had been waiting in tense expectation through the night for this moment, and their joy knew no bounds.[105] They waved palm branches and sang the praises of Yahweh, who had not forsaken their king, his anointed.[106] The king was exalted, carried along on a platform above the heads of the people.[107]

### The Enthronement Rituals

The procession moved through the temple gates for the great enthronement ceremony.[108] The ritual was equally one of covenant renewal, for in the reinstallation of the Davidic king on his throne, Yahweh's covenant with David and through him with Israel was reconfirmed.[109] When the king mounted the throne, a prophetic proclamation repeated the promises made to David, the king's forefather, and announced that they were now confirmed for his son.[110] Yahweh made him king in Zion on the throne of David.[111]

---

102. 1 Kgs 1:38–40; Ps 68:26. Steinmann, *David*, 144–45.

103. A. R. Johnson (*Sacral Kingship*, 110) suggests that this was an immersion into the water symbolizing death to the old and being raised to new life by his God.

104. Ps 118:15–21.

105. Ps 118:22–27a.

106. Ps 118:27–29.

107. 2 Kgs 11:14.

108. Ps 118:20–21.

109. Note that this does not necessarily imply the renewal of contractual relations between king and people at regular intervals. Kraus, *Worship in Israel*, 223.

110. 2 Sam 7; Ps 132.

111. Pss 2:6; 18:50; 89:3, 20, 35, 49.

A second prophetic announcement spoke the words of adoption that made the king Yahweh's "son."[112] He was Yahweh's vice-regent on earth. God's blessings for the land would be realized through him.[113] Yahweh's rule over the nations would be accomplished through him.[114] It was not simply the kingdom of Israel that had its seat in Zion. It was the kingdom of Yahweh of Hosts, ruler of heaven, the universe, and the world.[115] The newly (re)enthroned Davidic king had a key role to play in the universal kingdom as well as in Israel.

A third element of the enthronement ceremony was performed by the priests. The Davidic king was installed as priest-king after the order of Melchizedek.[116] Succession to the ancient priesthood of Jebusite Jerusalem belonged here. It symbolized the deeply religious role of the king in Zion. His office was not primarily administrative or military, but religious. It was a sacral kingship.

Scarcely were the official enthronement ceremonies in and over Zion complete before prophetic announcements proclaimed the king's rule "over the nations."[117] Those who had so recently been hounding him through the city streets now bowed submissively at his feet,[118] and all other kings of the land were called upon to follow their example.[119] The king's reaction to rebellion would be swift retribution, for he was the agent of Yahweh.[120] Rebellion against him was understood to be directed against Yahweh, his God.

The ceremonies looked to the future.[121] The truth in these cultic acts and words was in the proclamation of Yahweh's determination to bring all nations and peoples in submission to him, to make his kingdom supreme in all the land and the world.[122] Israel, Zion, and their king had

---

112. Pss 2:7; 110:3.
113. A. R. Johnson, *Sacral Kingship*, 58–59.
114. Ps 110:2.
115. A. R. Johnson, *Sacral Kingship*, 124–26.
116. Ps 110:2. Kraus, *Worship in Israel*, 223.
117. Ps 2.
118. Ps 18:43–45.
119. Ps 110:2.
120. Pss 2:9; 21:9–10; and others.
121. A. R. Johnson, *Sacral Kingship*, 124: "Cosmogony, however, gives place to eschatology."
122. Ps 22:27–31.

key roles to play in the establishment of that kingdom. When prophets stood up to proclaim that cultic imagery would become historical reality, they were drawing upon these rituals for their visions.[123]

The enthronement ceremonies ended with Yahweh's blessings being pronounced on the king, on Israel, and on the nations that submitted to Yahweh and his anointed in Zion.[124] The ark moved into the holy of holies, the symbol of Yahweh dwelling in Zion. The great festival had come to an end. There remained only the farewell ceremonies and blessings with which the pilgrims were sent on their way home,[125] having experienced the enthroning presence of Yahweh in Zion, confident that their lives, their nation, and the world were under his rule and blessing. They went home aware of a deep obligation to obedient service to God and king.[126]

---

123. Isa 2; Mic 4.
124. Ps 121.
125. Ps 138.
126. See McCarthy, *Old Testament Covenant* or *Treaty and Covenant*, for a summary.

PART 2

Jewish Literature from Josiah to the Late
Persian Period

# 6

# Beginnings

## WRITING IN ISRAEL AND IN THE OLD TESTAMENT

As S. A. Nigosian informs us,

> Almost all the collections in the Old Testament were originally written in Hebrew by Israelite authors (ancestors of modern Jews) who lived in ancient times in a small territory known as Canaan, Palestine, or Israel, bordering on the Mediterranean Sea. This piece of land was geographically and historically a small part of a vast area known today as the Middle East, and in earlier times characterized as the ancient Near East. One of the most lasting achievements introduced by the peoples of the ancient Near East was the art of writing.[1]

Three systems of writing were used in the ancient Near East.

(1) Cuneiform employed a wedge-shaped instrument to produce combinations of triangles and lines in tablets of soft clay, each representing a syllable of a language and was used by the Sumerians around 2800 BCE.[2]

(2) Hieroglyphics employed symbols that stood for words, a pictographic system of writing. This system appeared in Egypt about the same time that cuneiform appeared in Sumeria. It developed more fluid signs for pen and ink in the form of hieratic writing.

(3) An alphabetic system was used by the northwestern Semites of the Sinai, Phoenicia, and in nearby Syria-Palestine in the form of

---

1. Nigosian, *From Ancient Writings*, 1.
2. Ibid., 2.

Aramaic, by at least 1400 BCE.[3] Ugarit's temple had its myths recorded on clay tablets in a cuneiform alphabet. Ugarit is a Semitic language, a form of Canaanite. But other peoples in the area used letter-forms derived from Egyptian hieratic writing for their alphabets.

Israelites joined other Semitic groups in adopting the alphabet. The court of David and Solomon was the first to have the strength and affluence to be able to afford a system of scribes and scribal training. They likely depended on Hiram of Tyre (Phoenician) for aid in developing these skills, just as they depended on his builders for the temple (2 Sam 5:11; 1 Kgs 5, 9). Solomon's widespread economic enterprises and international relations would have required extensive scribal skills and activities. Second Samuel 20:25 and 1 Chr 2:55 record a clan of scribes.

The Israelite scribes first used a style known as primitive or round Hebrew letters. Scribes in the sixth and fifth centuries BCE turned to the use of Aramaic or square letters. Only the Samaritan Pentateuch continues to be written and read in the older style.

Early Hebrew undoubtedly had several dialects. In Hezekiah's reign, Hebrew culture and traditions came to be centered in Judah since it was all that was left of the twelve tribes, and the language of Judah became the standard Hebrew, which shaped the Scriptures.

Biblical Hebrew uses two words to designate writing and things written. The first is *katabh*, "write." The second is *safar*, "count or write." You see the related noun, *sefer*, translated as "scroll." These words are found frequently in virtually all the books of the Hebrew Bible, and particularly in the titles of scrolls. See appendix A for named scrolls, many of which use these Hebrew words in their names.

The related word *sofer* means "scribe." These scribes were not simply secretaries in the modern sense. They were "counters" (BDB "enumerators"). There was much around the royal court that needed counting: money, supplies, army musters, the king's age, and much more. These results of counting needed to be written down and filed. It is no wonder that the Old Testament has so many lists and numbers. That is precisely what the scribes were trained to do. Even in the ninth century CE, as they produced many copies of the Hebrew Scriptures, their method of quality control lay in counting words and letters.

The chronicler is particularly concerned that readers know he is using written documents. He repeatedly uses the question "Is it not

3. Ibid.

written in (*ketubim*) . . . ?" (see 1 Chr 9:1: "written in the *scroll* of the kings of Israel"—note that the Chronicler here has access to records from northern Israel). Another word, *devarim*, "words, speeches, sayings, acts," in the title of scrolls is appropriate where the written scroll is a transcript of things that had been transmitted and presented orally. The term is used of Moses in Deut 1:1; of a song in Deut 31:1; 32:44; of David in 2 Chr 29:30; and of the wise in Prov 1:6; 22:17; 30:1; 31:1; Eccl 1:1; 9:11; 12:11; Jer 1:1; Amos 1:1; Neh 1:1. The word appears again in 1 Chr 29:29: "The *words* of David the king . . . behold them written in . . . the *words* of Nathan the prophet and in the *words* of Gad the visionary." The Chronicler thinks of Nathan and Gad as being in David's retinue in much the same way that a scribe would be in later days. Both of them had written scrolls that the Chronicler uses. In two instances he even cites midrashes (commentaries) on these scrolls: "The rest of the *words* of Solomon . . . written on the *words* of Nathan the prophet[4] and on the prophecy of Ahijah the Shilonite[5] and in the vision of Iddo the Visionary[6] concerning Jeroboam the son of Nebat" (2 Chr 9:29). See further named scrolls from the Chronicler and beyond in appendix A.

A frequent word used for speaking of words, writing, or reading, especially the words of God, is *torah*. The word means "instruction" or "direction." Moses, the one who hears, receives the *torah* and writes and reads "the words of Yahweh," for example in Exod 24:3, 4, 7.

Ezra is called a scribe and is a specialist in *torah*, which is then defined in terms of laws and decrees, as in Ezra 7:11 and 9:4.

*Torah* can refer to one of the codes of law. There are three of these in the Pentateuch: the Covenant Code, the Deuteronomic code, and the Priestly Code. In the Pentateuch, Torah is always related to Moses, to the words of God, and to having been written down. Moses is never called a scribe, but he is pictured as writing the laws (e.g., the Ten Commandments, Exod 34:27, 28). The Covenant Code is spoken by God (Exod 19:3) and spoken to the people (19:3; 24:3), but "the book of the covenant" is read to the people (Exod 24:7): "Moses wrote down this Torah and gave it to the priests" (Deut 31:9; see also 31:24; 31:22).

Torah becomes the name of the Pentateuch, the five books of Moses.

---

4. See further references to Nathan in 2 Sam 7:2, 17; 12:1, 25; 1 Kgs 1:10, 22, 34.
5. See Ahijah also in 1 Kgs 11:29; 12:15; 14:2, 4, 6.
6. See also 2 Chr 12:15 for mention of Iddo.

The code of the covenant also employs the word *torah* along with other words that describe Yahweh's communication of instruction to his people. The word *torah* appears in the Deuteronomic code in Deuteronomy, in the writings of the Deuteronomist in Kings (and Joshua?), and in the Deuteronomistic sources in Chronicles.

## HEZEKIAH'S JUDAH: SEEDBED FOR LITERATURE

Hezekiah's reign (725–687 BCE) stands out in the Hebrew Scriptures. He came to rule at the time that Israel, his northern neighbor and rival, was being taken into exile. He survived because of an arrangement made by his father with the Assyrian conquerors, an arrangement that left him his throne and realm in exchange for tribute and loyalty.

Hezekiah received refugees from Israel, including priests, prophets, scribes, and wise men. Until his time, Israel had been the stronger and more culturally advanced of the two kingdoms. Judah was strengthened by this influx of population and by the skills and tradition that they brought with them.

Hezekiah recognized the value of the intellectual traditions and encouraged their cultivation. Whole villages of priests and scribes sprouted on the Judean countryside. While Jerusalem still honored the songs and traditions of David and Solomon, the priest and Levite villages brought reminders of the older Mosaic faith and culture. Since the move had torn the traditions from the roots, the bearers of those traditions set about conserving them in writing. Unemployed scribes abounded and were put to work. The king encouraged and supported these endeavors but insisted that they maintain standards of a common language: the Judean dialect as known and practiced in that day. Many scribes worked for the royal establishment, where they were schooled in the niceties of the language.

Some scribal villages specialized in Mosaic materials from Gilgal, Shiloh, Hebron, or Shechem. Their sources and advisors were priests, Levites, narrators, prophets, and singers who had worked in those places. Other villages housed former royal scribes from Israel who had brought with them records from Samaria's archives. In Jerusalem, Hezekiah oversaw his favorite project, the collection of wise sayings from Solomon's day, including some from neighboring countries. The temple singers had their own scribes who were busy transcribing psalms from temple ritual and royal festivals.

Leather scrolls were processed for the writing, and inks of various kinds were available. Archives of finished materials were in the palace, in the temple, and in the scribes' own schools.

This did not mean that the people at large learned how to read and write. That would come much later. Both writing and reading were specialized skills practiced by professional experts, but reading aloud to the people in the court and in the village gate became widely popular.

This book portrays the oral culture that supported the production of written literature and sketches the process by which the Hebrew Scriptures came into being, as well as its Greek translation and supporting documents that lay behind the New Testament.

## EDUCATION IN ISRAEL

Moses is the Hebrew Bible's ultimate model of the teacher and educator (as is illustrated in Exodus through Deuteronomy). He not only receives the law from God but also teaches it to the people.

Deuteronomy models the way that "all Israel" was to be instructed in the way God wanted them to live. It also instructs families in the education that they should provide family members (Deut 6:20–25), telling them how they should converse about the laws (Deut 6:7), should use the laws as symbols for prayers and devotions (Deut 6:8), and should display them prominently in their homes (Deut 6:9).

The story of Samuel (1 Sam 1–3) demonstrates how priests instructed candidates for their highly select vocation in their own homes and how Samuel continued this through a lifetime.

Ezra is presented as one highly trained in torah. His presentation of the written torah to all the people was a continuation of this ministry of teaching. The prophets from Elijah to Jeremiah and beyond were also involved in the education of the people in how to be the people of God. Wise men and the practitioners of wisdom played their role as well.

The annual festivals were occasions for such instruction and exhortation. The sacred places associated with ancient persons also played their roles. The entire structure and process help "enculturate" the people into being the unique and separate people that were called of God and used of God to reveal himself and his will. Carr is correct about this. The written Scripture and its public reading served this function to extend the ministry of prophets, priests, festivals, temples, and storytellers. There was an unbroken chain of tradition dedicated to that end.

## ENCULTURATION OF ELITES

Carr's concept of enculturation was introduced in chapter 2. As we begin discussion of the literary period, it is helpful to consider Carr's notion of enculturation as it applies to the educated elite of Judaism in relation to such developments in neighboring cultures.[7] In these cultures writing and the oral reading of written texts functioned as a means of enculturating an elite group into the secrets and foundations of the unit. This was true for the priests of Egyptian temples as well.

The insight that the reading of texts is educational in purpose and effect and that the ultimate goal is shaping the hearts and minds of a people, unifying them and identifying them in distinction from others, is accurate. The process is universal and takes different forms in various places. It usually involves a distinctive language. It often defines the elite in terms of a dominant culture and the education as a means of functioning in that culture. Latin served that purpose in Europe through the Middle Ages, being the language of the universities, the church, and the courts. In the cantons of German-speaking Switzerland, "high German" serves that purpose for a people that have dialects as their native tongue.

Sometimes a culture has to assert itself within a population. In seventeenth-century England, a strong movement with political implications worked to standardize English as the official national language. With the encouragement of the crown, the Bible was put into a good English translation so that its reading in the services every Sunday could school the people in the proper use and pronunciation of the medium. Shakespeare's plays performed the same function for a different audience. English people were enculturated into a unifying language.

Colonial administrations did the same thing in French, or Spanish, or English, in many parts of the world. Chinese ruling classes imposed a language and culture on a region that was used to many dialects. Usually these have been means by which ruling or dominant cultures have shaped the people under their control. A major ancient movement of this kind was that of Hellenistic rulers who followed the military conquests of Alexander the Great by establishing *gymnasia* where the Greek language and Greek games and way of life would be learned. They established an elite culture that flourished throughout the region and continued in Roman administration for centuries.

---

7. Carr, *Writing on the Tablet of the Heart*.

Israel faced this problem when it entered Canaan. It was a small and scattered people who used a dialect of Canaanite similar to those spoken by its neighbors. It tried to establish a religious form for itself different from its neighbors. Its efforts at enculturation in that early period were less than successful, as the biblical story shows, even as it gained political ascendancy in the region.

When larger nations (Assyria and Babylon) occupied the area, the problem was redefined. As exiles in foreign lands and a subject people at home, the Israelites had to find a means to help maintain their identity and respect. The Assyrian refugees from the kingdom of Israel apparently did not succeed. We have no records of their continued existence as a people.

The language of enculturation (Hebrew) was defined by the efforts of King Hezekiah to assemble scholars and scribes to his small kingdom to record the traditions of the twin kingdoms and of the people who had preceded them. Records and memories were assembled from sanctuaries and sacred places throughout the land.

A century later under King Josiah, a book of the Torah of Moses was found, and he had it read aloud to all the people. The covenant that it proposed was renewed, and its festivals were reconstituted around the worship of Yahweh alone.

Just over two decades later, King Jehoiachin and three thousand of the elite of his kingdom were banished to Babylon. Those who went with him must have included priests and scribes, who were permitted a high status and respectable living in Babylon. They used this privilege profitably to work toward an acculturation of Jews in a form that would perpetuate their faith/culture. Hebrew and the traditions that the royal scribes had gathered from Canaan were transcribed and read aloud. They emerged from exile led by an Aaronide priesthood consciously prepared to assume control of the new temple being built and of the cultural and religious life of a reconstituted people. The basis for this effort was written in a scroll called the Torah of Moses, which incorporated to itself traditions of covenant and their laws from at least three different groups: a narrative of Israel's exodus from Egypt under Moses and the trip to Sinai/Horeb through the wilderness on the way to Canaan; the story of their patriarch ancestors; and an account of creation and the beginning of human history.

Persian approval for the building of the Jerusalem temple opened the door for Jewish self-assertion. But it was Ezra's return with the Torah in his hands that began the process of enculturation that would allow Second Temple Judaism to achieve the goals of monotheistic worship and a distinctive way of life under Torah that the preexilic Israelites had never achieved despite having their own temple and king.

Judaism succeeded in establishing its identity and lifestyle as it lived among the nations in the following centuries. The Hebrew language and the literature (Torah, Prophets, and Writings) made this possible. Read and sung in the temple and in gatherings that became the synagogues, in festival occasions of national and village provenance, they enculturated/educated Jews. Priestly leaders in the temple and rabbinical leaders in the synagogues took the work of scribes and promulgated them among the people.

But the goal in all this was not to develop an elite group in Israel but to enculturate all Jews in the lifestyle and faith that would preserve their distinction among all other cultures. Their methods followed the methods of Moses, Joshua, Samuel, Josiah, and Ezra in having readings for *all the people.* If there is an elite group, it is made up of the entire people. Perhaps they function as an elite among the nations. But there is no elite inside Israel. All the people needed to learn Hebrew and hear the Scriptures read and prayers sung in Hebrew.

In time, the pressure from a dominant culture (Hellenist) led to translation of the Scriptures in Greek. This proved to be a fruitful basis for Christian growth. But Judaism clung to the Hebrew language for synagogue worship, even after the destruction of the temple in 70 CE.

The process continued for Christians with pressure to translate the Scriptures into Latin, the *lingua franca* for western Christianity, only in time to have Latin become an elitists' language for the priests in the church. The Reformation brought the translation into current languages (German, French, English, Spanish, and so on). In each case the translation and reading of the Bible helped to establish the various cultures in Germany, England, and elsewhere.

And the process has continued as the twentieth-century Bible societies and mission agencies have translated the Bible into most of the languages of the world. Thereby, they have allowed the reading of the Bible to help enculturate each of these peoples into a sense of identity and purpose as Christians.

## THE BEGINNING OF A LITERARY ERA

The finding and public reading of the scroll of Torah in the temple in 620 BCE marks the beginning of a literary era. Other works grew up around Deut 5–26 to form the Deuteronomistic History. By the time Judeans went into Babylonian exile with Jehoiachin in 598 BCE, they could take with them many scribes and their handiwork and records. They continued their work in the far land. The skills of the scribes proved valuable to the people in exile who found ready training and employment in government (Nehemiah, Ezra, Daniel and his friends, Mordecai, and many others). Scribes in Canaan were also active. The work that Hezekiah had begun over a century before was coming to fruition.

By the time Ezra, a skilled scribe in the Torah, came back to Jerusalem around 440 BCE, he brought with him a Torah book (or scroll) very close to the Torah that has been handed down to us, including priestly instructions for the temple and its services. By that time, prophetic books had been produced: Jeremiah in Canaan, Ezekiel in Babylon, Isaiah and the book of the Twelve Prophets in Canaan. The people that rallied to Ezra and Nehemiah were called Jews, and would become known as the people of the book.

7

# Introduction to a New Paradigm

A PARADIGM IS AN example or pattern. It is used as a model around which other thoughts and ideas may be clustered or displayed. In Old Testament study, to speak of a paradigm is to relate to the customary way in which the period and books of the Old Testament are portrayed, the dates of composition and of the history, and the usual ideas of authorship. To call for a new paradigm is to suggest that these need to be rethought and reformulated to bring them into line with new research.[1]

To speak of a new paradigm presumes that there was an old paradigm. Actually, there have been several. The traditional paradigm is displayed in the names and openings of the books and in their order in the canon. It dealt with the "implied authors" of books from Moses to Isaiah to Daniel. It was used by the rabbis, apostles, and scholars, both Jewish and Christian, down to the nineteenth century. It still is a pattern for many. It thinks of the Torah as the earliest writing, followed by the Prophets, and finally the works of Wisdom.

Historical criticism in the nineteenth century raised questions about the historical framework of this paradigm and called for revision. Julius Wellhausen proposed that the prophets preceded the Priestly Code. Rendtorff[2] describes this paradigm and the way it has been used, adjusted, and undermined in Old Testament studies throughout the twentieth century. Wellhausen called his book *Prolegomena zur Geschichte Israels,* "A Prolegomena to the History of Israel." He assumed that questions

---

1. Rendtorff, "Paradigm Is Changing," 34–53; Schniedewind, *How the Bible Became a Book;* Carr, *Writing on the Tablet.*
2. Rendtorff, *Old Testament,* 1–14.

concerning the origins and history of the literature of the Old Testament needed to be dealt with before one could seriously deal with the history of Israel. This approach has dominated the paradigm ever since.

Wellhausen suggested that four documents lay behind the Pentateuch: J, the Yahwist's account, to be dated in the time of Solomon; E, the Elohist account, to be dated in the time of Elijah; D, Deuteronomy, to be dated in the time of Josiah; and P, the Priestly work, to be dated in the fifth century after the exile. Further studies began to undermine this "documentary hypothesis" almost from the beginning. Herman Gunkel looked behind the writings using form criticism. Gerhard von Rad and Martin Noth turned to redaction criticism, viewing the history of the canon as a process of never-ending editions rather than as an establishment of fixed documents. Nevertheless, the Documentary Hypothesis remained the framework for most scholarship on the Pentateuch through much of the twentieth century.

Now there is a need for a new definition of the paradigm. Studies redating several of the crucial Old Testament books and focusing on the emerging literature, rather than its origins, call for a redefinition. The treatment of the literature is still basic to history. But the question is: which history? Wellhausen concentrated on the early history of the monarchy with a little spillover into the exile and the postexilic period. The new dating calls for concentration on the exilic and postexilic periods, i.e., on the beginnings of Judaism. To study the emergence of Hebrew literature is to relate it to the history of the Jews—and of Christianity, as John Barton has done in *Oracles of God*. For him "after the exile" continues until about 200 CE.

*Jew* is a term that originally designated someone from the territory of Judah. But it came to mean one who lived according to Jewish customs and worshipped in a specific way, no matter where one lived. Jews are Israelites in the periods that followed the destruction of Jerusalem in 587 BCE.

*Judaism* designates the way of life, of belief, and of worship practiced by Jews. This way of life was in process of formation during the Babylonian and Persian periods when the Hebrew Scriptures were being formed. The choice and writing of the Scriptures have a great deal to say about the way Judaism emerged and about the groups that joined together to become Jews as well as those who were excluded or separated themselves.

The Torah, the Prophets, and the Writings are the Scriptures of the Jews. Jews are the people of the book in a way and to an extent that pre-exilic Israel never was. Ancient Judaism related to the preceding history just as one does today: through its Scriptures.

The writing, editing, and publication of those Scriptures were intimately related with the early history of Judaism, a history that is neither well documented nor illumined, except through the Scriptures that it produced and that shaped it. Even the powerful and influential groups within proto-Judaism are unknown except through the books. They are identified today by the books they produced: the Deuteronomists, the Yahwists, the priests, the wise, and others.

I suggest that the new paradigm be called *Prolegomena zur Geschichte Judentums*, "Prolegomena to the History of Judaism," in contrast to Wellhausen's *Prolegomena to the History of Israel*. The history to be presented here is that of Judaism, beginning with the last decades of the Judean monarchy in the seventh century BCE and the early sixth-century exiles of Jews to Babylon. It will cover the Persian period in which much of the Scripture was published.

The writings produced in this period are different from those known before. While writing was known before this, the results were preserved in archives. So far as we know, they were not made available to the public. The first account of publishing a book widely is found in 2 Kgs 22–23. A book of Torah is found in the temple. It is read to the king, and he has it read to an assembly of the people. This reading leads to a radical reform of religious practices. The reform is led by the king and supported enthusiastically by the people. Things were never quite the same again.

A similar event is recounted in Neh 8, some 175 years later. Again there is a public reading of a book of Torah. It again has powerful results in the organizing and reform of the temple and its worship. These accounts mark out major historical benchmarks for the study of the history of the publication of Judaism's Scriptures. A final marker must be placed on the book of Sirach (or Ecclesiasticus) in the early second century BCE. He speaks of three groups of books: the Torah, the Prophets, and the Writings. This indicates that the books now in the Hebrew Bible were present and known.

## OUTLINE OF THE NEW PARADIGM

The heart of the new paradigm builds on the same ground covered by the older paradigm.[3] Since the beginning of the nineteenth century, the book of Deuteronomy has been identified as "the law book found in the temple" in Josiah's day. Dating Deuteronomy to the end of the seventh century BCE continues as in the old paradigm.

Dating the Priestly edition of the Pentateuch in the fifth century before the coming of Ezra also remains substantially the same. Wellhausen dated the non-Priestly portions of the Pentateuch to the tenth and ninth centuries BCE. This gave the historical early anchor for the paradigm. He also placed much weight on the eighth-century dates for the prophets Isa 1–39, Hosea, Amos, and Micah.

The new paradigm proposed here will change both of these assumptions from Wellhausen. It will suggest that all the parts of the Pentateuch were being edited and written at the same time, parallel to each other in the fifth century, and that the prophetic books of Isaiah and the Twelve Prophets were subsequent to this. The order of appearance of the books will be approximately like the following:

- Late seventh century: the book of Torah found in the temple (Deut 5–26)
- First half of the sixth century: the Deuteronomistic History, i.e., Deuteronomy–2 Kings, Jeremiah
- Second half of the sixth century: Ezekiel, Isaiah, and book of the Twelve Prophets
- By ca. mid-fifth century: the Pentateuch

Thus by near the end of the Persian period the Torah and the Prophets would be in place. (This date could be extended a century without damaging the paradigm.) The major groupings are:

- During the Babylonian period (605–539 BCE): the destruction of Jerusalem and the temple; Judeans taken into exile; Deuteronomistic History (including Deuteronomy) in Judah; Jeremiah in Egypt
- During the reigns of Cyrus and Darius (539–485 BCE): the first moves toward restoring the temple; Ezekiel; Isaiah and the book

---

3. Rendtorff, *Old Testament*, 159–63, 290.

of the Twelve Prophets

- During the reigns of Xerxes and Artaxerxes (485–427 BCE): the restoration of liturgical order in the temple by Ezra; the rebuilding of Jerusalem by Nehemiah

- During the rest of the Persian period and the first century after the invasion by Alexander (ca. 427–300 BCE): Psalms, 1 and 2 Chronicles, Ezra-Nehemiah, Proverbs, the five festal scrolls, and Job

The outer boundaries of the period are marked by the reign of Josiah (740–709 BCE), especially his reform in 726 BCE, and by the Hasmonean revolt (165 BCE). The book of Daniel is set at the outer boundary.

Of course Hebrew literature continued to be produced, as the Dead Sea Scrolls have demonstrated, down to the Christian era. But a core of literature had been marked off and separated for preservation. It could be and was translated into Greek as early as the third century BCE.

## INTRODUCTION TO THE NEW PARADIGM: JEWISH LITERATURE BETWEEN JOSIAH AND THE LATE PERSIAN EMPIRE

The four centuries that produced the literature that is the subject of this book were times of crisis, transition, and creativity for Israel and Judah. At the end of the eighth century BCE, the nation of Israel was sent into exile. A remnant sought refuge in Judah. Judah was reduced to the role of impotent vassal to Assyria. No published literature existed to pass on knowledge of the rich heritage and tradition, although undoubtedly archives of traditions and royal records existed.

By the end of the period, a sacred literature served as Scripture for the scattered communities who thought of themselves as Jews. The continued growth of that literature is reviewed in George Nickelsburg's *Jewish Literature between the Bible and the Mishnah*.

By 300 BCE, most of the literature that would later become the Scriptures of the Jewish people had already been written. This volume will trace the development of that literature in the period from Hezekiah to the end of the Persian period (ca. 715–333 BCE).

At the beginning of the period, the kingdom of Israel had already been devastated in the Assyrian invasions and its people sent into exile. Hezekiah began the hazardous experience of learning to exist as an

Assyrian vassal in a strategic border area. The century that followed was disastrous for Judah but ended in the reign of Josiah with a little window of freedom and a seed of hope.

This tranquil period was short lived. Assyria lost its place to the pressures of Egypt, Media, and Babylon. Judah was directly and traumatically involved in the struggle for power between Babylon and Egypt, eventually having Jerusalem destroyed and a group of Jews sent into exile.

Less than half a century later Babylon collapsed before Cyrus and Persia's two-century rule began. By the end of Persian rule, groups of Jews in Mesopotamia, in Palestine, and in Egypt were living conscious of their heritage, devoted in their worship, and faithful in their religious and moral observance. They were united by their recognition of the rebuilt temple in Jerusalem and by their adherence to the Scripture, the Torah and the Prophets.

The period is not well documented after the fall of Jerusalem. However, bits of literature mark out the major events of the period: the fall of Jerusalem in 586 BCE, the return of Jews under Persian patronage to rebuild the temple by 515 BCE, and the returns of Ezra and Nehemiah under Artaxerxes, which resulted in the organization of temple practice under the Torah and the rebuilding of the city of Jerusalem, including its walls by Nehemiah. It is this unlikely period that produced the published literature, building on the traditions and archives of previous centuries.

## PROLEGOMENA TO THE HISTORY OF JUDAISM

Julius Wellhausen wrote *Prolegomena zur Geschichte Israels*, in which he proposed to place the various writings of the Old Testament in their historical setting. He placed the J document of the Pentateuch in the time of Solomon (tenth century BCE), E in the time of Elijah (ninth century), D in the time of Josiah (seventh century), and P in the exile or early postexilic period. He placed Hosea, Amos, Micah, and Isaiah 1–39 in the eighth century and Malachi in the fourth century, with Joel, Obadiah, and Daniel later still. With this, the historical framework of the history of Israel was laid out. He never got around to writing that history. But the historians of Israel since that time have worked within that framework, assured that they were working with documents from those periods that made their work authentic.

Recent scholarly research has affirmed Wellhausen's dating for D and P, but it is increasingly uncomfortable with placing other written works before that time. When Deuteronomy was read to the people in Josiah's time as the book found in the temple, there were no other known books. Plenty of traditions preserved various locations, some of them in writing, but apparently there were no scrolls in the form of books. Israel's literary age begins with Deuteronomy, just as historical Israel, what we tend to call Ancient Israel, was about to end its history.

The exile of 587 BCE marks the dividing line between Ancient Israel, the age of the kingdoms and before, and the age of Judaism, when there is no state and existence involves a remnant in "the land" and a diaspora of scattered peoples in Mesopotamia, Egypt, and elsewhere. The way in which that scattered people recaptured its sense of identity and survived as a religious and ethnic entity after it had forfeited its place as a nation is a remarkable story. It is a story that is intertwined from the beginning with the growth and acceptance of a body of religious literature that captured its ancient traditions and presented them in the books that we now know as Torah, Prophets, and Writings—or, to Christians, as the Old Testament.

So a prolegomena to the history of Judaism is perforce a history of the literature of Judaism. One is unthinkable without the other.

## ISRAEL AND JUDAISM

Israel is the people who occupied a portion of Canaan in the thirteenth century and came to be organized as first one and then two kingdoms from the tenth to the sixth centuries BCE. It worshipped Yahweh and other gods, as Morton Smith amply documented in *Palestinian Parties and Politics*.

The name *Israel* is claimed in succeeding centuries by the Jews. But the Jews differ from preexilic Israel in that they insist that they are exclusively Yahwist. Morton Smith calls them "Yahweh only." While this distinction belongs to some Israelites before the exile, it comes to be the mark of all Jews and all Jewish Scripture. The process by which this happened was aided by and paralleled the development of the Hebrew Scriptures that is the theme of this book.

## THE AGE OF HEBREW LITERATURE

### The Language

Hebrew, a form of Canaanite (probably as spoken in Judea) written in alphabetic script—later adopting the Aramaic script for this purpose, was the language of the Scriptures. Aramaic loomed in the larger cultural background. The Assyrian Empire in the eighth century made Aramaic the official language of the empire. This was continued in the Babylonian and Persian periods. Ezra and Daniel (both of whom had been trained in the use of Aramaic by royal schools) have sections of their books written in Aramaic.

A classical period, when the books of the Torah and the Prophets were written using what is now called Classical or Biblical Hebrew (ca. Hezekiah to Ezra and later), was followed by another period during which the language evolved toward Mishnaic Hebrew, the Hebrew of the Mishnah (200 CE). From 300 BCE onward there was an increasing influence from Greek language and culture.

### The Monarchy from Hezekiah to Josiah and the Second Temple Period

Culture, religion, and history worthy of being written down or preserved to provide perspective and content until this time had been transmitted orally in festivals at sanctuaries by storytellers, singers, and judges.

Every great culture has some period when literature flourishes.[4] This is a time when great writers emerge who use the language in a particularly rich and powerful way. The Greek philosophers, dramatists, and historians in the fourth century BCE and the English dramatists and poets of the Elizabethan age who produced Shakespeare and the Authorized Version of the Bible were of this caliber. It is a time when the people are prepared to read and appreciate what is being written. Of course, in each case writing had been used before this flowering—for keeping records, sending bills, and much more—but literature and the imagination that can produce it are another matter.

The Old Testament speaks of a book being read publicly in 2 Kgs 22 when the book of the Torah was found in the temple and read to the king and the people. This occurs in the reign of Josiah about 725 BCE. A second account with literary content appears in Jer 36, where it is told that the prophet Jeremiah tries to avoid a royal order banning him from

---

4. Schniedewind, *How the Bible Became a Book*.

the court by dictating his messages to Baruch, a scribe, and having him read to the people in Jerusalem. We are later told that Jeremiah had all his messages written by the scribe as a witness to a future generation that God's word had been received in that time. The written words would preserve the oral words for future readings. The event described in Jer 36 occurs shortly before the fall of Jerusalem in the reign of Jehoiakim just before 600 BCE.

A third account that witnesses to a literary period is found in Neh 8, which describes Ezra being asked to bring out the book of the law of Moses and read it to the people. By this time, the book is larger, takes longer to read, and includes priestly requirements that must be enforced for the temple ceremonies. The date is somewhere about mid-fifth century BCE. These accounts speak of Israel's and early Judaism's use of literature. The literature was about the traditions of Israel, about God's word to them in those traditions and through the prophets God had sent. It is not difficult to identify in these accounts elements of the Pentateuch and the beginnings of the Prophets.

The end of this process that produced the Torah and the Prophets is marked by references in Sir 49:10, where the work is named as "the Torah, the Prophets, and the other books." This tripartite work is still what the Hebrew Scriptures present today. The literature continued to develop, but by this time there was a body of literature to treasure and cultivate. John Barton[5] has summarized the present state of scholarship on the distinction between "Scriptures," revered writings, and "canon," an approved and limited collection. The major contributors to this work are Shnayer Z. Leiman[6] and Albert C. Sundberg.[7] So the period beginning with the reign of Josiah and continuing through the Persian period into the Hellenistic period was Israel's literary age. In this period, the literature of the Hebrew Scriptures was produced, recognized, and copied.

The work of scribes was intense in this literary period. Judah's rule by Assyrian, Babylonian, Persian, and Hellenistic kings necessitated the use of scribes to engage the imperial bureaucracies. The exile put the Jews in a position where scribal skills opened doors to employment and advancement in the empires of Babylon and Persia. Daniel and Ezra are examples of such scribes. They were the foundation on which scribes

---

5. *Oracles of God*, 30–34.
6. *Canonization of Hebrew Scripture*.
7. *Old Testament of the Early Church*.

*Introduction to a New Paradigm* 99

among the priestly circles, the prophetic groups, and the wise could produce the literature that emerged.

In their professional capacities, scribes worked with all the groups that made up Israelite society. The most natural place for them to have been trained was among the wise. But only in a later period were scribes thought of as a separate group entrusted with the interpretation of the Scripture as in the New Testament. These references that I have cited above also give us the points of reference in describing the way that Israel's literary corpus came into existence.

The first distinguishable group of Jewish scribes may be called the Deuteronomists because Deuteronomy dominates their corpus. It includes the book of Deuteronomy (or Deuteronomy–Joshua) first, then the Deuteronomistic History (Judges–2 Kings), which was followed by the book of Jeremiah.

The book of Ezekiel stands alone. A prophet from Zadokite priestly circles, his work apparently was complete toward the end of the sixth century in Mesopotamia. The groups of scribes who produced the strands of the Torah that are called JE and P must have been active in this period. The product of their joint labor is apparent in the book that Ezra reads to the people of Jerusalem. This "book of the Torah of Moses" is considered by many to have been the Pentateuch.

Near this time prophetic circles produced Isaiah and the book of the Twelve Prophets. Other scribes worked for the singers in producing the magnificent hymnbook that we know as the Psalms. Scribes working for the wise produced Proverbs, Job, and the small scrolls of Song of Songs, Ruth, Lamentations, Ecclesiastes, and Esther.

All these witness to the diversity and strength of Judaism in the Persian period. In Babylon, Palestine, and Egypt, Jewish scribes were hard at work. The books they produced portrayed the work of God from creation to their own time. They pictured the life of their fathers in the land and outside it. The books made it possible for Jews to keep their identity and their faith while living in the pluralistic setting of the empires.

This literature was written in Hebrew, a Canaanite dialect spoken in Israel and Judah during the monarchies. It flourished in a golden age (from Hezekiah to Ezra) that produced the Deuteronomic canon and the Torah and in a silver age (from ca. 450 to 300 BCE) that produced the Chronicler's canon, the Writings. It gradually became a sacred language separate from the everyday languages of Aramaic, Greek, or Latin and was still being used in the time of the Dead Sea Scrolls. The oral reading of Scripture in worship was made possible by the synagogue schools.

## THE LAW AND THE PROPHETS: AN ALTERNATIVE APPROACH

The foundation and heart of the Hebrew Bible is the part known as the Law and the Prophets. This seems to have preceded the other books in being considered canon. This portion has also been granted a higher authority.

This literature consists of three blocks: the Torah (five books or Pentateuch), the Former Prophets (four books [or six]: Joshua, Judges, 1 and 2 Samuel, and 1 and 2 Kings), and the Latter Prophets (four books [or fifteen]: Isaiah, Jeremiah, Ezekiel, and the book of the Twelve Prophets).

In the following discussion, I propose to deal with the Old Testament (the Hebrew Bible) in terms of these three blocks of material. Current scholarship identifies the sixth and fifth centuries BCE (or a little later) as the period when these three blocks obtained their present form. These centuries represent the Babylonian period and the Persian period, when Jews were divided between Palestinians and exiles in Babylon and Egypt.

Current scholarship also recognizes that the literary processes that brought these works into existence were complex. A rich tradition of writing that archived significant literary and oral works in Palestine in the late monarchy lies behind this literature. All the finished works have made use of these archives and traditions, often inserting sizable units directly into their manuscripts. I intend to concentrate on these finished works that have come down to us, looking only one or two steps back of them to preceding literary work.

### *Deuteronomistic History*

The Deuteronomistic History includes Deuteronomy and grows from Deuteronomy. It enlarges Deuteronomy by adding a frame in chapters 1–3 and 27–34. It adds Joshua, including the boundary lists. It adds Judges, including narratives and poetry. It continues with 1 Samuel (Samuel, ark, and Saul narratives), 2 Samuel (David narrative), 1 Kings (Solomon, division of the kingdom, divided monarchy [prophetic stories]), and 2 Kings (divided monarchy continued, prophetic stories, end of Israelite monarchy, end of Judah-Jerusalem).

## Torah (Pentateuch)

Torah (the Pentateuch) appropriates Deuteronomy and develops its implications for the following ages. It grows in two stages: The first stage develops the narratives and laws of the JE, and the second stage inserts the P narrative, laws, and genealogies. The introduction of the Priestly influence comes with P, although undoubtedly other priests were involved earlier. The narrative describes the wilderness journey, including Sinai. Other narratives with Moses contain the Law codes at Sinai (Decalogue, Covenant Code, Holiness Code) and the exodus narrative. The narrative extends backward to include the Joseph story and the patriarchal narratives (including genealogies). The primeval story (creation, flood, sons of Noah [including genealogies]) comes to introduce all that followed.

## Latter Prophets

The Latter Prophets form a unit to themselves. Jeremiah (the scroll of Baruch and 2 Kgs 25) is first followed by Ezekiel (which includes the law of the temple, Ezek 40–48), addressing the situation of the exile. Isaiah (including Isa 36–39 from 2 Kgs 18–20) and the book of the Twelve Prophets (including Amos and Haggai-Zechariah) address the returned Judeans and others who would come to the rebuilt temple.

## Conclusion

The Law and the Prophets at this stage constituted the Scriptures of incipient Judaism. Deuteronomy dominated the collection. The time of its production and publication came in the Persian period. It is likely to have been the scroll read by Ezra and the law filed with the Persian authorities for the new temple.

The influence and authority of the Pentateuch stepped into the breach left by disappearance of a Davidic king in Jerusalem. Because of this, Moses became the most important founding figure in Judaism.

There is ambiguity toward the prophets. They are included in the canon, but many portions of Judaism, like the priests and Sadducees, held only to the authority of the Torah. The Samaritans also held to Torah only.

The attitude toward Jewish nationalism is also ambiguous. The canon includes monarchical literature but still includes Deuteronomy's warnings about a king and also the Deuteronomistic History's account of the kingdom's failures.

The role of the new temple in the process is vital. The Torah is the basis of its worship, but singers also sing the psalms.

"The people of the land" were the kind of people who still held firmly to Deuteronomy and its canon while the priests tended toward the larger Torah and the wider canon. The role of the book in the faith and worship of Jews was vital. After the destruction of the temple in 70 CE, only the Tanak (that is, the threefold canon of Torah, Prophets, and Writings) remained for all Judaism to hold on to, to be taught from, and to proclaim.

## THE WRITINGS

In time, elements of the literary tradition that had been suppressed re-emerged and took a place in the canon of literature. What made this happen? The taboos against the monarchy, royalty (at least from Jerusalem), and the wisdom that had been associated with it were softened. Perhaps a period came when the overlords were not threatened by the writings about Jewish national traditions. Perhaps the temple required something more than Moses' law to fill out its worship and mystique. In any case, the ancient positive works about David and Solomon reappeared and were rewritten. Israel's Camelot could be told again. This produced the Writings.

The first and most important book was the Psalms. The new temple needed its hymnbook. The psalms of the Davidic era and the succeeding services in Jerusalem echoed there again.

Wisdom had emerged again in Judaism with a sizable following. Witness Ben Sirach. The Proverbs of Solomon were published, with additional sections. Job and Ecclesiastes challenged the assumptions of wisdom. Ruth listed her descendents down to David. Historians issued revisions of Israel's history in which the monarchy was written romantically. David's Jerusalem was eulogized. David and Solomon, Hezekiah and Josiah, were vindicated and praised.

Jews in the Persian period needed words about their roots. Ezra-Nehemiah supplied essential orientation about Jerusalem and the temple. Esther told of life in Susa. Stories of Daniel and his friends supplied narrative from the Babylonian and Persian periods. Slowly the gaps were filled. Other stories, not in the canon, also existed. We know of additions to Daniel and of the story of Tobit. Josephus wrote of other stories, like that of Zerubabbel in the king's guard. These stories tell of Jewish life that lay outside the streams of Deuteronomic piety and Priestly devotion found in the Law and the Prophets.

## DEUTERONOMISTIC AND CHRONICLER'S CANONS

The Deuteronomistic canon is the twenty-one book canon of sacred Scripture of the sixth century BCE (the Torah and the Prophets: the Pentateuch, Joshua, Judges, Samuel, Kings, Isaiah, Jeremiah, Ezekiel, Hosea, Joel, Amos, Obadiah, Jonah, Micah, Nahum, Habakkuk, Zephaniah), which marks the true beginning of the canonical process. The same work may be counted as thirteen books if the Book of the Twelve is counted as one.

Deuteronomistic writers and editors produced the primary history that extended from creation to the exile. This was blended with the Priestly history and cultic law and extended by the addition of the Latter Prophets. The whole was a blend of prophetic and Priestly literature. Moses was the connecting and dominant symbolic figure. The whole comprises the Law and the Prophets. The Law gives the whole a stable and abiding foundation. The prophetic works provide the dynamic view of a continuing and growing work of God still to be done. The goal has yet to be reached. The scope is that of "all Israel," twelve tribes. Moses is law-giver, leader, and prophet. David is messiah, anointed and promised ruler.

The Chronicler's canon consists of the Writings. The central figures are David and Solomon. Jerusalem is the center of these books. They presuppose the existence of the Law and the temple, but emphasize neither. The dominant genre in this canon is Wisdom. It sees the historical sweep of Scripture as complete with the accomplishments of Ezra and Nehemiah.

In the new temple, the songs of David and the wisdom of Solomon give testimony to the beneficence and power of God. Neither David nor Solomon is portrayed in continuing ruling roles. Their contributions lie in psalmnody and wisdom.

The Hebrew canon thus consists of three bodies of literature with three worldviews, built on the same traditions and history. One gathers around the law. Another focuses on the prophets. A third turns to wisdom and its intellectual potential. They represent different elements in Jewish life.

In Second Temple Judaism, the temple and the Torah bound the people and their literature together. After 70 CE only the Tanak, the three-part Scripture of the rabbis, remained. The priests no longer had a temple. But the law, the prophetic group, and the wise each have a center within the larger canon. Christianity took over the Tanak in a Greek form, expanded and rearranged it with prophecy as its interpreter, and added the New Testament. Paul put the law into a subsidiary position. Wisdom had its own influence, but the denial of a place for Gnosticism limited it severely. Priestly influences continued to be felt in Christian rituals in both Catholic and Orthodox circles.

## JUDAISM

Postexilic Judaism was built on three preexilic traditions, available to them in books. Each tradition had geographical centers and claims.

One was of covenant renewal ceremonies at Gilgal, of the twelve tribes occupying the land and their life in the land, of the monarchy's history to its end. This was made up of Deuteronomy, the former Prophets, and the Latter Prophets. Its center was first Gilgal and then Jerusalem. Moses was the founding character, followed by Samuel.

A second was of the ancestors of the twelve tribes of Israel in Canaan, based on the stories of Abraham, Isaac, Jacob, and his twelve sons. The stories that carried the traditions were related to places in Canaan where the patriarchs were reported to have lived. Its center may have been in Shechem. It continued with the exodus from Egypt. This spoke of covenant, law, and Moses. It came to them through Torah (Genesis–Numbers).

The third centered in David, Jerusalem, and the temple. It was based on the books of Samuel and Kings (1 and 2 Chronicles) with traditions from Shiloh and Hebron, and the songs sung in the temple (Psalms). The continued existence of a Davidic monarchy until shortly before its recording added to its power.

But Judaism was formed in a time when none of these could be applied in full. Considerable adaptation was necessary. Persian dominance allowed no king. The political shape of the Near East did not usually allow independent sovereignty over the ancient territories of Canaan. The Latter Prophets, especially the Twelve and Isaiah, show how these adaptations took place.

Israel needed to be redefined. Judaism, as it came to be called, no longer had just territorial significance. It designated people in many places who gathered around Torah and worshipped in the temple in Jerusalem.

The Jews seized on the significance of Jerusalem, especially the new temple being built there. Isaiah called for it to be open to people of all nations who wanted to worship Yahweh. Ezra brought Torah to be the law of the new temple.

The hopes of recovering the earlier realities of a united Davidic kingdom, or of a land made up of twelve tribes in their territories, or even of a people living under a comprehensive covenant of those twelve tribes, continued in some form. But reality rarely allowed anything of the sort. Judaism in fact came to be centered in local schools (synagogues) in which Torah was taught and in the temple (until that, too, was destroyed in 70 CE).

The Scriptures were centered in Torah, but added the Prophets, the Psalms, and some other books (e.g., of wisdom). The teaching about election was applied to those who coalesced around Torah wherever they might be. Their leaders were teachers of Torah, rabbis. David's legacy was celebrated in the temple, and the sacrificial laws were observed there. Leaders were priests, Levites, and singers. Hopes for a new David and an independent kingdom were projected into the future. And in these forms Judaism thrived. The legacies on which Judaism was based were preserved in Scripture.

# 8

# The Beginning of Jewish Literature: End of the Assyrian Period

SOMETHING NEW APPEARED IN the mid-seventh century at the end of the Assyrian period: a literature and a following that defined Israel as exclusively Yahwistic, eschewing syncretism—that is, Judaism appeared. In this period, scrolls were composed—a textualization of traditions, which until then had been transmitted orally (cf. the Introduction above).

The growth of literary capability came in Hezekiah's reign. Nigosian[1] identifies "three concurrent stages... through which particular selections of Israelite writings came to be regarded as sacred": (1) authorship and the creative task of writing; (2) editorial function: assembling, arranging in sequence, clarifying and developing consistency; and (3) the selection process and the inclusion of specific items in a final collection. Philip R. Davies[2] puts this between the sixth and third centuries BCE. I see the creative stage starting earlier and including much oral composition and presentation as a stage of writing, editing, and publishing written texts, followed by recognition of authoritative status.

## THE BOOK FOUND IN THE TEMPLE
## (2 KGS 22:1—23:2; 2 CHR 34-35)

The tradition of Moses' speeches and repetition of the law had been maintained through repeated festival meetings of "all Israel" through the years as Deut 31:10-13 prescribes. The same chapter of Deuteronomy

---

1. Nigosian, *From Ancient Writings to Sacred Texts*, 8.
2. *In Search of 'Ancient Israel,'* 94-154.

tells of Moses writing a copy of "the law" and commanding that it be placed beside the ark of the covenant. The place of those gatherings was probably Gilgal, which appears prominently in the books of Joshua, Judges, 1 Samuel, and the eighth-century prophets.[3]

Note the speeches of Moses (in Deuteronomy) spoken beyond the river but repeated at gatherings in Gilgal and written in a book to be kept with the ark (Deut 31:22, 24-26), the speech of Joshua (Josh 24) spoken in Shechem, and the speech of Samuel (1 Sam 12) spoken at Gilgal.

The book found in the temple (2 Kgs 22:1—23:2 and 2 Chr 34-35) is the first recognition of the writing and publication activities of the scribes that Hezekiah had assembled after the deportation of the people from the northern kingdom. Some of these scribes were apparently related to persons who had served in Gilgal and Shechem at the amphictyony's celebrations, perhaps even the spokesmen who delivered the speeches of Moses on those occasions. They produced transcriptions of the major speech now appearing as Deut 5-26. They appended Deut 4:44-49 to introduce the speech. Noth suggested that this constituted "the book found in the temple."

## THE AGE OF JOSIAH AND "THE PEOPLE OF THE LAND"

### The Decline of Assyria

The decades just past the middle of the seventh century BCE witnessed the gradual decline of the Assyrian Empire.[4] After reaching its zenith in power and territorial authority in Palestine and Egypt under Ashurbanipal (669-633 BCE)—while Manasseh was the wretched king in Jerusalem (697-642 BCE)—by the time Manasseh died, Assyrian campaigns in Palestine became fewer and weaker. Assyria had conquered Egypt in 671 BCE, but by 663 under a new pharaoh, Psamtik I, Egypt was in the process of rebuilding its own autonomy and power.

For all the turbulence and violence of his reign, Manasseh died a natural death and was succeeded by his young heir, Amon, who is described in both Kings and Chronicles as continuing the policies and religious attitudes of his father. Then he was assassinated by officials of his

---

3. For example, Josh 4:19-24; 5:10; Judg 2:1-4; 1 Sam 7:15; 11:14—12:24; 13:7-15; 15:12, 33; Hos 4:15; 9:15; 12:11; Amos 4:15; 5:5; Mic 6:5.

4. Na'aman, "Kingdom of Judah," 3-71.

court, presumably princes of Jerusalem. These princes and their families were the traditional powers in Jerusalem and thus in Judah.

It had been like this since the beginning of the kingdom, with David and Solomon. Under Rehoboam, leaders of the ten tribes had rejected Jerusalem's rule over them but had not been able to unseat the young king. But with the death of Amon, a new power showed its strength in Judah. The people of the land (*am haaretz*) rose up against the princes, killed the assassins, and installed Amon's eight-year-old son, Josiah, as king. A new political force had made its appearance, and one of the signs of Israel's new age had appeared. Once before, after the reign of Athaliah, "the people of the land" had played a role in installing a new king (2 Kgs 11:17-20).

## The People of the Land

Lipiński summarizes fairly the results of intensive study on the subject of "the people of the land."[5] The Hebrew phrase *am haaretz*, "the people of the land,"[6] was used in Judah during the monarchy to describe an assembly of citizens that is to be distinguished from the population of the royal city Jerusalem.[7] That city's population was composed mainly of mercenary soldiers, functionaries of the palace, priests, and temple personnel. The people of the land stood over against the king and the princes.[8] They might confront the king and his ministers,[9] or leaders, priests, and prophets.[10]

The people of the land were composed, then, of the population of the territory outside the city. Nonetheless, the group's political power appeared from time to time. It sometimes chose and installed a king, as in the case of Joash,[11] after the priests had conspired with the temple guards to dethrone the usurper Athaliah. They decided to execute the Baal priest Mattan and the fallen Queen Athaliah.[12] They thus seem to

---

5. Lipiński, "עם," *TDOT* 11: 163-78.

6. Depicted in 2 Kgs 21:19—23:30; 2 Chr 33:21—36:3; Jer 3:6; Isa 28-33 (?); Zephaniah (see bibliography in *IDB* 2:999); Sir 29:1-4.

7. 2 Kgs 11:20; 14:21; 23:30; cf. Jer 25:2.

8. 2 Kgs 16:15; Ezek 7:27; 25:45; Dan 9:6.

9. Jer 37:2.

10. Jer 1:18; 34:19; 44:21; Ezek 22:24-29.

11. 2 Kgs 11:14, 18; 2 Chr 23:13.

12. 2 Kgs 11:18, 20; 2 Chr 23:17, 21.

have been native peoples resisting foreign usurpation of power. Their motive in resisting the officials who assassinated Amon[13] is not defined.

Then there is the case of Josiah.[14] Josiah's kingship had a political base in the people of the province, not in the royal establishment. His introduction to the people of the scroll of Torah found in the temple fits that picture as well. Josiah was not a king who owed his throne to the princes of the royal establishment or to the patronage of a foreign emperor. This popular base set Josiah apart from most of his predecessors.

### The Book of the Law

A second feature of the reign of Josiah was the emergence of "the book of the torah."[15] The treatment accorded the discovery indicated a level of literacy not previously recognized in the books of Kings. The priest reported the find to Shaphan, a scribe in the service of the king, who read the scroll, first for himself and then for the king. Their reaction, after checking its authenticity with the prophetess Huldah, was to call a meeting in the temple to have the scroll read publicly.[16] This time the scroll was called "the scroll of the covenant."[17] This represented a response to a literary piece not before described in the kingdom period, but which would be repeated in the following centuries.

What is remarkable here, in addition to the king's response to the people, is the level of literacy and literary sophistication (i.e., the response of the population at all levels to the reading of a book), the king's response to the reading of the scroll, the use of the scroll in the renewal of covenant, and the influence of the scroll on cultic reform. Piety, devotion to the Lord or to the temple, has often been listed as an occasion for renovation or reform in the temple. But here for the first time is the direct literary influence of the reading of a scroll. A new age had arrived in Judah.

---

13. 2 Kgs 21:19-26; 2 Chr 33:21-25.

14. 2 Kgs 21:24; 2 Chr 33:25.

15. Berry, "Code Found in the Temple"; Budde, "Deuteronomium"; Dietrich, "Josia und das Gesetzbuch"; Freed, "Code Spoken Of"; Gieselmann, "Sogenannte josianische Reform"; Granild, "Einige Voraussetzungen"; Gressman, "Josia und das Deuteronomium"; for more bibliography, see Hobbs, *2 Kings*, and Dillard, *2 Chronicles*.

16. 2 Kgs 22:3-20; 2 Chr 34:8-33.

17. 2 Kgs 23:2.

There is no reason to doubt that writing and recording had been a part of government and business life in the region for a long time. Very ancient documents of myths and religious liturgies have been found. But there is no evidence that anyone found it profitable or necessary to read these aloud to the people and expect response from them. (An exception is Exod 14:7, which uses language very near that of 2 Kgs 23:2. Note that in the narrative this precedes the giving of the tablets of the law.)

### The Reform of Josiah

Josiah's reforms[18] respond to the exhortations of Deuteronomy, as does the prophetic speech of Huldah. So the reform has the unique element of being the first to specifically respond to the requirements of Deuteronomy. But there is no suggestion that the priesthood was reformed on the basis of Deuteronomy. The destruction of the high places did help to achieve the requirements for the centralization of worship that Deuteronomy requires.[19]

### Josiah's Political Response to Assyrian Decline

Josiah's reign experienced that window of opportunity that existed between the Assyrian regime and the application of power by the succeeding powers. The declining years of Assyrian power gave opportunity for aspiring successors to prepare themselves for the struggle to come to determine who would be Assyria's heir. There were plenty of ambitious nations, all well instructed in the ways of tyranny by the Assyrians. These included Egypt, Babylon, and Media. However, before any one of them could make its move, years of preparation, securing of its own power base, and preliminary steps were necessary before they would be prepared to challenge the old lion. Josiah's thirty-two-year reign existed in this calm "eye of the storm."

Assyrian tyranny had by this time crushed every small power in Palestine. Aram and Philistia showed no signs of life. Ammon, Moab, and Edom were dormant. Even Tyre and Sidon would need decades to rebuild their trade and economies. Judah survived better than any of them.

---

18. Lohfink, "Bundesurkunde des Königs Josias"; "Cult Reform"; "Gattung der 'Historischen Kurzgeschichte'"; "Zur neueren Diskussion."

19. See Dillard, *2 Chronicles*, 277, for suggestion that reform began before the discovery of the book of the law.

Josiah appears to have used the response to the finding of the scroll of the law to give his people a renaissance of self-conscious piety and national identity. But it is to be noted that Deuteronomy is not a Judean scroll, nor is the national consciousness it aroused purely one of Judean sensibilities. It brings a rebirth of the dream of Israel, all-Israel, and the promises concerning the land that are assumed there.

Deuteronomy does not stand alone in the Jewish Bible. It is joined to Joshua in many ways. The language and ideology are similar if not identical. Deuteronomy looks forward to what Joshua fulfills. Dueteronomy was separated from Joshua when it was joined to the other "books of Moses." But Joshua is equally different in tone and message from the following books of the Former Prophets. Is it not far more likely that Deuteronomy and Judges existed as a single work? And, if so, that they both influenced Josiah's expansion to fill the vacuum left by Assyrian weakness and retreat?

Josiah applied his reform in Bethel and Samaria. He defended his land at the last at Megiddo, far outside Judean territory. Second Chronicles 34:5–7 records acts of reform "in the towns of Manasseh, Ephraim, and Simeon, as far as Naphtali . . . throughout Israel." No Judean king since Solomon had ranged so widely. So it seems that the vision of restored covenant also included the conquest of the promised land, and that both of them were in a large measure fulfilled.

### The Legacy of Josiah's Reign

Josiah's reign introduced a number of important elements to the life and experience of Judah, elements that were to be of decisive value for the age to come. In that sense this reign may be viewed as the opening of a new era in history.

It was the beginning of a literary age in which scrolls and the reading of scrolls would play decisive roles in maintaining Israel's self-consciousness and integrity. Deuteronomy-Joshua became a major and decisive part of Israel's life. The idea of covenant as the basis of the people's relationship with God with its concomitant sense of responsibility for the continuance of covenant lay the foundation for prophetic careers and scrolls. The idea of law in covenant that came from Deuteronomy laid the foundation for the day when Ezra would introduce the larger Torah and Judaism would come of age.

The influence of Deuteronomy-Joshua, with the success that Josiah enjoyed in expanding the borders of his kingdom, reintroduced "Israel" and "all Israel," rather than the narrow confines of Judah, as the underlying concepts of the people's heritage and self-understanding. But these concepts did not hinder the continuation of the importance of Jerusalem's influence.

The rise of political activism on the part of the "people of the land" raised the possibility of alternative centers for leadership outside the narrow royal circles that would be largely wiped out in succeeding years.

Religious and cultic reforms on the basis of Deuteronomy gave a precedent for using the Torah in this way and make possible respect for the priesthood when its function includes interpretation of the Torah in addition to its cultic functions. Such a priesthood could exercise powerful leadership in a new society, as it actually would.

### *Judaism: Ethnic Survival*

The beginning of the twenty-first century provides several reminders of the struggles of ethnic minorities to survive over centuries. The Armenians, the Kurds, and the Serbs are such examples. Many minorities have not been able to preserve their distinctive identity in a pluralistic environment. They have simply been absorbed.

Israel in the late seventh century BCE faced these problems of survival. Judah was the only surviving part of "all Israel." It was a miracle that it had managed to keep a semblance of political and ethnic integrity during the century-long Assyrian rule.

A century earlier the armies of Tiglath-Pileser and his successors had swept into Canaan, subjugating the small kingdoms. Syria and Israel were among those who became Assyrian provinces. Their populations were redistributed to other parts of the empire.

But tiny Judah's rulers managed to come to terms with the conquerors and were allowed to remain on their thrones, although their territory was severely reduced. The small Transjordanian countries were also spared.

In the latter half of the seventh century, Assyria's powers began to wane. Its emperors no longer campaigned far from home. But there were no obvious successors to their power and territory. In the chaotic situation that ensued, Judah was in the fortunate position of having an unusual leader. Josiah had been placed on the throne by a group of citizens from the countryside outside the capital when he was just a boy. A priest was named regent.

Josiah was the first king in a century that had the opportunity of reigning without the oppressive oversight of an emperor. He had the insight and character to take full advantage of the opportunity. His power became such that he was able to assert his authority over much of what had earlier been Israel. He pushed his borders to the sea between the Philistine territory to the south and the territory of Tyre just north of Carmel. He took Gilead and recovered the Negev from Edom.[20]

His greatest achievement in the light of history was the recovery of a sense of religious identity for his people. His enthusiasm for the temple in Jerusalem was not surprising in light of his being raised by a priest. This led to projects of renovation and expansion of the temple.[21]

During that work, a scroll was found. They called it the scroll of the law.[22] This scroll called for exclusive allegiance to Yahweh, who had brought Israel out of Egypt. The worship of Yahweh had been carried on throughout the history of the temple, but it had never been an exclusive policy, and many Israelites found spiritual support in the worship of other gods as the books of Kings amply document. Josiah is recorded to have approved the exclusivity of Yahweh's claim and acted vigorously to support that requirement.

A group called "the people of the land" enthusiastically supported that policy. The following kings fell back into a more tolerant mode despite Jeremiah's exhortations. But the party dedicated to Yahweh-only worship survived in the person of Jeremiah and his followers. Most of these believers were apparently among the exiles to Babylon. Some undoubtedly remained in Palestine. The group that went to Egypt, despite Jeremiah's presence among them, apparently did not support this view.

### Chronological Turning Points in Isaiah and the Twelve Prophets

Modern study of the prophets using historical criticism has usually thought of a crucial turning point in the history of Israel/Judah in terms of the destruction of Jerusalem by Babylonian forces in 586 BCE. This is founded on the end of the book of 2 Kings and on the prophetic books of Jeremiah and Ezekiel.

20. 2 Kgs 22; 2 Chr 34–35.
21. 2 Kgs 22:3–7.
22. 2 Kgs 22–23.

But this does not hold true for Isaiah and the book of the Twelve Prophets. Interpretation has been badly skewed because interpreters have tried to apply it in the same way, resulting in "First and Second Isaiah" and an outline that put all of the Twelve from Hosea through Zephaniah on one side with the turning point coming in Haggai-Zechariah. But neither Isaiah nor the Twelve picture the scenes of the fall of Jerusalem as Jeremiah does.

Instead, the Twelve put Micah with a dated prophecy in the reign of Hezekiah at the turning point, and Isaiah, by dating the prophecy down to Hezekiah's time and by having the scroll of Isaiah's prophecy (Isa 36–39) read to introduce the new age, puts its center of gravity in the same place. The turning point comes in Hezekiah's reign. Monarchy is no longer the key to divine planning. (Even the Deuteronomistic History recognizes that in Josiah's reform and reintroduction of Torah.) We need to look for a new paradigm.

The new paradigm for Isaiah is the Persian Empire, the new temple, and "the servants of Yahweh." In the book of the Twelve Prophets the emphasis is on the new temple and a new piety. The year 586 BCE marks the end of the monarchy, but the preparation for the new order had been going on since the days of Hezekiah. The rebuilding of the temple in 515 and the reading of the Torah by Ezra in 445 or 400 mark moves toward accomplishment of the new order. The role of written scrolls being read is another sign of the new order of things.

## THE READING OF THE SCROLL; REFORMS THAT RESULTED

Second Kings 22 tells a remarkable story of Josiah having a scroll read to him. It had been found while the workers were repairing the temple. The "scroll of the law" made a profound impression. He understood the words to be directed toward himself and his generation (2 Kgs 22:13). The prophetess Huldah confirmed that impression, specifying the transgression that incurred the wrath of God: "because they have forsaken me and burned incense to other gods and provoked me to anger by all the idols their hands have made" (2 Kgs 22:17 NIV). She then conceded that Josiah's response to the reading led the Lord to postpone the judgment beyond his death (2 Kgs 22:19–20).

The king, however, approached the issue more aggressively. He called a convocation of the elders of Judah and Jerusalem to listen to a reading of "the book of the covenant" (2 Kgs 23:2, 21). The narrator makes certain that we know that this is "the law of Moses" (2 Kgs 23:25). (See appendix A.)

The narrative continues with a description of Josiah's actions in response to this reading. He does thirteen things, each of which is noted in Deuteronomy and condemned in the prophets:[23]

- removes from the temple articles made for Baal and Asherah and the heavenly host (2 Kgs 23:4; Deut. 4:19)
- removes the "idol priests" who burned incense in the high places (2 Kgs 23:5; Hos 10:5; Zeph 1:4).
- removes the Asherah pole from the temple of Yahweh and burns it (2 Kgs 23:6, Deut 16:1).
- destroys the quarters of the (male) prostitutes (2 Kgs 23:7; Deut 23:18–19).
- desecrates the high places (2 Kgs 23:8–9; Deut 12:2–3).
- desecrates Topheth (2 Kgs 23:10; Lev 18:21; 20:2–5; Jer 7, 19).
- removes the horses at the entrance to the temple dedicated to the sun (2 Kgs 23:11; Deut 4:29).
- removes altars from the temple (2 Kgs 23:12; Zeph 1:3; Jer 19:13).
- removes high places east of Jerusalem (from Solomon's time?) (2 Kgs 23:13; Deut 7:5; 12:3; 16:21–22; Hos 9:10; Jer 7:30).
- destroys the altar at Bethel that was built by Jeroboam (2 Kgs 23:15).
- celebrates Passover (2 Kgs 23:21; Deut 16).
- gets rid of the mediums, the spiritualists, the household gods, and the idols in Judah and Jerusalem (2 Kgs 23:24; Deut 18:9–12).

Second Kings 23:24 explicitly relates the actions to the "torah that Hilkiah the priest had found in the temple of Yahweh." In the next verse it is called "the torah of Moses."

What was this "scroll of the covenant" found in the temple? It obviously contained *torah*. It was torah recording a covenant, and it was related

---

23. Hobbs, *2 Kings*, 320.

by the historian with Moses. Judaism knows a Scripture that it calls Torah. It recounts the story of Moses freeing the Israelites from Egypt, leading through the wilderness toward Canaan, making covenant with them and Yahweh at Sinai, and renewing that covenant on the border of Canaan.

This Torah contains three different collections of *toroth*, instructions given by God through Moses to be part of the covenant agreement that sealed the relation of Yahweh with his people, the children of Israel. One collection is in Exod 20:1—23:19, which we call the Covenant Code. It contains in Exod 20:1–17, what we call the Ten Commandments. It is embodied in the narrative of Israel's stay at Sinai.

A second collection is in Lev 17–26. Lev 19:1–19 contains apodictic laws like the Ten Commandments. The whole echoes with the refrain "I am Yahweh, I am holy," which has caused us to call this the Holiness Code. It is also understood to be spoken by Moses. It breathes the essence of covenant, including the promises for keeping covenant and the threats for not doing so (Lev 26).

A third collection is found in Deut 12–26, which is preceded by the Ten Commandments (Deut 5) and followed by covenant blessings for keeping covenant and curses for those breaking covenant (Deut 27–28). This is all part of the second speech of Moses in Deuteronomy.

Covenant traditions were cultivated in Israel in places that were already known to host covenant-renewal celebrations before the monarchy. These were Shechem, Shiloh, Gilgal, and perhaps Hebron. The coming of monarchy shifted the cultic centers to Jerusalem, which took control of the ark of the covenant for its temple, and Samaria, Bethel, and Dan. But the old sanctuary personnel continued in these amphictyonic sanctuaries, and repetition of their ceremonies may be presumed, though without the large attendance known before the monarchy. Perhaps the recorded codes of torah were those from different sanctuaries. As noted above, the most likely of these to have been in the scroll of Torah presented to Josiah was from Gilgal and became what we know as Deuteronomy.

## THE SCROLL (DEUT 5–26)

"The scroll" is described as "torah" and from "Moses." In late seventh-century Judah, where did it come from? How, where, and by whom was it written? The story only tells us that the scroll was read.

The books of Kings and Chronicles record the appearance of torah at the temple in Jerusalem on a number of occasions. But up until this

*The Beginning of Jewish Literature: End of the Assyrian Period* 117

time it was not called a scroll or book. We have noted that there are various forms of covenant laws in the Pentateuch. We have also noted that Josiah's response to the reading of the scroll suggests that the version he heard is from Deuteronomy. It is not likely that the scroll included the entire book of Deuteronomy. The essential torah is contained in the second speech of Moses (Deut 5–26), and the commands to which Josiah responded are found there.

We have noted in part 1 that ancient traditions were preserved in old sanctuaries. Four of these specialized in covenant-renewal ceremonies of the old amphictyony. Deut 4:45 places the speeches in "Beth-peor east of Jordan." Josh 4–6 tells of the crossing of the Jordan river, making camp at Gilgal, and important ceremonies designed to help future generations know the meaning of these events (Josh 4:21–24). Men were circumcised, and Jericho was overcome by ceremonial marches around the city for seven days. Gilgal became a place for regular gatherings to remember and renew covenant.

Deuteronomy reproduces the speeches made at these gatherings in the name of Moses. Scribes from the time of Hezekiah on had worked to put these into writing. The first result, Moses' speech of covenant renewal (Deut 5–26), is their work, ready to be presented to Josiah by the "people of the land" to inspire reforms to bring the kingdom more in line with amphictyonic standards.

The speech begins with a reminder that this is not the first time that Yahweh had made covenant with the twelve tribes. That was at Horeb. Moses stresses that the covenant obligation continues for the succeeding generations, as surely as it had applied to the first generation. Moses defines his role: he as the mediator "stood between Yahweh and you" (Deut 5:1–5). The recital will frame the commandments (Deut 5:22–27),[24] repeating Yahweh's words that had first been inscribed on stone, the Ten Commandments (Deut 5:6–21). These are followed by a series of hortatory homilies that urge the people to keep the covenant and obey the commands (Deut 5:28—11:32).

---

24. Watts, "Deuteronomy," 206.

## THE BEGINNING OF A LITERARY ERA: JOSH 1-12

Josh 1-12[25] fits the era of the closing decades of the Assyrian period.[26] It also fits the background of Gilgal.[27] It is narrative that tells of the initial movements of Israelite tribes into land west of the Jordan. There are references to "the whole land" (*kol haaretz*) in Josh 2:24; 6:27; 9:24; and 11:16, 23 that matched Josiah's interest in reuniting the whole land under his rule.

The narrative develops around a series of episodes:

- preparations for the march on the land (Josh 1:1–16)
- Rahab's help for the spies (Josh 2:1–24)
- crossing the Jordan to begin the conquest (Josh 3:1—5:1)
- circumcision at Gilgal: the wilderness journey officially over (Josh 5:2–15)
- the fall of the walls of Jericho (Josh 6:1–27)
- consequences of breech of *herem*, "ban" (Josh 7:1—8:29)
- Gibeonites' negotiation of a compromise (Josh 9:1–27)
- the sweep of the southern cities (Josh 10:1–43)
- the campaign through the north (Josh 11:1–23)
- the list of the conquered (Josh 12:1–24)

This section gives the impression that Joshua's victories were complete and that all Canaan now belonged to Israel, though later additions will correct this view. The unit matches the challenge found in Moses' second speech (Deut 5–26), which called for total devotion and promised total vistory. It also matches the picture of unity for all Israel under a single God.

---

25. Butler, *Joshua*.
26. Rose, *Deuteronomist und Jahwist*.
27. Eckart, *Mazzotfest in Gilgal*.

## THE TEACHINGS OF THE SCROLL OF DEUTERONOMY AND INCIPIENT JUDAISM

Major doctrines of Judaism are proclaimed in Deut 5–26 and echoed in the book of Joshua.[28] These doctrines include

- the singleness (exclusiveness) of God (Deut 6:4, the Shema)
- the requirement of complete love for God (Deut 6:5)
- God's covenant with Israel, which continued to be applicable (Deut 5:2–4)
- the revelation of God on Sinai: the Ten Commandments (Deut 5:6–21)
- Yahweh's oath that Canaan would belong to the descendants of Abraham, Isaac, and Jacob, conditioned on their keeping covenant (Deut 6:10–12)
- Israel's devotion to only one temple (Deut 12)
- The list could be extended. Judaism built its faith on Deut 5–26. The book of Joshua gave an example of covenant loyalty and the blessings that flow from it.

The marks of Deuteronomistic writing[29] show, in the exhortations to loyalty and covenant obedience, the sense of Israel's place in history at any given time (in Deuteronomy: between the wilderness journey and the occupation of the land) and the recognition of fate being both a gift of inheritance and a result of personal choices and actions. These are true in life because God is as he is. God works with goals. He is loyal to his own, but he expects obedience and loyalty from his own as well.

God (and the people) expect resistance and opposition from enemies (Canaanites, Egyptians, etc.). But a great deal of their trouble comes from their own: persons and groups inside the tribes as well as from kindred peoples (Edom, Moab, Ammon). God has to act as judge in both areas. The people and their leaders have to do the same.

---

28. For further discussion of Deuteronomic theology see Herrman, "Die konstruktive Restauration"; McConville, *Law and Theology*; idem, *Grace in the End*; Perlitt, *Bundestheologie*; von Rad, *Das Gottesvolk*; Rose, *Der Ausschliesslichkeitsanspruch Jahwes*; Watts, "Deuteronomic Theology."

29. Examples are Deut 6:1–3; 11:31–32; 12:8–12; 26:16–19; Josh 1:2–9; 24:2–28.

# 9

# Jewish Literature of the Babylonian Period

## NEBUCHADNEZZAR'S CONQUESTS AND OPPRESSION

FROM 609 UNTIL AFTER 587 BCE, Israel/Judah was caught up in the struggle for succession to the Assyrian empire after Nineveh fell in 612 BCE. That had been made possible by an understanding between the Babylonians and the Medes, which allocated the north and east to Media while Babylon could concentrate on Mesopotamia and Palestine. Egypt was left out of the agreement but arrived too late in the war to affect the consequences for Nineveh. When Egypt's armies did arrive for the last battles against Assyrian armies in Haran in 609 BCE, Babylonian armies met and defeated them at Carchemish in a decisive battle.

Egyptian armies had to cross Palestine on the way to that battle. Josiah was killed when his forces met them at Megiddo. Egypt then controlled the area for a period. They had moved about Palestine almost at will for some time as Assyria's hold on its frontiers relaxed. There can be no doubt that Egypt intended to reassert its authority in Palestine. The march of their large army through Palestine on the way to Haran coupled with the final demise of Assyrian power left Palestine totally within their realm of authority.

It looked as if Judah's Assyrian period would be followed by an Egyptian period. Josiah had managed to work with both the Assyrians and the Egyptians during this difficult period. But for some incomprehensible reason he decided to forcefully oppose Pharoah Neco's march at Megiddo[1] and died in the battle.

---

1. 2 Kgs 23:29 / 2 Chr 36:20–24.

"The people of the land" put Josiah's younger son, Jehoahaz, on the throne. But when Neco returned, he took Jehoahaz into exile and placed his elder brother, the natural heir, Jehoiakim, on the throne. Judah was in the awkward position of not knowing who would ultimately win out in Palestine. Egypt lost the battle at Carchemish to the Babylonians, but it claimed Palestine. Jehoiakim was subject to Egypt until Nebuchadnezzar came in 605 BCE to claim his heritage of formerly Assyrian territories. Judah, as a border territory, continued to be torn between loyalty to Babylon and to Egypt.

Nebuchadnezzar, Babylon's general-king, got around to establishing his authority in Palestine in 605 BCE and was back in the region in 598 BCE. On the latter occasion, he took Jehoiakim's successor, Jehoiachin, and his family into exile with a number of the leaders (apparently including Ezekiel and Daniel of later fame), and placed Zedekiah on the throne. The following years were uneasy ones until Nebuchadnezzar returned in 587 to sack Jerusalem and take a larger number of the people of the city and the countryside into captivity in Babylon and surrounding lands.

These years and events are portrayed in the Bible in several places and ways:

- the fall of Nineveh: Nahum
- the history of the period: 2 Kgs 23:29—25:26; 2 Chr 35:20—36:21; Ezekiel; Jeremiah
- the coming of the Babylonians: Habakkuk
- the fall of Jerusalem: Lamentations; Isa 34:8–15

The extensive coverage of this relatively short period shows its importance in the thinking reflected in Scripture and also the rapid expansion of literary activities. The account of these events in 2 Kings may well be virtually contemporary. It is generally agreed now that the writing of the history (called DtH or Deuteronomistic History because of its obvious dependence on the teaching of the book of Deuteronomy; it includes the books of Joshua, Judges, 1 and 2 Samuel, and 1 and 2 Kings) was completed shortly after this period. Scribes still had access to court records in Jerusalem or those taken into Babylon from Jerusalem, but they also wrote under the threat of doom echoed in Huldah's prophecy (2 Kgs 23:16-20). This magnificent explanation of how God could, indeed had, given his people into the hands of their conquerors, played a major role in making survival of faith possible for the exiled and devastated people.

The second great literary piece of this period is the book of Jeremiah. The prophet's career runs from the time of Josiah's reform until after the fall of Jerusalem. His prophecies are placed in important positions through all those reigns. Jeremiah also breathes the spirit of Deuteronomy. His testimony to God's calls for repentance addressed to king and people that constantly fell on deaf ears provided for the exiles the best explanation possible of why God allowed his sacred precincts to be overrun. Jeremiah also sounded a note of hope in the assurance that God had not gone down with his city and that his plans for his people were not over.

Evidence of the growing influence of literacy is shown in Jeremiah in the work of Baruch, his scribe and companion, who on occasion was called upon to present the prophet's messages in writing to be read to the people and to the king when the prophet himself was physically unable to present them orally (Jer 36). On one occasion Jeremiah sent a message in writing to the exiles in Babylon (Jer 29:1–28). And in Jer 30:2 Jeremiah is commanded to write his words in a book. This was clearly the beginning of a genre of written prophecy. Alongside Deuteronomy-Joshua and the Deuteronomistic History, the people of the exile heard the words of Jeremiah read. Their faith and knowledge of God were shaped by these books, which fed the faith of those who survived the devastation of Jerusalem and who flourished in exile.

Ezekiel, as a book, probably derives from a later period. But its prophecies are set in the period between the first Judean exile of 598 and the final fall of Jerusalem in 587 BCE.

## JUDAH AND JEWS UNDER THE BABYLONIANS

### Between 587 and 540 BCE

This period is largely blank in biblical presentation. Part of Jeremiah spills over into this time (Jer 52:31–34) that tells of the treatment of Jehoiachin in exile. Second Kings 25:27–30 reports the same events. And Daniel from a much later perspective reports various experiences from the Babylonian period.

Jewish experience was now divided. Exiles in Mesopotamia and in Egypt settled into a new existence. The miserable groups left in a devastated Palestine struggled to come to grips with their lives or, better, to simply stay alive. Nebuchadnezzar died in 562 BCE. Nebuchadnezzar's successors proved unworthy of the power and privileges passed on to them. We are uncertain of the conditions in the following decades.

Nabunaid held the throne in Babylon from 550 to 539 BCE but apparently was absorbed in deep religious meditation in his secluded sanctuary during much of that reign, while Belshazzer, his wastrel son, partied his life away in Babylon.

The remnants of the Israelite deportations of 722 were still to be found in upper Mesopotamia and Media. The center of active Jewish life, however, was in Babylon. Judah's deportations in 598 and 586 had brought Judeans to villages near Babylon and further east near Susa. Jehoiachin and his family were in "house arrest" at the palace in Babylon. Some of the most promising young men were trained for civil service in the government (Dan 1). Most of the families were settled in villages in territories south of Babylon. Among them were Levites and priests who, of course, had no temple in which to serve. No doubt some of "the people of the land" who had welcomed the reading of the book of the law were among them.

The hope for the future for Jews lay in Babylon after 587 BCE. The chaotic conditions in Judah after the fall of Jerusalem are pictured in Jer 40–43. The appointed governor was assassinated, and a group of people, including Jeremiah and Baruch, fled to Egypt. Parts of Judah were assigned to Philistine administration while other parts were put under the administration of Samaria.

Jeremiah's words to the Egyptian refugees (Jer 43:8—44:30) do not picture a Judean community that had much promise for the future. Judean communities in Egypt were typically composed of mercenaries who lived in separated towns.

There are some biblical descriptions of the era. These look back on it from a later time. Descriptions of the time in Babylon are found in Dan 1–6 (esp. Dan 5:25–31), 7, and 8; Prayer of Azariah; Song of the Three Young Men; and Susanna. Isa 40–44 looks at the very end of the period in anticipation of the entry of Cyrus. By the end of this period Jews were using the book of Deuteronomy, the Deuteronomistic History, and the book of Jeremiah.

*The Composition of the Tetrateuch*[2]

The sanctuaries and festivals of Israel and Judah had cultivated the traditions of their history. They were rehearsed at the festivals at intervals, annually or otherwise. Storytellers and liturgists developed elaborate versions of the stories related to a particular sanctuary or to a festival. Since some of these festivals were celebrated at more than one place, these versions were often variants on a theme.

After Deuteronomy had published the covenant speeches from Gilgal and since the exile of the northern kingdom had threatened the existence of several sanctuaries, scribes related to the sanctuaries or to the groups responsible for them began seriously to try to preserve their religious treasure. Thus began the work that led to the composition of the Torah.[3]

Deuteronomy had looked at these traditions from the viewpoint of those entering the land. The new work looked behind that perspective to the things that were only hinted at or barely mentioned in Deuteronomy. Priestly scribes completed the work in Babylon, but they worked with versions of the larger story that had been developed before in the land.

The scribes worked with covenant traditions, as Deuteronomy had done, but placed them in the setting of Sinai, or Horeb as it was sometimes called. These traditions included what is now Exod 19–24, which includes a version of the Decalogue in Exod 20:1–7, very similar to Deut 5:6–21. A collection of laws, which is now called the Covenant Code, in Exod 21:1—23:19, is parallel to Deut 12–26.

Deut 1–3 had told the story of the journey from Horeb to the land. The new work tells the story of being slaves in Egypt and of the work of Moses in setting them free, Exod 1–12, which is probably taken from traditions recited at Passover celebrations. Exodus then tells the story of the journey from Egypt to Sinai (Exod 16–18). Deuteronomy refers

---

2. Martin Noth (*Überlieferungsgeschichte des Pentateuch*) coined the term for the first four books of Torah when Deuteronomy is considered the opening of the following Deuteronomistic History. More recent thorough studies of the Pentateuch are those of Erhard Blum: *Studien zur Komposition des Pentateuch* and *Die Komposition der Vätergeschichte*.

3. Donald Akenson (*Surpassing Wonder*, 21) thinks of this work being done in Babylon by "a young religious genius." He uses the term "invention" (p. 24) "for the product of a great and nimble mind" who uses "what is to hand, then adds something of their own genius, whether it is new ways of recombining old elements, or tiny improvements in existing parts."

to a rebellion of the people while still at Horeb (Deut 9:8). Exod 32–34 tells the story in detail. Numbers continues the story of the journey to the land.

Deut 32 and 33 speak of Jacob. Deut 1:6, 6:10, and 30:20 speak of a promise made to Abraham, and Deut 9:27 speaks of Isaac. The new work prefaces the stories of Israel with those of the patriarchs. The Jacob story is found now in Gen 25–50. The story of Abraham is found in Gen 11–24. Many places in Canaan were related to the patriarchs, and stories of their visits there were told through the years. The Jacob stories were gathered into the collection we now know first in Shechem. The Abraham stories come mostly from Hebron. The Joseph story in Gen 37, 39–48, and 50 is of a different type, parallel to the other stories in Hebrew literature of Israelites who become influential and powerful, such as the stories of Moses, Daniel, Nehemiah, and Esther.

Then the work adds a preface concerning beginnings that Deuteronomy does not know. It tells a story now found in Gen 2:4b—9:28 of the creation of Adam and Eve and their descendants down to the great flood and Noah's ark. We have no idea where the traditions came from for these stories, but they are oriented toward Mesopotamia. They imply that God had control of that part of the world, not just over Canaan. Priestly scribes in Babylon during the exile found the great story valuable and arranged and edited it to make it adequate for their purposes as Torah. They prefaced a new beginning in Gen 1:1—2:4a in which God (as understood by the Israelites) is the causative force that created the universe and all that is in it. It is the first of a number of lists of generations *(toldoth)* that they used to structure the work. These lists occur in Gen 1:1—2:4a (heavens and earth), 5 (Adam), 10 (Noah's sons), 11:10-16 (Shem), 11:27-32 (Terah), 25:12-18 (Ishmael), 25:19-20 (Isaac), 36:1-43 (Esau), and 37:2 (Jacob) and Exod 1:1-6 (sons of Jacob). The Priestly propensity for lists continues in Num 1–4 with the census of the tribes participating in covenant at Sinai.

In the larger work, massive priestly inserts occur in the Sinai section with instructions concerning the building of the tabernacle (Exod 24–31, 35–40), narrative about the priests in Lev 1–16, and a body of laws that is now called the Holiness Code (Lev 17–26, 27), which has threats in chapter 26 about not keeping the covenant, threats similar to those in Deut 27–31. The Holiness Code makes the third group of laws in the Pentateuch. Other priestly laws are promulgated through the continued stories in Numbers.

The final stabilization of the text would have to wait a long time, but there is no reason this work cannot be considered to be "the Torah" that Ezra had read to the people in the rededication of the temple and that he filed with the Persian authorities as the law governing the temple and its territory. Accepting the Deuteronomistic History and the Prophets alongside this work unified the people, the exiles and "the people of the land," the priests and the prophetic parties. A version of Torah with significant variations even served the Samaritans. It gave Jews the basic canon of the Torah and the Prophets that would govern them for a long time. The rich tradition that had sustained Israel and Judah since before the time of David had now been put into a book. Through it, Judaism became a religion of the book and Moses became the central figure in revelation.

## Building the Pentateuch from D

If Deuteronomy, the Deuteronomistic History, and the Prophets were the first canon for Jewish people rebuilding Jerusalem and Judah and for the Diaspora attempting to found a satisfactory and enduring Jewish faith, the building of the temple brought new challenges. The Jews were working under the approval of the Persian government, and they wanted the empire to recognize the legitimacy of their temple's laws.

The Deuteronomic corpus was not planned for this eventuality, although Isaiah's book provided some basis for claims about the nature and authority of Yahweh's rule. The scribes set to work to frame an adequate expansion for Deuteronomy to fulfill these purposes and needs. The goal was to unite all Jews under one law and to pose the claims for universal authority for Yahweh as he was recognized in the Jerusalem temple. The role and function of priests needed to be laid out, as well as the requirements for the building of the temple.

There existed in the archives of Jewish scribes records of traditions and requirements that could be brought together for these purposes. The work is not shy about creating redundant systems, duplicating things already found in Deuteronomy. Many of them are mentioned or hinted at in Deuteronomy and the History.

There are three groups of general laws in the Pentateuch: Deut 12–26 is the Deuteronomic Code. Exod 21:1—23:19 is often called the Covenant Code and is presented as a part of the narrative of Israel at

Sinai. Lev 17-27 is called the Holiness Code because of its oft-repeated admonition to be holy as Yahweh is holy. It is in many ways unique in style. It has similarities to Deuteronomy.

There are three records of the "ten commandments." Each of the Law collections contains a version: Deut 5:6-21, Exod 20:1-17, and Lev 19. In Deut 27:1—28:68, 30:1-19, and Lev 26, there are parallel treatments of the eventuality that Israel would break covenant. Deuteronomy tells of an earlier covenant at Sinai: Deut 5:2-5, 9:1-29, and 31:1. Exodus tells that story in full: Exod 19:1-25, 24:1-18, and 31:12—35:3.

Deuteronomy recounts the journey from Horeb to the Plains of Paran: Deut 1:1—3:29. Num 20:13—32:32 covers the same ground but includes various instructions for the priests to use.

Deut 26:5-10 and Josh 24:2-10 give summaries of earlier history from Abraham to the Egyptian sojourn. Gen 11:10—38:30 tells the story of the ancestors. Gen 30-Exod 2 tells of the stay in Egypt. Exod 3-15 tells of the exodus out of Egypt. The story of the journey through the wilderness to Sinai is told in Exod 16-18 and Num 20:13—32:32.

Deut 32:7-8 speaks of human origins. Gen 2:1—11:9 provides a full narrative. Deut 12:4-14 orders the setting of one central place of worship. Prescriptions are provided for:

- the tabernacle: Exod 25:1—31:11; 35:4—40:38
- sacrifices, priests, and atonement: Lev 1-16
- census and departure: Num 1-10
- land allotments: Num 32:33-42 (Josh 13-21)

Deut 7:1 is aware of the various ethnic groups in the land: Hittites, Girgashites, Amorites, Canaanites, Perizzites, Hivites, and Jebusites. Josh 3:9 and 12:8 follow suit. Josh 13:2 adds Philistines and Geshurites to Canaanites, Hittites, Hivites, Perizzites, Girgashites, Amorites, and Jebusites. Gen 10 details a full table of the nations over the entire Near Eastern territory. Amos 1-2 and the prophets add Assyria, Babylon, and Egypt to the political units in the land: Aram, Gaza (Philistines), Tyre, Edom, Ammon, Moab, Judah, and Israel.

Gen 1 gives the whole a cosmic dimension that only Isa 40 can match. Yahweh's authority over the Persian ruler Cyrus is matched by Moses applying Yahweh's power to the pharaoh in Exodus. His victory over the pharoah is emphasized by his victory over Assyrian and Babylonian rulers in Isaiah and other prophets.

In these ways the Torah is drawn together to provide the necessary instructions for the temple and the priests as well as the worldview needed for a Jewish constituency that stretched around the Persian Empire and the Mediterranean basin. The whole is based on narrative that moves from "the beginning" of everything to the time when the Israelite tribes stand ready to enter the territory west of the river Jordan, i.e., the point at which Deuteronomy takes its departure. When added to the narrative that follows, Deuteronomy covers the story from the beginning to the end of the exile, the anticipation of the new Jerusalem and the new temple. The P redaction works these into the narrative, plus lists and laws that lead up to Deuteronomy as a second giving of the law. Together they form the Torah as used in Judaism.

## *The Torah and the Prophets Are Complete*

Priestly participation in the new edition of Scripture was decisive for the shape of the Torah. In no part was that more true than in the Sinai and following sections. They added to the narrative the cultic laws for the tabernacle (Exod 25:1—31:11; 35:4—40:38). The major sections on sacrifices (Lev 1–7), concerning priests (Lev 8–10), on clean and unclean (Lev 11–15), and regarding the Day of Atonement (Lev 16) provided the program of worship needed for the restored temple worship. The so-called Holiness Code and other Priestly laws (Lev 17–27; Num 5–6, 9:1—10:10, 15, 18–19, 28–30) were of little use in exile; they were essential for plans to make the temple the center of Jewish faith and identity.

A census of the Israelites leaving Sinai (Num 1–2) and one later in the journey (Num 26) establish the identity of the tribes. A remarkable feature of postexilic writing shows the Jews consciously reestablishing an identity of twelve tribes after two centuries of the divided monarchy and the occupation and exile by the Assyrians that appeared to have ended the existence of the northern tribes.[4] The accounts of distribution of land to the tribes (Num 32:33–42; Josh 13–21), along with the fixing of the rights of Levites and priests to land rights, offerings, and jobs, were essential to the return to Judah.

---

4. Williamson, "Concept of Israel in Transition," 141–62.

The Deuteronomistic History had already established the presence and preeminence of the book of the law for the community. All of this set the stage for Ezra's reading of Torah in Jerusalem (Neh 8). Ezra and Nehemiah leave no doubt that two documents were basic to Jerusalem's renewal. One was the edict of Persian emperors, renewed at least twice (Ezra 1:1-4). The second was the "the book of the law of Moses that Yahweh had given to Israel" (Neh 8:1).

Persian policy allowed the existence of temple cities, which could operate under their own laws, of course approved by the Persian authorities. Ezra's instructions from the emperor were to administer "the law of your God and the law of the king" (Ezra 7).[5] The temple before the exile was Solomon's temple under the administration of Davidic kings and their appointed priests. What influence Mosaic law had in it is difficult to assess. The priesthood was known to be Zadokite, as it still was in Ezek 40-48. Ezra established the supreme role of Torah and Aaronide priests in the new temple. See Neh 12:47 for the explicit mention of "the descendants of Aaron." Nehemiah apparently did not apply the rules of Torah that reserved the rights of Kohathites, Gershonites, and Merarites (Num 4:17-33) to the positions of workers in the temple (Neh 7:73; 11:19-23). These and their positions are explicitly related to royal appointment from David and Solomon (Neh 12:45-46). Ezra's policies excluded foreigners from the temple (Neh 10:28-31; 13:1-3, 23-27), apparently on the basis of strict Deuteronomic injunctions. Most of these developments build on things mentioned in Deuteronomy. The Torah allows redundant accounts and legal groupings.

## The Origins of the Prophetic Literature

Erich Bosshard-Nepustil has summarized the view that the prophetic corpus grew in stages from the eighth century down into the Greek period.[6] Douglas Stuart[7] summarized the view that the prophetic judgment speeches and hope speeches were rooted in the covenant judgment sections of Deuteronomy and Leviticus. Other research has established the way that the books of the Latter Prophets relate to the Torah and to the Former Prophets. The constellation of land/people that is basic to the pro-

---

5. Blenkinsopp, *Pentateuch*, 240.
6. Bosshard-Nepustil, *Rezeptionen von Jesaia 1-39 im Zwölfprophetenbuch*.
7. Stuart, *Hosea-Jonah*, xxxi-xxxii.

phetic works is fundamental to Deuteronomy and the Deuteronomistic History (Joshua–2 Kings).

Is it fair to remind ourselves that we must account for the place of Deuteronomy in the scheme before we begin to describe how the other works came into existence? The Deuteronomistic canon runs from Deuteronomy to the Former Prophets and the Latter Prophets. The literary appropriation for the reader requires that Deuteronomy be read and known to understand and follow the two prophetic corpuses.

Deuteronomy lays out God's conditions on which Israel was granted the right to live in the land. It spells out the way that Israel's compliance to those laws would be tested (Deut 27–32) and foresees the possibility that Israel would lose her status in the land, would be punished with a series of curses, and later would be restored to blessings in the land. The Former Prophets (Joshua–2 Kings) trace the history of Israel's reception of the land, her failures to fulfill God's provisions, and finally the judgments that deprived her of the land. The Latter Prophets portray Israel's (and Jerusalem's) apostasy and the devastations of people and land brought about by the Assyrian invasions of 740–609 BCE and by the Babylonian invasions of 605–560 BCE. Isaiah and the Twelve Prophets move beyond that to restorations accomplished under the Persian regime.

The prophetic corpus (Former + Latter Prophets) depends on Deuteronomy, both for its reading and understanding and for its production. One cannot solve the issue of dates for the various layers of the Latter Prophets[8] until one solves the issues related to Deuteronomy (the book or the traditions behind the book). One cannot propose a long literary history for this period without also proposing a view of the scribal system and history needed to produce such a work as well as the way that the work would have been presented to its readers (hearers).

Is this possible? I think it is. There must be a separation into two periods: the actual period of *literary* development and the period dominated by traditions (oral and written) located and cultivated around temples and monarchies. Then we will need to be alert for the hints within the text concerning its history.

---

8. Bosshard-Nepustil, *Rezeptionen von Jesaia 1–39 im Zwölfprophetenbuch*.

## Deuteronomy's Story: The Second Stage

Josiah's reformed kingdom was overtaken by events on the world stage. The Assyrian Empire was already crumbling when his reform took place. Ambitious heirs were lurking in the wings. Media, Babylon, and Egypt were prepared to compete for the vacant throne. Media and Babylon besieged and destroyed Nineveh. Egypt pressed northward to join the fray, defeating and killing Josiah on the way and taking control of all Palestine.

Egypt eventually had to retreat within its boundaries. Babylon agreed with Media that they would divide the Assyrian territories: Media would rule areas east, north, and northwest of Mesopotamia (Persia, Armenia, and Anatolia) while Babylon would inherit all of Mesopotamia and Palestine.

It was not long before Nebuchadnezzar arrived to claim his booty in Jerusalem and Judah's long night of the soul began. The political opportunities that Josiah enjoyed were gone. The bright hopes that the book found in the temple had nourished were snuffed out. Deuteronomy looked forward to life in the land of Canaan. The first decades of the sixth century under Babylon changed that prospect forever. The people were scattered. They had no political integrity. The prospect for the unity and riches that Deuteronomy and Joshua envisioned was dimmed.

What happened to the book? Did it die and go away? Far from it! It became the cornerstone for a new faith called Judaism.[9] Its central appeal "Hear, O Israel: Yahweh, our God, Yahweh is One!" became the heart of faith for a people without a land, and for a long time without a temple. They followed the instructions of Deut 6:8 to "tie them as symbols on your hands and bind them on your foreheads. Write them on the doorframes of your houses and on your gates" (NIV). And Jews remained a separated and distinct people, even in foreign lands, because of Deuteronomy.

---

9. See discussion of the development of Deuteronomistic History in the following literature: Begg, "Bible Mystery"; idem, "Non-Mention of Amos"; idem, "Non-mention of Zephaniah"; Dietrich, *Prophetie und Geschichte*; Freedman, "Deuteronomic History"; Friedman, *Exile and Biblical Narrative*; Halpern, *First Historians*; Hoffmann, *Reform und Reformen*; Nelson, *Double Redaction*; Noth, *Deuteronomistic History*; O'Brien, *Deuteronomistic History Hypothesis*; Peckham, *Composition of the Deuteronomic History*; Person, "II Kings 24:18—25:30 and Jeremiah 52"; Provan, *Hezekiah and the Books of Kings*; Radjawane, "Das deuteronomistische Geschichtswerk"; Smend, "Das Gesetz und die Völker"; Westermann, *Die Geschichtsbücher des Alten Testaments*; Wolff, "Kerygma of the Deuteronomic Historical Work."

But the continued effect of the book, now copied many times over and read wherever Jews lived and gathered for worship, was much greater than that. The same scribes that had produced Deuteronomy, perhaps some related to Shaphan, who read the book to Josiah and to whom the book was entrusted afterwards (2 Kgs 23), used the book to show how God had fulfilled what was announced in Deuteronomy.[10] Richard Nelson studied the possibility of two editions of the history.[11] Claus Westermann has published a denial of the entire concept in which he exalts the role of oral tradition in the process of transmission.[12]

The genre of Deut 5–26 is that of sermon or exhortation in expounding the law, calling for obedience, and warning against disobedience. The next stage began to look at the book as a prophecy. The warnings had been ignored, and the results that Moses had predicted had come to pass. Prophecy interprets history in terms of God's work. Deuteronomistic prophecy interpreted the history of Israel from the time it entered Canaan until the exiles left for Babylon and Egypt. These interpreters are called Deuteronomists because they built the book of Deuteronomy into their history and used it as a basis for interpreting the history. God dealt with Israel in accordance with his covenant as enunciated in the book of Deuteronomy. Martin Noth[13] established the essential unity of the history that begins in Deuteronomy and goes through 2 Kings and is now called DtH, the Deuteronomistic History. A major study of the relation between Deuteronomy and DtH is Moshe Weinfeld's, *Deuteronomy and the Deuteronomic School*. This work first expanded the book found in the temple. It prefixed a speech of Moses (Deut 1:1—4:43).[14] Josef Plöger[15] followed with a detailed study of the beginning chapters, including a lengthy introduction (Deut 1:1–5) that placed Moses and the people at the end of the period of wanderings, poised to cross the Jordan. The conquest of the countries on the east bank of Jordan is complete. It also notes that forty years of wanderings is at an end.

10. Noth, *Überlieferungsgeschichtliche Studien*; Weippert, "Das deuteronomistische Geschichtswerk"; Wolff, "Kerygma des deuteronomistische Geschichtswerks."

11. *Double Redaction*.

12. Westermann, *Die Geschichtsbücher des Alten Testaments: Gab es ein deuteronomistisches Geschichtswerk?*

13. *Überlieferungsgeschichtliche Studien*, first published in 1943.

14. Noth, *Überlieferungsgeschichtliche Studien*, 14.

15. *Literarkritische*, 11–58.

The speech begins with a recital of the journey from Horeb to Paran (Deut 1:6—3:29). Its tells the stories of appointment of judges (Deut 1:9-18), of the abortive experience of spies sent to search out the land (Deut 1:19-46), of travels and victories in the land east of Jordan (Deut 2:1—3:17). It tells of promised help for the conquest that lies ahead and of pleas from Moses (Deut 3:18-29).

The portion closes with a powerful sermon on the first commandment (Deut 4:1-40). The sermon exhorts the people to keep the law that is Israel's supreme wisdom (Deut 4:1-13). Then it singles out the great commandment (Deut 4:14-20). It exhorts the people not to forget the covenant. It warns that if the Israelites in the future fall into idolatry, they will lose the land that they are now going in to possess and they will be scattered among the nations (Deut 4:25-28).

After the introductory passage (Deut 1:1-6a), the speech is presented without interruption through Deut 4:40, just as chapters 5-26 are presented in uninterrupted fashion after the introduction (Deut 4:44-49) and the narrative interlude (Deut 4:41-43). These (Deut 1:1—4:40 and 5:1—26:19) are presented as two speeches, each of which can stand on its own feet.

The closing paragraph of the opening speech (Deut 4:29-31) looks beyond such judgment: "If from there [in exile] you seek the Lord your God, you will find him if you look for him with all your heart and with all your soul" (NIV). The last phrases echo Deut 6:5. The possibility of returning to Yahweh and obeying him is affirmed: "For the Lord your God is a merciful God; he will not abandon or destroy you or forget the covenant with your forefathers, which he confirmed to them by oath" (NIV). In these words the positive message of the prophets in the exile and afterward is enunciated, from Jeremiah to Zechariah.

This speech, then, looks beyond the entry into the land, sobered by reminders of the golden calf at Horeb and of the terrible experiences with the spies, to recognize that judgment for infidelity and idolatry will certainly come. But it also looks beyond that to God's continued purpose for the people founded on the same promises to Abraham on which the first entry into the land was based. The hallmarks of Deuteronomistic theology are laid out. There is promise based on covenant. Blessing will follow obedience to covenant. Failure to obey invokes curses that include invasion and exile. But the opportunity for covenant renewal continues through the eternal purposes and grace of God and the promises made long before to the patriarchs.

The scribes then extended the book at the end. Plöger[16] presents a detailed study of Deut 28 in this connection. Noth[17] treats Deut 27-30 as a part of Deuteronomistic History. He had already dealt with Deut 31[18] and connected it to the beginning of Joshua. Deut 27-28 is introduced by the words "Moses and the elders of Israel commanded the people" (Deut 27:1a RSV), marking it as a separate speech. Deut 29-30 is similarly introduced in 29:1, marking this as another speech. Deut 31 is narrative containing several smaller speeches.

Deut 27-30 spells out issues related to covenant judgment and covenant renewal. These chapters are just as pessimistic about Israel's ability to live faithfully in covenant as Deut 4 was.

Deut 31 narrates measures being taken to make possible succession of Joshua to take Moses' place. Deut 4 had already recognized that Moses would not be allowed into the West Bank. With this chapter, it is clear that the writing will continue beyond Moses. The law is written down, and provisions for its regular reading are given. But before Moses dies, two more works from Moses are included. Deut 32 is introduced as a song (Deut 31:30) that pictures a heavenly judgment on Israel. Deut 33 is introduced (Deut 33:1-2a) as a blessing spoken on each of the tribes. Deut 32:48-52 and 34:1-12 tell of the death of Moses.

The book of Joshua continues the story.[19] It tells of the conquest of Canaan in Josh 1-12. Josh 13-21 recounts the distribution of the land, recognizing that the entire land was not subdued. These are tribal boundary and city lists. In chapter 22 Joshua sends the representatives of the eastern tribes who had fought alongside their brethren back to their homes. A farewell address from Joshua follows in chapter 23. A narrative of a covenant ceremony at Shechem closes the book.

Many features in Joshua parallel those in Deuteronomy. The books end with a finality that builds no bridges to subsequent events. When the story is resumed in Judges, it begins all over again.

Imitating Deut 1:13-18, which tells how Moses appointed judges from all the tribes foreshadowed the coming age, the book of Judges

---

16. *Literarkritische*, 130-92.
17. Noth, *Überlieferungsgeschichtliche Studien*, 17-18.
18. Ibid., 13.
19. Polzin, *Moses and the Deuteronomist*.

recounts the period between Joshua and Samuel in terms of judges who led Israel, one from each of the tribes. But the book begins by recognizing that the conquest had not been complete. The task of living with the Canaanites still in the land was a problem.

The signs of Deuteronomistic interpretation are everywhere. "The people did evil in the sight of Yahweh" accounts for repeated disasters as God reacts to this evil. But Yahweh heeds repentant pleadings from the people of the land and raises up saviors or judges for them. These are all set within a chronological frame. The work of judges followed by periods of apostasy tend to run to about forty years (six times). The book ends with narratives from the period.

One narrative tells of a migration of a family of the tribe of Dan to a northern location and the employment of a Levite to be a priest for a family's idol (Judg 17–18). The second tells of an atrocity in Benjamin in which a woman is killed and the resulting tribal war (Judg 19–20).

Deuteronomistic History so far has made the point that Israel tends to apostasy. It all began at Horeb with the golden calf and continued in Israel's reluctance to enter the land when the spies brought their report. The book of Judges tells of the cycles of apostasy and repentance that continued throughout the period. All these illustrate the Deuteronomic teaching that warned of judgment on apostasy but promised God's openness to those who seek to reenter covenant with him afterward on condition of their full repentance and whole-hearted faith.

Samuel was the last of the judges. But his book, 1 Samuel,[20] takes a different turn. During Samuel's lifetime, Eli's death brought an end to his line as priest and judge, Saul was made the first king against Samuel's better judgment, and David was singled out to be Saul's successor.

Israel crossed the line from being a loose confederacy of tribes to trying to be a kingdom. Saul took the title of king but did little to change the political or social nature of Israel. This story and that about the rise of David in 2 Samuel were inserted into Deuteronomistic History and do not directly reflect its theological concerns.

David's story is high drama in which he rises from being a leader of a band of outlaws to king of Judah in Hebron to finally being king of all Israel in Jerusalem.[21] His military expertise and his winsome personality did unite the tribes and provide them with substantial security. The

20. Polzin, *Samuel and the Deuteronomist*.
21. Carlson, *David the Chosen King*; Veijola, *Die ewige Dynastie*.

story tells of David's election by Yahweh, the blessing that followed his life up to the point of his affair with Bathsheba, and then the curse that lay heavily upon him and his family for the rest of his life.

First Kings picks up the story. The promise that God made to David (2 Sam 7:14) is kept.[22] The author/editors found the story lacked something to deal with the succession of David's son to the throne and therefore needed the first two chapters of 1 Kings to be complete.

David's son Solomon succeeds to the throne, but the succession is difficult. Solomon proves to be a strong king. His diplomacy and commercially astute policies, with his ability to organize and build up, make Israel into a rich and envied nation. But his ruthless rule, while it achieved those goals, leaves a restless and dissatisfied people who divide the kingdom rather than live under David's son.

So 1 Kings recounts the doleful narrative of the two kingdoms and their kings who are not pleasing to God. The story continues with the appearance of prophets, from time to time, whose message from God speaks the Deuteronomic message of warning from God. The prophetic narratives about Elijah and Elisha in 1 and 2 Kings are the highlights of the prophets. The story tells of the invasions of the Assyrians that led to the fall of the northern kingdom with the first heavy deportations of Israelites. The story continues with Judah alone, including the story of Josiah's reign, which has already been surveyed. The book ends with the narrative of the Babylonian destruction of Jerusalem and the deportations that constituted the definitive exile of Jews in Babylon. The kingdoms are at an end, although Jehoiachin's family still lives under house arrest in Babylon.

The Deuteronomistic History has enfolded Deuteronomy into a continuing account that extends the message, and the application is incendiary as was the book found in the temple. It is more reflective. But the impact is devastating. It is a story of lost opportunity, a story of divine patience, a story of remarkable realism in showing human nature in all its forms, but also a story that speaks of God's persistence in sending prophets to call the people to repentance.

The massive work must have been completed, copied, and published soon after so many of Judah's best leaders trekked to Mesopotamia and so many others fled to Egypt. It became the standard way that the people of the exilic age knew and read Deuteronomy.

---

22. Whybray, *Succession Narrative*.

## The Book of Jeremiah

The book found in the temple influenced another writing. Jeremiah was a young prophet in Judah when Josiah's reform took place. Some of his prophecies reflect his own disenchantment with the reform. The detailed experiences with kings and officials throughout the Babylonian period of the kingdom are reflected in the book of his prophecies. His work was recorded by Baruch, the scribe. Other scribes of that time are listed as sons of Shaphan. Baruch may well have been a relative trained in the same schools for scribes.

Jeremiah marks the change from personal oral prophecy to written prophecy. The book tells the story of Baruch having to take dictation from the prophet and to read what was dictated in the temple, indeed to redo the whole thing when the first copy was destroyed. Jeremiah's book echoes many of the Deuteronomic themes, including God's mercy and the requirement of whole-hearted seeking in order for God to respond to repentance.

Jeremiah develops as a book in close correlation with the life of the prophet. It tells of his early call and messages he gives through phases of his life that correspond with the reign of Josiah (and the finding of the book of the law in the temple), with the following reigns of Jehoiakim and Jehoiachin, and finally with the reign of Zedekiah, which ends with the destruction of Jerusalem in 587 BCE. Jeremiah's story continues into the next period before he finally goes into Egyptian exile.

Jeremiah is called "the prophet to the nations," and his book contains a substantial number of prophecies aimed at the nations, beginning a trend that is followed in Ezekiel and the book of the Twelve Prophets.

There is warmth and deep feeling to be found in Jeremiah's prophecies. The book also provides the first evidence of the way prophets and scribes worked together to produce their books. Jeremiah may well have appeared as a book before the end of the Babylonian period to stand alongside Deuteronomy and the Deuteronomistic History.[23]

The relation between Jeremiah and the Deuteronomistic History is sealed by having the last chapter of Jeremiah (chapter 52) be a copy of 2 Kgs 24:18—25:30. Certainly Deuteronomy, the Deuteronomistic History, and Jeremiah were circulated together, and probably the same group of scribes copied and published the two books. Together they

---

23. See Craigie et al., *Jeremiah 1-25*; Keown et al., *Jeremiah 26-52*.

formed the Bible for Jews both in exile and in Judah. Exilic faith was built around them and their message.

### The Book of Ezekiel

Ezekiel purports to be the record of visions seen by a priest/prophet in Babylon beginning in the fifth year of Jehoiachin's exile (593 BCE). The first vision (Ezek 1–7) showed God's chariot appearing in Babylon announcing the end of Judah as judgment on the people. A second vision (Ezek 8–24) took him to Jerusalem to witness the glory of the God of Israel abandoning the temple. Varying prophecies follow, ending with an account of the death of Ezekiel's wife.

Foreign prophecies follow (Ezek 25–32), culminating with prophecies against Tyre and Egypt. Other prophecies follow in Ezek 33–39.

A final great vision of the new temple is dated in the twenty-fifth year of his exile (ca. 573 BCE) with an exact description of how the new temple should look (Ezek 40:1—47:12). The book closes with revelations of the boundaries for the land (47:13—48:38), including places for all the tribes.

Ezekiel stands on its own, apart from the Deuteronomistic literature and unlike the later Priestly literature. The temple that will be built does not conform to Ezekiel's specifications. The book is included in the growing Scripture, not for its priestly revelations but for its prophetic values.[24]

Ezra's Torah was read in Jerusalem ca. 445 BCE, and the temple was brought under Torah marking the distinctive turn of the Persian period. But two major prophetic books also marked this period: Isaiah and the book of the Twelve Prophets.

## THE CORPUS TO THIS POINT AND ITS ADHERENTS

The era of Nehemiah (mid-fifth century BCE) was a time when there was a strong Jewish presence in Babylon and a growing Jewish population in Judah. The temple was operational under Aaronide priests as Torah requires. Nehemiah had brought some stability to the province, and people were beginning to have economic viability. The religious community included Deuteronomists (the *am haaretz*, "people of the land"), active prophetic communities inspired by the prophetic books, and priests who were busy promoting the priestly establishment.

---

24. Allen, *Ezekiel 1–19*; *Ezekiel 20–48*.

The Scriptures were based on the full Torah of five books, which was gaining preeminent authority. Scripture also included the Former Prophets (Joshua–2 Kings), which were the surviving remnant of the Deuteronomistic History (Deuteronomy–2 Kings) after Deuteronomy had been separated to join the rest of Mosaic Torah, and the Latter Prophets (Isaiah, Jeremiah, Ezekiel, and the book of the Twelve Prophets). Uniting the various parts of Torah brought together the parts of Judah that were represented by them: Deuteronomy for the "people of the land" party, Leviticus and other Priestly portions of Torah to represent the priests and their party, and other portions of the Mosaic literature that represented the prophet parties. The uniting of these in Torah was the master stroke that, with the rebuilding of the temple, united Judaism.

The Scripture at this time was "Torah and the Prophets," a designation that continued into New Testament times.[25] Rainer Albertz[26] has a chart tracing various elements and traditions from early Israelite religion through the monarchy into the exilic period. They include the themes surveyed above, but he also sees a decisive role played by family piety. The following chapter elaborates the religious developments revealed by the biblical literature of the early Persian period.

---

25. Matt 11:13; 12:44; Luke 16:16; Acts 13:15.
26. Albertz, *From the Beginnings*, 107.

10

# Jewish Literature in the First Century of the Persian Period

THIS INTERPRETATION WILL LEAN heavily on the literary portrayals of the historical period.[1] There is not much that archaeology can tell us. The literary works will include the Hebrew Scriptures and whatever material is available from the archives of other nations involved.

## THE WORLD OF 539 BCE

World history was changing in 539 BCE. When Cyrus took control of Persia, uniting its two parts, he began a march of conquest that would stop just short of seizing the entire Eastern world. His is the first empire of this size. He was stopped just short of conquering Egypt and did not confront the Greek kingdoms. His successors would do both of these.

The events of 539 BCE were not unforeseen. Many would have predicted a half century earlier that Babylon was not up to governing an empire. The Medes were much too strong and too ambitious to be kept out of Mesopotamia, Egypt, and the Mediterranean coastlands for long. At the destruction of Nineveh in 612 BCE, which marked the effective end of the Assyrian Empire, the Medes had withdrawn their claim to a lion's share of the booty. They had unfinished business on the boundaries of their already swollen empire. Questions concerning Babylon's capabilities were pushed aside by the career of a remarkable general and leader known as Nebuchadnezzar. It was the power of his will and personality that had driven the Babylonian armies with their

---

1. See Ackroyd, *Exile and Restoration*; idem, *Israel under Babylon and Persia*.

allies and tributaries to victories over Assyria, Palestine, and Egypt. But this energy and vision did not outlive him. The years following his death witnessed a nation simply awaiting its demise.

The Babylonian years had been fateful for a number of peoples. Each had its own story. Some did not survive but were absorbed into the mass of Near Eastern peoples. Some did survive to rise to prominence and prosperity again. The people of Judah were one of the latter. Their vacillation between loyalty to Babylon and to Egypt led to a Babylonian campaign against Jerusalem in two stages eleven years apart that ended the kingdom and took many of their best people into exile in Babylonia.

But Babylon had not gone about the business of exile with the thoroughness that Assyria had shown in 721 BCE when it replaced virtually the entire population of Israel. This time only a few thousand were taken. The rest were left to fend for themselves. No effective Babylonian administration was introduced in the land. By 539 BCE, Jews were settled in Babylon, in Egypt, and, of course, still in Palestine. In Mesopotamia the original settlement of Israelites in 721 BCE had been in Gozan on the Habor river between Haran and Nineveh, in Halah near Nineveh, and in Media.[2] Many of them undoubtedly continued in those places. In 597 and 582 BCE, Jews were settled near the Chebar River in Babylon and Nippur. They lived in villages named Tel-aviv, Tel-melah, Tel-harsha, Cherub, Addan, Immer, and Casiphia.[3]

In Egypt, Jewish exiles settled in towns that were given privileges because they served as mercenary troops. The best known of these was Jeb on an island in the Nile near Syene. It is known today as Elephantine in southern Egypt, called in the Bible the land of Pathros.[4]

Palestine was not resettled by the Babylonians, so lands and villages vacated by the exiles were taken over by "the residue of the people" (Jer 40:11), a move not received happily by the exiles (Ezek 21–27). Edomites, who were already pressured by desert tribes, occupied what portions they could get in the southern hills near Beth-zur and Hebron.

Of these groups, those in Mesopotamia were probably the most prosperous. Some of them found their way into government positions.

---

2. Aharoni and Avi-Yonah, *Macmillan Bible Atlas,* 150; 2 Kgs 17:6, 24; 30–33; 1 Chr 5:26; Annals of Tiglath-Pileser III, Sargon II.

3. Aharoni and Avi-Yonah, *Macmillan Bible Atlas,* 163; 2 Kgs 24:11–16; 25:11; Ezra 2:59; 8:17; Jer 52:28–30; Ezek 3:15.

4. Aharoni and Avi-Yonah, *Macmillan Bible Atlas,* 164; 2 Kgs 25:25–26; Jer 42–45.

Daniel and his friends, Mordecai, Ezra, and Nehemiah are names known to have successfully done so in this and later periods. Most were peasants working the land and living in villages as they had in Palestine. Eventually more of them would move to the cities and develop mercantile occupations.

Without the possibility of temple worship, Jews at first wept, homesick for the temple (Ps 137). But they found other ways to maintain their loyalties to God and to his people. They developed "new and lasting forms for spiritual teachings that became the hallmark of Jewish life."[5] The biblical books of Deuteronomy and Jeremiah and the complex we call the Deuteronomistic History (Joshua, Judges, 1 and 2 Samuel, and 1 and 2 Kings), which came with them from the earlier period, were known and read in many places.

### *Dispersed: Judah, Babylon (Mesopotamia), Egypt*

The people in the Diaspora continued to be a people composed of several cultural groups. They had their roots in the monarchy, which continued to define the groups of Jews in the Diaspora. They included monarchists, the royal family, and those who had been a part of the court. There were priests, both from Jerusalem and from other places. There were Levites. But the vast majority were common people, villagers who tended fields and herds, craftsmen, and shopkeepers. This group is the *am haaretz*, "the people of the land," who came to political prominence in the reigns of Amon and of Josiah.[6]

These villager agriculturalists continued to be a substantial part of Jewish populations in Mesopotamia, Palestine, and Egypt in the Diaspora. Priests are documented to have been a substantial part of the population in Palestine.[7] The priests were not specifically listed among the captives taken to Babylon in 587 BCE, but they were certainly to be counted earlier among the leaders of the land taken in 598 BCE. Ezekiel was one of these, and the lists of those that returned always included priests and Levites. Princes and soldiers were also sent into exile. Israel was a steady source for mercenaries for various armies from the time of Solomon on. There were Jewish military colonies in Egypt. The royal

---

5. Raphael, *Road from Babylon*, 20

6. For a bibliography on *am haaretz* see *ThWAT* 6:178–79.

7. For bibliography on priests see *ThWAT* 4:62–63.

household was kept in house arrest in the palace in Babylon from 598 BCE to the end of the Babylonian period. Prophets and scribes were certainly among those that were taken.

Scribes[8] had a marketable skill and found employment abroad as well as at home in business, in government, and in the production of books for their own faith. They wrote for all the other groups.

### A People with a History

In Kings and Chronicles, Isa 1–39, Dan 1–6, and other books, the stories are told that made up the history of this people. Their sense of national identity was tied into a history filled with the names of heroes, judges, fathers, prophets, and kings.

### A People with a Tradition and a Literature

This history carried with it traditions of worship and of faith. It was told in a literature, thanks to the Deuteronomistic History and Jeremiah.

We complain of a television culture in the twentieth century that deals in "sound bites" and the narrow vision of the camera that does not show the surrounding scene. Our access to ancient history is similarly limited by the little glimpses of events that surviving literature affords us.

Historians complain that virtually no solid historical information exists for the Persian years. With the exception of the books of Haggai–Zechariah 1–8 and Ezra-Nehemiah, this is true. So to speak of our portrayal as history is to say too much. But there are two lines of investigation that can help shed light on this dark period. One of them is to utilize all the literary depictions of the period that we can find. The other is to trace the evidence that suggests that Judaism's literature emerged as literature in this period. Together they shed more light on the real existence of the people in this time than any other methods can.

It is indicative of the scarcity of our knowledge that we must name the groups that apparently produced the literature by referring to the works they produced. Deuteronomists are the people who produced Deuteronomy and the Deuteronomistic History. Priestly writers are those who produced the work we now call Priestly. Prophet circles are those who produced the works we call the Prophets. Wisdom writers are those who wrote what we call books of Wisdom. Psalmists are the

---

8. For a bibliography on scribes see *ThWAT* 5:922.

writers of the psalms. We use these terms because we simply do not know the persons or groups that did these remarkable things. We do the best we can to name the implied authors and editors of this remarkable literature. But, tentative as these designations are, they give us the best insight into the intellectual and spiritual life of this remarkable people in that remarkable age.

### *A People Accustomed to Imperial Domination*

The Jews were a people accustomed to imperial domination. The Assyrian, Babylonian, and now Persian Empires had left their stamp on this people. And they had learned how to survive under empires. They had learned the hard way, as the stories of 2 Kings show.

### *A People Accustomed to Hostile, Competitive Neighbors*

Throughout the Israelites' history in Canaan, the peoples of Edom, Moab, Ammon, Aram, Tyre and Sidon, and Philistia had competed with Israel and Judah for every advantage. In Judah and in the Diaspora after the exile, even under empire, this did not change. Esther and Ezra-Nehemiah record the struggles. But these were issues that their fathers had survived and conquered. They could do it again.

The tenure and stability of persons or groups dependent on royal favor (Daniel, Zerubabbel, Nehemiah, Mordecai, the Elephantine mercenaries) are tenuous and temporary at best. The settled village and town communities are the ones who survive and prosper over the long run. They are the bases and the refuges of the educated and the powerful, the religious and the literary. Ultimately it is to them that we owe continuation of the Jewish tradition. Even the temple's existence was interrupted. Judaism had had to find its own basis for existence before the temple was rebuilt, and it survived the temple's destruction in the Roman period. The Scriptures and the synagogue made survival and continuation possible.

### *A People Increasingly Identified Only by Their Faith*

Increasingly, Jews were known not so much by their ethnic identification, although this was not lost, but by their faith. Judaism and its institutions, the synagogue, the temple, and the "book," were linked together. At the beginning of the Persian period, 439 BCE, that book consisted of the Pentateuch, the Deuteronomistic History, and Jeremiah: Torah, history, and prophecy.

## CYRUS

Second Chronicles 36:22-23, Ezra 1:1-4, and Isa 41:25 and 44:28—45:7 all attribute the next step in Israel's history to Cyrus, king of Persia.[9] Chronicles uses the announcement to keep a door open to a hopeful future after the destruction of Jerusalem. Ezra cites Cyrus's order to rebuild the Jerusalem temple to support his own application for such support to complete the job a century later. Isaiah's references to Cyrus are set like jewels in the story of Yahweh turning a gracious eye toward the ruined city and its people.

One may remember that Media had made a pact with Babylon when they collaborated in the destruction of Nineveh in 612 BCE to concentrate on lands to the north and east, leaving Babylon free to exploit the areas of Mesopotamia, Palestine/Syria, and Egypt. Media succeeded in conquests of what is now Iran and moved toward the area of Turkey (Asia Minor). In the process it took control of Persian tribes in the high lands. Cyrus, a young prince of one of these tribes, in a brief decade (550-540 BCE) succeeded in consolidating his power over the Persian tribes, forcing Media to merge its power with his and tightening his control of Anatolia; subsequently he was ready to rethink the agreement with Babylon. His armies were marching by 540 BCE. A year later they stood at the gates of Babylon, which opened to him without a fight. In this way Cyrus acquired Babylon's lands and fiefdoms.

Cyrus with his Persian and Median armies appeared at the gates of Babylon in 539 BCE. His coming was not unexpected. He had been making his way slowly and carefully southward. But the Babylonian court had long since ceased to be militarily capable. The king of Babylon seemed perpetually to be on a religious pilgrimage or retreat. The king's regent never left off partying. The city's only chance was to throw itself on the mercy of the conqueror. Cyrus immediately set about organiz-

---

9. See Dan 6, 9, 10; Isa 40-57; Haggai-Zech 1-8; Ezek 40-48; Ezra; Josephus *Ant.* 11:228-34; Ackroyd, *Israel under Babylon and Persia*, 162-72; Bickerman, "Edict of Cyrus in Ezra 1," 249-75; Bright, *History of Israel*, 360; Hoglund, *Achaemenid Imperial Administration*, 1-28; Kuhrt, "Cyrus Cylinder," 83-97; McEvenue, "Political Structure in Judah," 353-64; Olmstead, *History of the Persian Empire*, 34-85; Raphael, *Road from Babylon*, 25-26; Yamauchi, *Persia and the Bible*, 65-92.

ing his new territories. He left them in pretty much the same shape and form that they had had under Babylonian administration. But he began to work to gain the favor of the religious minorities in Babylon and the territories. Judah/Jerusalem fit that category and was also strategically located on the trade routes through Palestine near the border.

Cyrus issued an edict that is quoted in 2 Chr 36:22–23 and in Ezra 1:1–4. Isa 45–48 tells a different version of these events. This edict was in accord with his policy of supporting temples and priesthoods of various selected religions.[10] It placed the restoration of Jerusalem's temple on the agenda of every Jewish group. The restoration of the temple and issues related to it came to dominate everything written in that period. It also drew the priests into the process. Priests normally are not interested in publishing their cherished secrets and laws for the laity to read. But the imperial sponsorship of the temple and its work required publication of the laws for its function. The common goal of restoring the temple and the people brought about the unlikely coalition of Deuteronomists, prophetic circles, and priests, which produced the Law and the Prophets in this period.

One gets a still different picture of this period from the narratives in Dan 6, 9, 10, and 11. Daniel is also portrayed working under the last Babylonian and the first Persian rulers.

With the annexation of Babylon and its territories "over the river" (the Euphrates), Persia became the largest empire the world had known. Its borders extended from India on the east to the middle of Asia Minor and from Palestine to the Caucusus. But for the Achaemenid kings, it was still not big enough. They lusted for control of Egypt and territory as far away as Greece, for control of the Aegean territories and those of the eastern Mediterranean. Palestine would play a key role in their endeavors to gain control of that larger territory.

Cyrus began laying plans for a campaign into Egypt. But it was his son, Cambyses, who carried out the campaign in 524–523 BCE. One of the principles of Cyrus's rule was religious toleration. He restored temples and priesthoods. The edict that permitted the first steps toward the restoration of Jerusalem and its temple is typical of his policies.

It is in line with these policies that Sheshbazzar was dispatched with some eager compatriots to begin restoring the temple in Jerusalem (Ezra

---

10. See Fried, *Priest and the Great King*; Tuell, "Nature of Persian Involvement," 78–102.

1:5—4:5). Jehoiakim had not lived to see that day. Sheshbazzar was probably the Shenazzar of 1 Chr 3:17, son of Jehoiachin. In 538 BCE this prince of the Davidic line led the first move toward restoration of Jerusalem and its temple. He was the first governor under the Persians. "The treasures of the house of the Lord" (2 Kgs 24:13 RSV / 2 Chr 36:18) that had been taken by Nebuchadnezzar were entrusted to him to be returned.

Two decades later little had changed in Jerusalem, perhaps because of opposition from Judah's neighbors regarding the project. The temple and its restoration became a major concern of Jews in this period, especially those in Babylon.

Of the actual reign of Cyrus very little is known within Scripture. And we know little else of the first expedition. The references in 2 Chronicles and in Ezra are about all there is. Sheshbazzar's expedition gained a foothold in ruined Jerusalem but accomplished little else.

Isa 40–48 dramatized the period. Cyrus's success was a sign of Yahweh's change of attitude toward Judah and Jerusalem. Cyrus had been called to this position by Yahweh (Isa 41:2–4) in order to restore the city and rebuild the temple. He was given specific instructions to do this (Isa 44:28). The call for Jews to leave Babylon (Isa 48:20) referred to a project like Sheshbazzar's. The existing Scriptures read by Jews in Palestine as well as in Babylon included Deuteronomy, the Deuteronomistic History, and Jeremiah. These were very successful in building faith and community, but they did not address the new opportunities that the Persian attitude toward restoration of sacred sites presented.

## JEWS UNDER DARIUS I (522–486 BCE)

The short reign of Cambysis brought the subjugation of Egypt. This guaranteed continued attention on Palestine. Darius succeeded to the throne in 522 BCE.[11] Zerubbabel had succeeded Sheshbazzar in Jerusalem. Haggai and Zechariah brought enthusiastic prophetic support to a revival of the temple project that was complete by 515 BCE. Elnathan succeeded Zerubbabel, possibly because of his marriage to Shelomith, the sister of Zerubbabel. He was followed by Seconiah, who was the first non-Davidic governor; however, his wife, a daughter of Zerubbabel, did

---

11. See Haggai–Zech 1–8; Ezra 5–6; Ackroyd, *Exile and Restoration*, 169–73; Ahlström, *History of Ancient Palestine*, 819–61; Bright, *History of Israel*, 367–75; Cross, "Reconstruction of the Judean Restoration," 4–18; Yamauchi, *Persia and the Bible*, 129–86.

come from a Davidic family (1 Chr 3:19). Until this time, persons of Davidic lineage had rather naturally assumed leadership in Jerusalem, but there are suggestions in Zechariah that their actions and policies in this period drew criticism and opposition.[12] The subsequent governors were not chosen from the Davidic families. Zech 7–8 witnesses to changing patterns of cultic worship in this period and to the growing influence that a reactivated temple gave to the leadership in Jerusalem. There are no witnesses to Jewish life in Mesopotamia or in Egypt during this period. Joshua was high priest in Jerusalem.

Darius consolidated Persia's hold in Egypt. He sponsored the collection and publication of Egyptian laws. He completed a canal between the Nile and the Red Sea. He pushed the eastern boundaries of the empire as far as India. He pressed north beyond the Black Sea into Scythia.

Cyrus had extended Persian benevolent rule over Ionian cities, usually ruling through Greek dictators, but at the turn of the century, troublesome revolts began on that frontier, including on the island of Cyprus. Persia had a dominant fleet involved there, manned by sailors who were probably from the area of Tyre and Sidon and whose ships were built there. This brought the conflict close to Palestine. Constant troubles with the Greeks were highlighted by the famous battle of Marathon in 492 BCE. Persian troubles with the Greeks were just beginning.

One of the outstanding accomplishments of this era was the building of a royal road that ran from Suza to the Dardenelles. The Persians also built roads in many other directions. Darius was also responsible for the organization of the empire into satraps or provinces. Palestine belonged to the satrap "over the river" (the Euphrates, of course).

## JEWS UNDER XERXES (485–465 BCE)

Xerxes was occupied during most of his reign with a great campaign against the Greeks, using massive forces.[13] The campaign was not successful in conquering Greece. The reference in Dan 11:2 is to Xerxes: "then a fourth [Xerxes], who will be far richer than all the others. When he has gained power by his wealth, he will stir up everyone against the kingdom of Greece" (NIV). Greek historians, like Herodotus, turn

---

12. Laato, *Josiah and David Redivivus*, 275 et passim.

13. Ahlström, *History of Ancient Palestine*, 856–61; Bright, *History of Israel*, 375–79; Hoglund, *Achaemenid Imperial Administration*, 51–85; Yamauchi, *Persia and the Bible*, 187–240.

much of their attention toward Xerxes. He had to begin by crushing revolts in Egypt and Babylon. Then he turned to his massive invasion of Greece. In naval and land warfare, the struggle was intense. The name of Thermopylae stands out as a battle site where a few Greeks held up the Persian advance. A major naval battle with some three hundred ships on each side was fought at Salamis, a disaster for the Persians. From then on, Persian dominance did not go unchallenged.

The book of Esther is a story of Jews of the royal bureaucracy in Susa. It tells of their troubles, connected with persecutions of Jews throughout the empire and of their vindication. Julian Morgenstern[14] drew upon the distressing news that began Nehemiah's efforts on Jerusalem's behalf (Neh 1:3) to suggest that the period of Xerxes had witnessed massive persecution against the Jews. Other historians doubt this depiction of the period, but we have no witness to other Jewish experiences in Mesopotamia, Palestine, or Egypt during the reign of Xerxes.

## JEWS UNDER ARTAXERXES (446-423 BCE)

Artaxerxes faced a strengthened Greek alliance called the Delian League, which, in time, became the Athenian Empire.[15] He faced a revolt in Egypt that drew Greek assistance. Greek intervention so far from home was disastrous. The rebellion was crushed by a remarkable satrap of the region named Megabyzus. But naval activity in the eastern Mediterranean continued for decades. Some stability was achieved in 449 BCE through an agreement called the Peace of Callas in which Persia agreed not to move too close to the Ionian coast, to stop trying to liberate Cyprus, and to stop intervening in Egypt.

In Egypt, this is the age of the Elephantine Tablets that document the life of the Jewish mercenary colony there. By this time Aramaic had become the language of the empire.

For Jews, a climactic period in the Persian era comes in the reign of Artaxerxes. Ezra went to Jerusalem in 457 BCE, and Nehemiah went in 445 and stayed until 425. This is the period of the successful rebuilding of the city with its walls. Successive expeditions under Sheshbazzar,

---

14. "Jerusalem—485 B.C."

15. Ezra 7–Neh 11; Isa 58–66; Malachi (perhaps also Zech 9–14); Ackroyd, *Israel under Babylon and Persia*, 173–96; Ahlström, *History of Ancient Palestine*, 861–88; Bright, *History of Israel*, 379–402; Hoglund, *Achaemenid Imperial Administration*, 86–248; Yamauchi, *Persia and the Bible*, 241–78.

under Zerubabbel, and finally under Ezra and Nehemiah had been dispatched to accomplish this, each with imperial approval. But only under Nehemiah was it finally successful. The temple and its services were put into good running order under the regulations of the Torah. The story is told in Ezra-Nehemiah and is portrayed in Malachi and in Isa 60–66. The same literary conditions are observed in this account.

In Neh 8, Ezra is asked to bring out the book of the law of Moses before the people. This is done. The book is read aloud before all the people for seven days. As Ezra reads, Levites stand beside him to help the people understand, an act that may have included translating into Aramaic for those who did not understand Hebrew. The people react to the reading by immediately observing some of the cultic laws, such as observing the Festival of Booths. This leads up to a great prayer of confession (Neh 9). The implications of their reaction to the law suggest that they are reacting to the book of Leviticus. So, by this time, the book of the law of Moses meant the Pentateuch, probably including Deuteronomy. Between the reading of Deuteronomy in Josiah's day and the reading by Ezra, "the law" had grown from Deuteronomy to all the Pentateuch, including the priestly cultic requirements. The presence of sections that fit this period in the book of Isaiah and of Malachi in the book of the Twelve Prophets suggests that these books also were circulated, read, and heard in Jerusalem. With Isaiah and the Twelve Prophets, the Scriptures—Torah and Prophets—were complete. The classical period of Hebrew literature had climaxed. There had been intense literary activity during the period, which actually came to be seen as the golden age of Hebrew literature. Virtually all of it was focused on issues relating to the temple, the nature of its service and its officials, and the significance of the temple for Jews throughout the empire. The resultant work, the Torah and the Prophets, became the core Scriptures for Judaism.

## THE TEMPLE AND SCRIPTURE

The Bible is much more related to the temple than we have usually realized.[16] We have been too much interested in the preexilic existence of

---

16. See Braun, "Solomon," 581–90; Busink, *Tempel von Jerusalem*; Clements, "Deuteronomy," 300–312; idem, *God and Temple*; Haran, *Temples and Temple Service*; Hayes, "Tradition of Zion's Inviolability," 419–26; Kraus, *Worship in Israel*, 179–236; Mettinger, *Dethronement of Sabaoth*; Noth, "Jerusalem," 132–44; von Rad, *Old Testament Theology* 2:155–69; idem, *Studies in Deuteronomy*, 37–44; Roberts, "Davidic Origin,"

Israel to notice. The Bible was written, for the most part, with the so-called Second Temple in view. Much of its writing was done with a view to defining what the temple should be and how it should operate. The temple of Zerubabbel[17] and Ezra was clearly distinct from the temple of Solomon, in almost every way except its location. After the city of David and the temple of Solomon were thoroughly destroyed in 587 BCE by Babylonian invaders, no efforts at restoration were made as long as the Babylonians held power. Such efforts would probably have been seen as seditious. Judeans were thoroughly cowed during this period. Hope was reduced to smoldering embers. The idea that they were responsible for their own fate weighed heavily on them. The accession of Cyrus the Persian raised hopes for return and restoration. Almost a half-century had passed since Jerusalem and the temple were destroyed. The book of Ezra records the story. In accord with his standard practice of religious toleration, Cyrus issued an edict enabling the first efforts to restore Jerusalem and its temple. A small band led by Sheshbazzar set out about 530 BCE. They found the situation more depressing, the task more daunting than they had imagined. It is likely that the regime of Cambysis was not as sympathetic as his predecessor had been. The accession of Darius in 522 BCE occasioned a new attempt, led by Zerubabbel, that did manage to erect a temple structure by 515 BCE. Its operation was hampered by the lack of urban infrastructure: the city lacked walls and other necessities. It was open to vandalism. And it lacked an economic base to support the temple.

After a break of some eighty years, during the rest of Darius's reign and the unsympathetic reign of Xerxes, a new beginning was achieved under Artaxerxes by Ezra, the scribe, and by Nehemiah, the emperor's cupbearer. This time, by about 430 BCE, they succeeded in restoring the city, its economy, and its administration. The temple would have shared in this rebuilding. It also was probably put on a sound administrative basis, using the Torah of Moses to model the order for priests and Levites and the sacrifices to be offered there. But the arrangements went beyond Torah. Choirs and singers were part of the services, and the calendar of

329-44; Schmidt, *Prophet und Tempel*; Weinfeld, *Deuteronomy*, 191-209; Westerholm, "Significance of the Temple," 767-68; idem, "Temple," 759-76.

17. See Ackroyd, *Exile and Restoration*; idem, "Temple Vessels," 166-81; Bickerman, *Studies in Jewish and Christian History*, 1:72-108; 2:86-104, 159-99; Galling, *Studien zur Geschichte Israels*; Gelston, "Foundations of the Second Temple," 232-35; de Vaux, "Decrees of Cyrus and Darius," 63-96.

feasts added to the three required by the Torah. With Ezra, Judaism had achieved a stable element in its understanding of itself and its cult. It was a faith built around worship in the temple. Jerusalem was its center, ideally if not in geography. All Jews wanted to go to Jerusalem at least once in their lifetimes. They longed to die and be buried there. It was during this period that the Law and the Prophets came into existence as published literature and canonical Scripture. And virtually every book is involved in thoughts of what the temple should be and how it should be run.

The following age of Hellenism found the temple continuing to play a central role. The temple and events around it were the center of the war against the Seleucides in 165 BCE, the rise of the Hazmonian priest-kings, and their turbulent reign that continued until the accession of the Romans a century later.

Herod, serving under the Romans and inspired by the temple-building prowess of the Hellenists, made the rebuilding of Jerusalem's temple the centerpiece of his reign. Herod's temple became by far the largest, most elaborate, and most beautiful of all the structures that had stood on that spot, only to be destroyed by Roman legions in their wars with Jewish zealots in 70 CE. It would not be rebuilt.

Jesus prepared his followers for that destruction, and the book of Hebrews turned temple ideology into a Christology. Early Christianity functioned without a symbol like the temple. But this would not last for long. Rome, the Vatican and its temple area, became Christianity's Jerusalem. By the middle ages Saint Peter's Basilica had become Christianity's temple with all the trappings. But divisions within Christianity both before and after that prevented it from symbolizing the total unity it might have had. In this, it followed in the footsteps of Israel's temples: Solomon's temple lost northern Israel; Zerubabbel and Ezra's temple lost the Samaritans. Herod's temple lost Christianity. So Rome lost the Eastern churches, and later Westminster and all of Protestantism.

Deuteronomy and Joshua had not challenged the temple order of Josiah's time. They made claims for a Levitical priesthood and insisted on a single sanctuary for the realm where only Yahweh would be served. Jeremiah's criticisms of idolatrous worship supported this, but did nothing to lay a foundation for a new form of temple worship. The same may be said for Deuteronomistic History. The book of Ezekiel[18] made the

---

18. Eichrodt, "Der neue Tempel," 37–48; Elliger, "Die großen Tempelkristeien," 79–103; Gese, *Verfassungsentwurf*; Levenson, *Theology of the Program of Restoration*;

first move toward a redefinition of temple worship. It established the one essential to be the presence of Yahweh manifested in the temple. It went on to present an elaborate picture of the temple, its relation to Israel's tribes and to worship. Its priests were Zadokite, as those in the preexilic temple had been.

Haggai and Zech 1–8 encouraged the building of the temple, but did little to settle the open issues of the day related to the temple except to establish the role of the priest beside the governor through prophetic oracle. The book of the Twelve Prophets insisted on a priesthood responsible to law (Malachi). The book of Isaiah called for a temple open to all, a place of worship less concerned with priestly rituals than with spiritual worship (Isa 55, 65–66).

It remained for Aaronide priests in the Diaspora to prepare the definitive regulations for the building of the temple and for the rules about priests serving there. The narrative of the tabernacle (Exod 25–31, 35–40), the rules for sacrifice (Lev 1–7), narratives about priests and worship (Lev 8–16), and a restatement of the law in terms of achieving holiness as a people (Lev 17–25) laid out a charter for the new temple and the age that it represents.

Psalms and Chronicles later consolidated the place of singers and gatekeepers in the order of things. The *Temple Scroll* found at Qumran shows that disputes about the temple continued in Judaism. The Gospels show how Jesus entered into the discussion, while the book of Hebrews gives a Christian reinterpretation of the role of the temple. The Revelation of John projected the holy city and its temple into a heavenly setting.

## THE BOOK OF ISAIAH (IN JUDAH)

Prophetic scribes in Judah collected narratives concerning the prophet Isaiah, who had lived in the eighth century and been a confidant of Judean kings.[19] They first found the stories that 2 Kings reported (2 Kgs 18:13—20:19 = Isa 36–39) and inserted the Psalm of Hezekiah (Isa 38:9–20). They found other stories, as well, which became Isa 7:1–17 and 20:1–6. They then gathered prophetic poetry around each of these stories to make a great prophetic book.

---

Mackay, "Why Study Ezekiel 40–48?" 155–67.

19. See my commentaries *Isaiah 1–33* and *Isaiah 34–66*.

Isa 7:1–17 began a unit that dealt with the survival of the Judean monarchy and its capital in the Assyrian invasions of the eighth century (Isa 7–12). Ahab survived the threats of his time, and his son, Hezekiah, was enthroned in Jerusalem to take his place. The unit ends with a psalm (Isa 12) celebrating Yahweh's care for his king and his house.

Isa 20 becomes the centerpiece in a unit (Isa 13–27) that deals with Yahweh's sponsorship of the international events that led to the death of Nebuchadnezzar and the collapse of Babylon in ca. 539 BCE, events that made it possible for Judah's Babylonian exiles to return to Jerusalem (Isa 13:1—14:23). The entire territory had been laid waste by two centuries of Assyrian and Babylonian invasions (Isa 24–27). The period of those invasions is portrayed in the material that is inserted in Isa 14:24—23:18.

Isa 36–39 is cited as evidence in the great work of Isa 34–62, which is a *riv*, a complaint against God by the exiles and by Jerusalem in the presence of the gathered nations. These chapters constitute God's defense. They begin in Isa 34:1–7, which summons the nations and announces Yahweh's reasons for his bloody actions against them. In Isa 34:8 the speaker explains that Yahweh had a day of vengeance, a year of retribution for his *riv*, "complaint" or "charge," relating to Zion. Isa 34:9–15 describes the destruction of Jerusalem in 586 BCE. Isa 34:16 calls for a reading of the "scroll of Yahweh," followed by the reminder that Yahweh himself had allotted Israel its portions in the land (Isa 34:16b–17). When the record from 2 Kgs 19:34 is read, it is clear that Yahweh had promised to save Jerusalem in the future as he had in the past. The clear evidence from Isa 34:9–15 shows that he has not done so.

Isa 40 and following presents God's defense. Yahweh proclaims his care and concern for the city (Isa 40:1–11). He challenges his accusers, saying that they are incapable of understanding things this complicated (Isa 40:12–26), implying that they are comparing him to the idols (Isa 40:19–20). He cites Israel's complaint in Isa 40:27 and will return to Israel's complaints repeatedly through Isa 49:5. He reveals that he has already made arrangements for Jerusalem's salvation and renovation through bringing Cyrus to take over the empire (Isa 41:1–6; 42:1–4; 44:24—45:8, 13; 49:5–8). Yahweh turns to the complaint of Zion (Isa 49:14) and then moves in Isa 55:1—56:8 to declare his new temple open to all peoples who seek him.

These prophet-scribes are intensely aware of the problems that the dreadful history of the eighth to the sixth centuries, the periods of the

Assyrian and Babylonian Empires, had laid on Israel, Judah, and all the countries of Palestine. They see these as judgments from Yahweh and portray these in the opening chapters of the book (Isa 1–6) and in the middle unit of the book (Isa 28–33). In the closing chapters they portray the first movement to rebuild the temple and Yahweh's return to it (parallel to Ezek 40–48) along with the approach of devotees from the nations.

Isaiah portrays a new existence for Jerusalem and the Jews who look to the temple in the Persian Empire without a king and without other temporal power. The temple functions and the city exists under the good will of the emperor.

## THE BOOK OF THE TWELVE PROPHETS (IN JUDAH)

Another group of prophetic scribes was at work in Judah, also building upon prophetic traditions. They had in hand two books. One was the book of Amos. A second was a collection of prophecies from Haggai and Zechariah, who prophesied during the first attempt to rebuild the temple under Zerubbabel (Haggai–Zech 8). They were much more strongly influenced by the prophetic traditions of Jeremiah and the Deuteronomistic History than was the Isaiah group. Like Isaiah, they traced the history of Israel-Judah from the mid-eighth century down to the mid-fifth century through the prophetic word.

Zech 7:7 refers to "words that Yahweh proclaimed by the former prophets" who worked when Jerusalem and its region were inhabited and prosperous. Deuteronomistic History tells of a number of such prophets, including Elijah and Isaiah. These prophetic scribes had a book from one of those prophecies (Amos). With this they set out to present a prophetic view of events from Amos to Zechariah and beyond.

How much of the material they produced already existed to be used by them and how much they wrote themselves is not possible to determine. They picked up from Amos the theme of "the day of Yahweh." Amos thought of the Assyrian invasions. Joel and Zephaniah look to the destruction of Jerusalem in 586 BCE. Zech 14 looks well beyond those events. The book of the Twelve Prophets takes Amos's idea and develops it into a key for understanding Israel's experience in the period. Amos had also prophesied against the nations around Israel and Judah (Amos 1–2). This probably predates Jeremiah's prophecies against the nations, as well as those in Ezekiel. Prophecies against nations in the Twelve speak against Edom (Obadiah), against Nineveh (Nahum and

Jonah), against the Chaldeans (Habakkuk), and against Hadrach and Aram (Zech 11).

The scribes composed a frame around these prophecies: Hosea, Micah, and a final triad of Zech 9–11, 12–14, and Malachi. Like Isaiah, they campaigned for an open temple (Mic 4:1–4) in a demilitarized and depoliticized land. Like Isaiah, Jeremiah, and Ezekiel, they taught that the future center of God's activity lay in Jerusalem's temple. Like Isaiah, they thought of God having to work with unwilling and often corrupt persons and priests (Malachi). But they, like the other prophetic books, proclaim the amazing persistence with which Yahweh continues to seek out people who will worship and serve him. The book ends (Mal 4:4–6) with the admonition to "remember" Moses, the laws from Horeb, and the promise from God that he will send Elijah, the prophet, before any final day of judgment. No better summary of the contents of Judaism's faith (the Law and the Prophets) could be imagined.

The outer frame of the Twelve (Hosea and Malachi) emphasizes the persistent love of God for Israel. Hosea's acted parable of marriage to an unfaithful spouse leads up to God's speech to Israel. In it he pleads for her to turn away from her lovers. His intention is expressed by these words: "Therefore, behold, I will allure her, and bring her into the wilderness, and speak tenderly to her. And there I will give her vineyards, and make the Valley of Achor a door of hope. And there she shall answer as in the days of her youth, as at the time when she came out of the land of Egypt" (Hos 2:14–15 RSV). Malachi begins on the same tone: "I have loved you, says Yahweh." It also speaks to a people who do not believe this and dispute it. The prophets share the grim view of Genesis that humankind tends to sin and pride, which ultimately leads to disaster. This is also true of Israel. Yet God's concern for the people he created and saved and led continues. He tries new ways to win at least some of them to himself. The last verses of Malachi, and hence of the Twelve and the Latter Prophets (Mal 3:22–24), calls upon Israel to "remember the Torah of my servant Moses" and announce the sending of Elijah "before the great and terrible day of Yahweh." See the table illustrating a chiastic representation of the book of the Twelve Prophets.

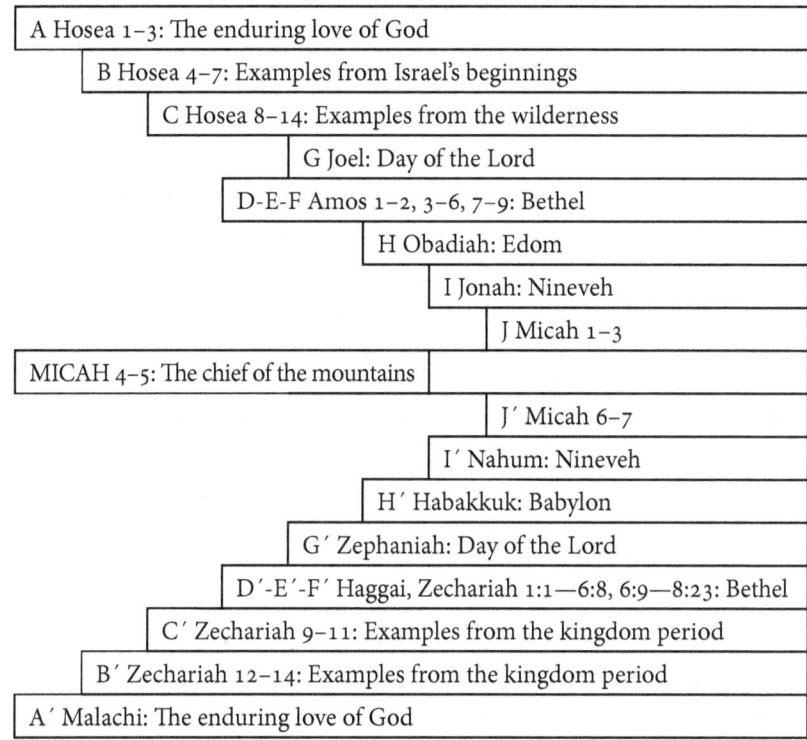

## EZRA-NEHEMIAH
## (DIASPORA LEADERSHIP IN JERUSALEM)

Ezra-Nehemiah[20] is the only report of historical events related to Jews in the fifth century. As I reported earlier, a major listing of books in the third section of the Hebrew canon, the Writings, lists Chronicles first and Ezra-Nehemiah last. In this way Ezra-Nehemiah ends the Tanak, effectively defining the the biblical period ending with the time of Ezra. Jewish tradition thought of Ezra as the second Moses and even suggested that Ezra wrote the Torah from memory and under inspiration after it had been lost in the exile.[21]

The books were originally viewed as one. After the Middle Ages, they were treated separately. The books look at the postexilic period from the viewpoint of Ezra (mid-fifth century). But they recite the events of the beginning of the Persian period in the fifth century and the return

---

20. Williamson, *Ezra-Nehemiah*.
21. Babylonian Talmud, *Baba Batra* 14b/15a.

from exile (Ezra 1–6). This includes the first rebuilding of the temple in 515 BCE. The alternation of Hebrew and Aramaic sections is remarkable: Hebrew in Ezra 1:1—4:7 and 6:19–22; Aramaic in Ezra 4:8—6:18.

In Ezra 3:2-3 Joshua and Zerubbabel begin rebuilding the altar for burnt offerings "in accordance with what is written in the Law of Moses the man of God" (NIV). In Ezra 3:4 they celebrate the Feast of Tabernacles "in accordance with what is written." In Ezra 3:10 we learn that when the foundation of the temple was laid "the priests in their vestments and with trumpets, and the Levites (the sons of Asaph) with cymbals, took their places to praise the Lord, as prescribed by David king of Israel" (NIV). The joint authority of Moses through Torah and of David the king is recognized. Darius orders the vessels taken from the first temple returned (Ezra 6:5).

When the temple is completed, the priests and the Levites are installed in office "according to what is written in the Book of Moses" (Ezra 6:15-18 NIV). The returned exiles celebrate the Passover and the Feast of Unleavened Bread. The story has been at pains to show that the priests in Jerusalem had Torah as well as David's orders about the temple before Ezra arrived. They knew the rules about the priests and the Levites. And they knew about the institution of the Festivals of Tabernacles and Passover/Unleavened Bread.

Ezra enters the scene in chapter 7. In the midst of the narrative of Ezra's trip to Jerusalem, an Aramaic section tells of the documents that made it possible (Ezra 7:13-26). It is a remarkable document, recognizing Ezra as "the priest, a teacher of the Law of the God of Heaven," a teacher of Torah, "a man learned in matters concerning the commands and decrees of the Lord for Israel" (Ezra 7:11-12 NIV). Artaxerxes is particularly interested in this expertise. He grants Ezra authority in all matters related to the temple (Ezra 7:18-20). Ezra is also named to appoint magistrates and judges of Judea according to the Torah, and he is to "teach any who do not know those laws" (Ezra 7:25-26). Instructions for applying the law are given along with penalties for failing to obey it. Following are a list of royal contributions for the temple, a list of those returning follows, and a narrative of the journey.

Ezra identifies the first problem in the marriages that had been arranged with non-Jewish wives. He demands that this be remedied. After a long prayer, the people of the land agree to dissolve such marriages (Ezra 9–10).

Then Nehemiah appears and begins the urgent task of rebuilding the walls of the city (Neh 1–7). The book of Nehemiah is titled "the words of Nehemiah" and is, to a large extent, written in the first person. Nehemiah reports hearing of a disturbing situation in Jerusalem while still cupbearer to the emperor and requests leave to go and investigate the report. He reports on external opposition to the work of the Jews and is determined to rebuild the city walls to make the city defensible. Opposition develops with the population of the city, but his building plans are completed anyway after fifty-two days.

After Neh 7, the first-person account breaks off. Ezra reenters the narrative leading to a reading of the Torah and a great recommitment to covenant and Torah. In the seventh month "they told Ezra the scribe to bring out the Book of the Law of Moses, which the Lord had commanded for Israel" (Neh 8:1 NIV). So Ezra, now also identified as "the priest" (Neh 8:2), brings the Law before the assembly, which is made up of men and women and all who were able to understand. He reads from daybreak until noon. "And all the people listened attentively to the Book of the Law" (Neh 8:3 NIV). This is presumably the Torah scroll brought back from Babylon. Jewish scribes in Babylon had been working on the scroll. The story has told of priests in Jerusalem following the rules of Torah in celebrating feasts, so they had a version of Torah, too. But were they the same?

Neh 8:14 notes that in the reading of Ezra's scroll

> the Lord had commanded through Moses, that the Israelites were to live in booths during the feast of the seventh month and that they should proclaim this word and spread it throughout their towns and in Jerusalem: "Go out into the hill country and bring back branches from olive and wild olive trees, and from myrtles, palms and shade trees, to make booths"—as it is written. (NIV).

This the people gladly do. But then the narrator notes, "From the days of Joshua son of Nun until that day, the Israelites had not celebrated it like this" (Neh 8:17b NIV). Apparently these provisions did not exist in the version of Torah that was being used in Jerusalem (cf. Deut 16:13–15). The new provision follows exactly the words of the Holiness Code (Lev 23:33–36, 39–43).

With Ezra's return, the newly enlarged and edited Torah is made the standard for the temple, as it is also the law of the land recognized by Persian authorities and administered by Ezra, priest and scribe. By this time Torah is virtually the same book that will later become the standard for Jews.

Neh 10 presents a written "pledge" to keep the law. It leads up to a series of reforms by Nehemiah (Neh 13) relating to mixed marriages, keeping Sabbath, providing firewood for the altar, firstfruits, and tithes for Levites.

The book ends with a series of lists, a description of the dedication of the walls and further reforms by Nehemiah. It ends with Nehemiah's words: "Remember me, O my God, for good" (13:31 RSV). The book is organized in a way to characterize the postexilic period with its concern for the purity of the community and the position of the Torah in liturgy and life. It recognizes the two pillars of Jewish religious commitment: the Torah and the temple.

## THE CORPUS TO THIS POINT (JESUS BEN SIRACH)

The Wisdom of Jesus ben Sirach is a second-century book that contains an extensive survey of what he calls "famous men." They begin with Enoch and Noah and continue through the patriarchs, Moses and Joshua, then to the kings and ending with Nehemiah and Simon, the Hasmonean ruler who restored the temple.

He witnesses to a grouping of books that included Torah and the Prophets. In another place he refers to Psalms. That his work is wisdom literature witnesses to the place of that kind of writing in his day.

## THE EARLIEST EXTANT TEXTS AND THE HEBREW CANON

The earliest Hebrew texts come from the fragments of the Dead Sea Scrolls from the second and first centuries BCE, which include Hebrew and Greek fragments. There are materials from a wide variety of canonical books, but also from some that are not in the canon. The presence of so many fragments from canonical books suggests that the Hebrew canon was very nearly complete at this time, although the earliest full texts of the Hebrew Bible still date from the tenth century CE. The tripartite collection of Torah, Prophets, and Writings held true. But the impression that these were three equal parts is misleading. Perhaps a listing like this would be more accurate: (1) Torah (Genesis, Exodus, Leviticus, Numbers), which was honored by all Jews and Samaritans; (2) the Deuteronomistic canon (Deuteronomy, Joshua, Judges, Samuel,

Kings), which was supported by the Pharisees and parallel parties; and (3) the Chronicler's canon (Psalms, Proverbs, Job, the five festal scrolls [Song of Songs, Ruth, Lamentations, Ecclesiastes, and Esther], Daniel, Ezra, Nehemiah, 1 Chronicles, 2 Chronicles), which was supported by Pharisees, the wise, and the singers.

## THE CORPUS TO THIS POINT AND ITS ADHERENTS

At this point the Torah was complete and was recognized in both Babylon, where it originated, and in Jerusalem, where Ezra had made it the law of the land. It must have included the books we now know, beginning with Genesis. It would have been composed of two narrative frames. One begins in Genesis and continues through Numbers and includes the law codes we know as the Covenant Code in Exodus and the Priestly Code found in Leviticus.

A second narrative provides the frame for Deuteronomy, including the Deuteronomistic code, and continues in Joshua through 2 Kings. This is the Deuteronomistic History that we have already recognized, which now had the earlier extended narrative beside it.

When Ezra made the Torah into the official law, recognized also by the Persian authorities, it may well have been separated from the following history, which had no relevance for the legal uses to which Torah would be put.

## 11

# Jewish Literature in the Late Persian Period

### PERSIAN HISTORY IN PALESTINE (423-332 BCE)

LITTLE HISTORICAL INFORMATION IS available for the rest of the Persian period (until 332, when Alexander the Great passes through and the Hellenist period begins).[1] The fourth century BCE was one of Persian decline. Its front against Greece in Asia Minor remained fairly stagnant until Alexander's campaign in 334. But the attention of successive emperors turned toward Egypt and the coastal area of Palestine, which were invaded repeatedly, though the interior cities of Palestine were hardly involved. In 401, Egypt won its freedom and was not conquered again until 342 BCE. During this period, Egyptian forces campaigned in Palestine. There were repeated battles against Persian forces, which also involved Phoenician and Cypriot units. Egyptian power could again be felt in Palestine. The strong states in Palestine were the coastal cities of Sidon and Gaza.

Artaxerxes I died in 423 and was succeeded by Darius II. The last known Jewish governor of Judah, Anani, held office in this period. Jaddas succeeded Johanan II as high priest in Jerusalem. Artaxerxes II succeeded to the throne in 404. Artaxerxes III became emperor in 358. Darius III came to the throne in 335. Alexander, the Macedonian, brought the Persian Empire to an end through his campaigns in 333-332.[2]

---

1. Ahlström, *History of Ancient Palestine*, 889-906.
2. See Bickerman, *Jews in the Greek Age*, esp. 3-65.

## The End of the Persian Period

The end of the Persian Empire is marked by the conquests of Alexander of Macedonia. He swept through Palestine in 330 BCE. But the life of Jews in Mesopotamia, Egypt, Palestine, and Asia Minor did not change significantly under the new rulers. When the Hellenistic kingdoms emerged after the death of Alexander, Palestine again became a boundary area. Ptolemy of Egypt established his control of Palestine by 301 BCE. A period of continued strife between the Seleucid and Ptolemaic kingdoms continued for almost a century.[3] Little is known about the period.

The end of the period was marked by Seleucid determination to take Palestine back from Egypt. Battles continued over twenty years. The issue was settled in 198 BCE when the Seleucid Empire annexed Palestine. The change was at first welcomed by the Jews.[4] Their privileges continued on much the same terms as those accorded by the Persians. Then a new factor entered the scene. The Seleucid Empire became embroiled in a war with Rome and was humiliated in 190 BCE. These reduced circumstances produced a petulant tyrant in Antiochus IV, badly in need of money. When the Jews under the Maccabees revolted against his arrogant atrocities, the period of the Persian Empire's arrangements for the Jews in Palestine was truly at an end. The intense struggle with Hellenism, the velvet glove that masked the imperial power of Rome, began. It would not end until the Zealots were totally repressed in 135 CE.

### SUMMARY: PERIOD OF CONSTANT UNREST

The last century of Persian rule saw the successful war of liberation of Egypt. This meant that the entire fourth century was dominated by military expeditions in Palestine, most of them in the coastal region and at sea.

The coming of Alexander brought more war, and the following centuries were filled with wars involving the Ptolemaic and Seleucid Empires. The period was not without its troubles for the Jewish population. Persian rulers became more concerned by the growth of Greek power. Jewish growth both in Babylon and in Judah continued. In Judah new groups began to be heard in the literature produced and used. This included the works of "the wise," the singers in the temple, and monar-

---

3. Nickelsburg, *Jewish Literature between the Bible and the Mishnah*, 45.
4. Josephus *Ant.* 12.3.3.

chists in Jerusalem and in village culture. The Diaspora leadership from Babylon continued to have influence in Jerusalem.

PART 3

Canons of Scripture

12

# Turning Points for the Jews: Fourth Century BCE to First Century CE

EVENTS THAT MARK TURNING points for the Jews in the five hundred years of history from the late Persian period to the early Roman era are not the changes of empires or the significant battles between the giant kingdoms. They are events that involved the temple.

The first was the restoration of temple and city under Ezra and Nehemiah in the mid-fifth century under the Persians. The second was the Samaritan schism with resultant building of a competing temple on Mount Gerizim sometime in the latter half of the fourth century or early third century. But the full breech between Jerusalem and Gerizim may not have occurred until the beginning of the Roman era.[1] Competing Jewish temples also existed in Egypt.

The third event was the desecration of the Jerusalem temple by the Seleucid emperor, Antiochus IV, in 165 BCE, which resulted in a Jewish revolt and Hasmonean kingdom. The fourth event was the destruction of the Jerusalem temple in 70 CE by the Romans in a brutal war between Jewish zealots and Rome.

The ironies of history include great events for which no credit is given. Over the decades beginning about 40 BCE, Herod the Great rebuilt the temple in which Jesus worshipped. But Jews gave him no credit for it, although they lamented its destruction in 70 CE.

The era of Ezra-Nehemiah marks the time when the Law and the Prophets were completed and functioning as scripture. Between that event and the Samaritan schism, the bulk of the Writings was

---

1. Ahlström, *History of Ancient Palestine*, 908.

composed and published. None of the Writings shows a concern or interest in the Samaritan issue. Yet all of them give evidence of being written in Palestine.

The early governors were princes of the royal house. Most of them were related to Jehoiachin and his family. But by the beginning of the fifth century this had changed. There is a series of enigmatic statements regarding David in the writings of the period that suggest significant resentment of the Davidic house. Antti Laato[2] finds criticism of the Jewish aristocracy in Zech 9–14 in the specific references to the "house of David" and shepherding in Zech 11:4-14 and 12:1—13:1.[3] The history by Josephus indicates more interest in the high priests and the beginning of the Samaritans than in other issues. He notes the marriage of Manasseh, the Jerusalem priest, and Nicaso, the daughter of Sanballat III of Samaria.[4]

The literature produced thus far, the Torah and the Prophets, suggests that Moses had been the authoritative figure most acceptable to Judaism in the period. The collapse of the kingdoms may well explain Jewish aversion to anything associated with royalty, including David and Solomon. The one exception was the temple, and even that was brought under the rule of Mosaic law and under the sponsorship of the Persian emperor.

Significant elements of the population, however, continued to revere the monarchy of David and ideals connected to him and to Solomon, despite the criticism and resentment. These included surviving members of the royal house. Jehoiachin's household had been taken to be "a guest of the king of Babylon" in 598 BCE (2 Kgs 24:12) and even flourished (2 Kgs 25:27-29 = Jer 52:31-34). Sheshbazzar is called "a prince of Judah" (Ezra 1:8). He was probably of the royal line. Zerubbabel was the grandson of Jehoiachin (1 Chr 3:17-18). He returned to Jerusalem with his family (Ezra 3:2). And five more generations of the royal family are chronicled (1 Chr 3:19-23). Under monarchy, several groups had enjoyed privileged and influential positions. One of these groups was the wise. They were teachers and advisers, chroniclers and archivists. They preserved the ideals of kingship. Since the destruction of Jerusalem, many of them had no doubt been active in other movements. Scholars

---

2. *Josiah and David Redivisus*, 275.
3. See Ezek 34 and the passages critical of the *nasi* in Ezek 40–48.
4. Josephus, *Ant.* 11.8.

have detected wisdom influence in Deuteronomy,[5] in the prophets, especially Isaiah and Amos, and in Gen 1–11 and the story of Joseph. But their traditional and central interests had been submerged.

A favorite group for David and in Solomon's temple had been the singers. Mosaic structures made no room for them. But Nehemiah's arrangements for the temple included the singers (Neh 7–12). Temple administration required a huge staff of workers at all levels. "Gatekeepers" included staff for a large number of maintenance and security functions. Undoubtedly many families had performed these functions for generations. They, too, were holdovers in Nehemiah's temple (Neh 7–12). There is no evidence that Nehemiah attempted to reestablish the Levitical claim to these places (Num 4:17–33). With the restoration of the city and of temple ceremonies, there apparently came a relaxation of the aversion to royal themes. The psalms of David and the temple singers came back into favor. Proverbs and wisdom literature associated with the name of Solomon returned to the schools. Another version of Israel's history, which treated the Davidic kings more kindly than did the books of Kings, appeared—the books of Chronicles. The five small books related to the annual festivals—Ruth, Song of Songs, Ecclesiastes, Lamentations, and Esther—appeared and were used enthusiastically. Two other books found their way into the third section of the Hebrew Bible, the Writings—Job and Daniel. They, along with Esther and Lamentations, are books in the Writings that are not related to David and Solomon. With these, the Hebrew literature that would come to be recognized as the canon of rabbinic Judaism was complete. While the literature gave David and Solomon a respected place, it was also careful to recognize the supreme place of Torah.

Some other Jewish writings dated to this period demonstrate two tendencies. The first is the beginning of apocalyptic writing in the parts of *1 Enoch* that were done in that time.[6] The other is a continuation of the wisdom traditions preserved in "the Wisdom of Jesus the son of Sirach," sometimes called Ecclesiasticus.[7]

Jews in Egypt prospered and grew in numbers. They were comfortable with using Greek as their basic language. The status of Jerusalem under the priests continued as before. Little is known of Jews in Mesopotamia

---

5. Weinfeld, *Deuteronomy and the Deuteronomic School.*
6. Nickelsburg, *Jewish Literature,* 46–55.
7. Ibid., 55–69.

during this period. Ahlström's picture of Jerusalem,[8] dominated by a small group of Jews from the Babylonian *Golah*, or Diaspora, who were in constant tension with Yahweh-worshippers who had remained in the land, some of whom became the Samaritans, leaves no room for the development of this Davidic literature. Yet the books are there in the Hebrew Bible. They show no influence from later Hellenistic periods. They achieved their present literary form and status during this period.

One caution is in order. It is difficult to place a terminus on this period. Alexander's campaigns are easy to date. But it was a long time before Hellenism made a mark on Palestine. One emperor's administration, Persian or Hellenist, was about the same as another to those who paid taxes and had to serve in military drafts. The historical reactions of Jews to Hellenism are to be seen in the Hasmonean revolts of the second century. Literary responses come first in Jesus ben Sirach, only a little earlier. The last of the biblical books, Daniel, usually is dated in the Hasmonean period. But this is due to understandings of Daniel's visions (Dan 7–12). There is no reason to date Dan 1–6 so late.

## THE SAMARITAN SCHISM

At the end of the Persian period, events of particular importance to Jews included the separation of the Samaritan community and the building of their temple on Gerizim.[9] Otherwise, the Palestinian community continued its way of life and worship on much the same track well into the Hellenistic period despite the troubled history of Palestine through the third century. Jewish interests were not directly threatened again until the reign of Antiochus the Great in the second century. The books of Maccabees tell of the Jewish revolt and kingdom that followed.

The "blank period," which Raphael defines as the period from Ezra to Hillel,[10] may be divided by the Samaritan disagreement and the Hasmonean revolt. The period from Ezra to the Samaritan break is the

---

8. *History of Ancient Palestine*.

9. See Josephus *Ant.* 11.8; R. T. Anderson, "Samaritans," 303–8; Bickerman, *Jews in the Greek Age*, 1–13; Bowman, *Samaritan Documents*; idem, *Samaritan Problem*; Coggins, *Samaritans and Jews*; Cross, "Aspects of Samaritan and Persian History," 201–11; Crown, *Bibliography of the Samaritans*; Kippenberg, *Garizim und Synagoge*; MacDonald, *Theology of the Samaritans*; Montgomery, *Samaritans*; Purvis, *Samaritan Pentateuch*; Rowley, "Sanballat and the Samaritan Temple," 166–98; Wright, "Samaritans at Shechem," 357–66.

10. Raphael, *Road from Babylon*, 28–29.

one most likely to have provided the opportunity for the Writings of the Hebrew canon to have been composed and published. None of them shows signs of the feelings engendered by the Samaritan break. They show minimal signs of Hellenization.

The book of Jesus ben Sirach is dated near the turn of the third to second centuries. It contains a list of biblical books showing a fairly complete three-part Jewish canon of "the Law and the Prophets and the others." My account of the literary developments in the period will have placed the origin of the Writings in the latter part of the Persian and the early part of the Hellenistic periods (the fourth and third centuries BCE).

The corpus builds on the foundation of "the Law and the Prophets." The Deuteronomist's narrative is prophetic to the core. To it were added the Latter Prophets, which, as we have seen, were already a part of the collection of works in Hebrew. They were Isaiah, Jeremiah, Ezekiel, and the book of the Twelve Prophets.

The Torah was recognized as authoritative by the Babylonian Diaspora and by the temple priests in Jerusalem. It would also be recognized by the Samaritan priesthood and by the Jewish party of Sadducees. The Pharisees also held it sacred and added to it the Former and Latter Prophets. With this, the basic theology of Pharasaic Judaism was established.

## 13

## The Renaissance of Davidic Culture in Jerusalem

THERE WERE ALWAYS TWO poles in Jewish culture as revealed in its literature. One centered in Moses and Sinai. The other was centered in David and Zion.[1]

In Deuteronomistic literature, the monarchy is brought under the authority of Mosaic law and judged for failure to obey it. In the Latter Prophets, an alternative in messianic teaching has Davidic promise supersede Mosaic law. In the Writings, a third alternative appears: Davidic liturgy (Psalms) and Solomonic wisdom build on a picture of Davidic kings who kept and taught the law to open new perspectives for Jews.[2]

The opportunity for prosperity continued to increase for Jews and other groups in Palestine, in Mesopotamia, and in Egypt.[3] The number of Jews at this time can only be estimated. The census ordered by the Roman Caesar Claudius in 48 CE found seven million Jews within the Roman Empire. That would mean over eight million in all. Of these there would have been about one million each in Egypt, Syria, Asia Minor, and Babylonia. There were more on the Iranian Plateau and in Yemen and Ethiopia, and two and one half million in Palestine.[4] Jewish institutions and writings grew throughout the period. Hellenization grew in influence and strength, especially from the third century on. Both Jews

---

1. Levenson, *Sinai & Zion*, 209-18.
2. See Pomykala, *Davidic Dynasty Tradition in Early Judaism*.
3. See Ackroyd, *Israel under Babylon and Persia*, 279-314; Ahlström, *History of Ancient Palestine*, 889-906; Bright, *History of Israel*, 2nd ed., 405-12; Talmon, "Emergence of Jewish Sectarianism," 165-201; Miller et al., *Ancient Israelite Religion*, 587-616.
4. Raphael, *The Road from Babylon*, 33.

and other groups were constituted in ways that allowed them a certain independence from having to control the central governments in order to prosper.

Ahlström notes that "the only historiographic information about this period in the Hebrew Bible consists of two genealogical lists: one is a list of high priests down to c. 400 BCE (Neh. 12.10–11, 22); the other gives the names of the Davidides through the Persian period (1 Chron. 3.17–24)."[5] Specific historical information about Jews in this period is scarce. From the Bible—none. One may extrapolate from the previous period that a substantial community continued to live and work in Mesopotamia. The work of Nehemiah assured a basis for community in Judah. A remarkable find of letters in Elephantine gives insight into a community of mercenary Jewish soldiers who lived on an island in the Nile in southern Egypt.

## MONARCHISTS IN JERUSALEM

### 1 and 2 Chronicles

The renaissance of monarchists in Jerusalem is most clearly shown by a revision of the "primary history" to put emphasis on the united monarchy and to put the entire monarchy in Jerusalem in a better light. First Chronicles[6] covers the history before David with an extensive genealogy beginning with Adam and continuing to the tribes of Israel. The genealogy of David's progeny continues to the fifth century BCE (1 Chr 3:17–24). The genealogy of high priests in the fifth century is found in Neh 12:10–11, 22. First Chronicles 9:2 jumps forward to the exile in order to give lists of those who returned first to Judah (1 Chr 9:3–44). The narrative begins with the death of Saul (1 Chr 10). First Chronicles 11–29 deals with the reign of David. However, the stories about David from 1 Samuel are omitted; instead the narrative begins in parallel with 2 Sam 5. The passage begins with his being made king in Hebron. The stories of Bathsheba (2 Sam 11:1—12:25) and the uprising of Absalom (2 Sam 14:25—20:26) are also omitted. First Chronicles emphasizes David's plans for a temple and the arrangements for staffing and funding it when Solomon builds the temple.

---

5. Ahlström, *History of Ancient Palestine*, 889.
6. See Japhet, *I & II Chronicles*; Kalami, "Die Abfassungszeit der Chronik," 223–33.

### Dissension among the Wise

In the Chronicler's canon only one book is included to speak of "days of old" before David. That patriarchal book is Job.[7] Its spokesman is not even an Israelite, although the narrative presents him as a worshipper of Yahweh.

The Chronicler's canon is well stocked with Wisdom books. Job obviously portrays a time before the existence of the Law or the temple. But even in the ancient times, there was a challenge to Wisdom's claim that the world was orderly and that all things happened in ordained ways that were both good and righteous guaranteed by the existence of God. Job's book shows that this was not true for Job. However, it insists that human beings cannot comprehend God and that God does eventually "make it up" to Job. Job's friends, wise men all, deny the reality of Job's claims. They insist that the righteousness of God's actions is immutable and that one must adjust his perception of other reality to fit that dogma. Wisdom of this sort is shown to be unrealistic, incapable of dealing with reality. God, however, is highly realistic, dealing with the needs of nature and of humanity. But the dilemma of why such clearly unfair things should happen to good people in God's created world is not answered.

The book is enveloped in a narrative (Job 1:1—2:14; 42:7-17) that tells of "a man in the land of Uz" who was "blameless and upright, one who feared God, and turned away from evil" (Job 1:1 RSV). He was successful and rich, with a large family. His children, in turn, were rich and had children.

When Yahweh's investigator reports that Job appears too good to be true, Yahweh allows him to test Job's impeccable character to see if he will be true to God even if he is not rich and successful. In time, all of his family except his wife are taken away through catastrophes, and he is even stricken with a painful disease. But he remains faithful to God.

Job's situation is a paradigm of humanity's ills, except that its sins do not play a part. Three wise men come to "comfort" Job (chaps. 3–28). They analyze his problem in depth, all arriving at the conclusion that none of this makes sense unless Job has in fact been a secret sinner, whose ungodly behavior necessitates these judgments from God. Job vigorously rejects this argument, in effect insisting that humanity's sin does not ac-

---

7. Clines, *Job 1-20*; idem, *Job 21-37*; idem, *Job 38-42*; Habel, *Book of Job*; Hartley, *Book of Job*; Janzen, *Job*; idem, "Place of the Book of Job," 528-37, also 504-6; Owens et al., "Job," 22-152; Safire, *First Dissident*; Terrien, "Yahweh Speeches," 497-509.

count for all the ills and catastrophes that befall it. Or, more precisely, that the fortune of any particular individual does not reflect his or her relative degree of piety or goodness.

A fourth younger wise man tries to solve the issue. Elihu (Job 32–37) acknowledges that the others have failed to deal with Job's real situation, but he finds Job also at fault for not being willing to confess his dependence on God and the possibility that he has sinned.

Job completes his presentation by turning directly to God (Job 29–31), giving a recapitulation of his case, taking an oath of innocence, and challenging God to hear his case and answer his complaint. Yahweh responds in two speeches that challenge Job's ability to understand the ways of God. Elihu had opened up this line of thinking (Job 37). Job is asked whether he has explored what God has done in creating and maintaining the world that he presumes to question how God does his work (Job 38–39). Is Job wise enough to question God? Then he is asked whether Job would presume to put God in the wrong in order to justify himself. He is asked whether he is strong enough to stand up to God (Job 40–41).

The book of Job does not answer the questions of theodicy, the existence of evil in the face of God's goodness. It does question the adequacy of wisdom to deal with the ultimate issues of faith and life. Job and Ecclesiastes are like bookends of the Wisdom collection. Both echo the same theme. Like Gen 1–11, Job stands outside the election/salvation experience of Israel. He speaks for all humankind. Gerald Janzen summarizes Jacobsen's understanding[8] of Job in this way:

> Jacobsen's comment on Job comes in the context of his characterization of three millennia of [Mesopotamian] religious understanding in terms of three fundamental metaphors for the gods: (1) the gods as powers immanent in the phenomena of nature, powers willing to come to specific form as the phenomena (fourth millennium); (2) the gods as royal divine figures transcending nature and society, creating nature as a complex artifact and humankind as slaves of the gods, and ruling nature and society by the display of 'absolute power . . . selfish, ruthless, and unsubtle' (third millennium); (3) the gods as 'personal' deities related 'parentally' to the individual family or clan head, responsible for birth, nurture, protection, and guidance, present to the devotees as the power within the individual for success,

8. Jacobsen, *Treasures of Darkness*, 121–63.

and sensitively responsive to the devotee's familiar, trusting petition for every felt need (second millennium).⁹

Jacobsen goes on to see the religion of the patriarchs beginning at this third level of Mesopotamian religion. In the first millennium BCE Mesopotamian religion reverted to the earlier forms. Only Israel continued and built upon the parental model, extending it through ideas of covenant to cover family, tribe and nation.

> As far as we can see, it is only Israel that decisively extended the attitude of personal religion from the personal to the national realm. The relationship of Yahweh to Israel—his anger, his compassion, his forgiveness, and his renewed anger and punishment of a sinful people—is in all essentials the same as that of the relation between god and the individual in the attitude of personal religion. With this understanding of national life and fortunes as lived under ultimate moral responsibility, Israel created a concept of history as purposive.¹⁰

The book of Job challenges the exclusive use of the personal metaphor, reminding the reader that the personal model is no substitute for the model of the God of Nature and the Sovereign of History, but is an addition to them. God does not become "my God" by abandoning his role as creator and sustainer of nature. He is not my advocate against nature or against history, but in the midst of natural courses and historical events Job's insistence to his friends that the things that happened to him are not due to his sin is correct. However, his insistence that God should stop the world to speak to his argument with the friends goes too far. The courses of nature and the events of history do not give unambiguous evidence of the caring parental oversight of God for the individual.

### *The Davidic Kingdom*

According to Chronicles, David is to be remembered in relation to the temple and especially as the founder of its music (1 Chr 21:18—29:22).¹¹ Second Chronicles 1–9 covers the reign of Solomon, featuring his build-

---

9. Janzen, "Place of the Book of Job," 523.

10. Jacobsen, *Treasures of Darkness*, 163.

11. Botterweck, "Zur Eigenart," 402–35; Im, *Davidbild in den Chronikbüchern*. Contrast with the characterization in the Deuteronomistic History: Gerbrandt, *Kingship*; Veijola, *Ewige Dynastie*; idem, *Königtum in der Beurteilung*; Whybray, Review of *Königtum*, 121–23.

ing of the temple (2 Chr 2–7). He is to be remembered for his wisdom. He prayed for it (2 Chr 1:10, 12) and was praised for it (2 Chr 9:1–9). His wealth and the prosperity of his reign are recounted (2 Chr 9:9–28).[12]

The keeping of the law is set as a condition for blessing the Davidides (2 Chr 7:17, 19). The following kings are judged on that basis. Rehoboam "abandoned the law of Yahweh" (2 Chr 12:1) and was judged accordingly. Asa "commanded Judah to seek Yahweh the God of their ancestors, and to keep the law" (2 Chr 14:4). Jehoshaphat "walked in his commandments" (2 Chr 17:4 RSV). Amaziah's story speaks of "what is written in the law, in the book of Moses" (2 Chr 25:4 RSV). Hezekiah's great festival of renewal, including keeping Passover, was done "according to the law of Moses the man of God" (2 Chr 30:16 RSV). His work was done "in accordance with the law" (2 Chr 31:21 RSV). In the account of Manasseh's sins, reference is made to Yahweh's words to Solomon that made his blessing contingent upon being "careful to do all that I have commanded them, all the law, the statutes, and the ordinances given through Moses" (2 Chr 33:8 RSV). And the finding of "the book of the law of the Lord given through Moses" (2 Chr 34:14 RSV) is reported in the days of Josiah. Only here the great reform had already been carried out (2 Chr 34:3–8). The renewal of the temple and the finding of the book of the law is a result of the reform, not its cause (as in 2 Kgs 23).

A major measure of the greatness of the kings is their devotion to maintenance of the temple. David, Solomon, Asa (2 Chr 14:8), Joash (2 Chr 24:4-14), Hezekiah (2 Chr 29:3—31:19), and Josiah (2 Chr 34:9—35:18) are measured in this way. These set the stage for the accounts of restoration in Ezra-Nehemiah.

The active role of priests is a feature of Chronicles. Aaronides are recorded to have served as soldiers with David (1 Chr 12:27), as well as Zadok with others of his family (1 Chr 12:28). They are installed under the king for service in the temple. It is a priest, Jehoiada, who organized the revolt against Athaliah that restored a Davidide to the throne (2 Chr 23) and the administration of the temple to the Levites (2 Chr 23:18). The priests challenge Uzziah's right to enter the temple (1 Chr 26:16-21). They are, of course, active in Hezekiah's and Josiah's reforms.

---

12. Braun, "Solomonic Apologetic," 502–16; idem, "Solomon," 581–90; Williamson, "Accession of Solomon," 351–61.

## Psalms and Singers in the Temple

Collections within the Psalter have been identified.[13]

- A Torah psalm and a royal psalm, Pss 1 and 2 (both without superscriptions)
- Psalms of David, Pss 42–49
- Psalms of Korah, Pss 51–71 (Ps 50 is a Psalm of Asaph)
- Psalms of David, Pss 73–83 (Ps 72 is a Psalm of Solomon)
- Psalms of Asaph, Pss 84–89 (except Ps 86)
- Psalms from different groups, Pss 90–110
- Psalms of David followed by a group beginning with "halleluiah," Pss 111–18
- An alphabetical Torah psalm, Ps 119
- Pilgrimage psalms, Pss 120–34
- Pilgrimage psalms followed by "halleluiah," Pss 135–37
- Psalms of David, Pss 138–45
- "Halleluiah" psalms, Pss 146–50

Later, the book of Psalms was divided into five books, each ending with *amen, amen* (Pss 41:14, 72:19, 89:53, and 106:48, with Ps 150 as the closing doxology). The five books are: Pss 1–41, 42–72, 73–89, 90–106, and 107–50. The five groups may reflect the five books of Torah.

Another grouping is marked by Torah psalms (Pss 1, 119) and royal psalms (Pss 2, 89, 110) with a group of halleluiah psalms (Pss 111–17) to form the first group. It is followed by the pilgrim psalms (Pss 120–34) and another group of halleluiah psalms (Pss 135–36). A single exilic psalm (Ps 137) intervenes before the last group (Pss 138–45), which is again followed by a halleluiah group (Pss 146–50).[14]

David's psalms[15] take us into a different world from that of Job, just as Abraham's sphere is different from that of Noah. The Pentateuch makes no provision for music in worship. Solomon's temple had a rich

---

13. Gese, "Die Entstehung der Büchereinteilung," 657–64, followed by Rendtorff, *Old Testament*, 247.

14. Rendtorff, *Old Testament*, 248.

15. Commentaries: Allen, *Psalms 101–51*; Anderson, *Psalms*; Craigie, *Psalms 1–50*; Scroggie, *Psalms*; Tate, *Psalms 51–100*; Weiser, *Psalms*.

history of such music under famed choirmasters like Korah and Asaph, a history that traced its origins to David's interest in music and his composition of psalms. The establishment of the place of singers in the temple by Nehemiah (Neh 10:27–30) opened the way for the temple's hymnbook to become a part of the growing Scriptures. This was the first sign that Davidic institutions would have a place in the Second Temple and in Judaism.

Nehemiah mentions "gatekeepers and temple servants" along with Levites in Neh 11:19–21 as well as singers in Neh 11:22–24. They are also listed as directed by "the king" (Neh 11:23–24) and "according to the command of David" (Neh 12:24, 45). Nehemiah carefully dodges the question of whether these come from Moses or David by listing both authorities. In the psalms, God's mountain is more likely to be Zion than Sinai. The primary voice is David's rather than Moses'. The focus of history is that of the united monarchy rather than the conquest. The wilderness is more likely to be that of David's flight from Saul than that of Israel's wanderings after the exodus. While psalms acknowledge royal sins in prayers for forgiveness, they portray God's protection for Jerusalem and the king rather than chronicling God's judgment on them as 1 and 2 Kings did.

The psalms represent a religious expression that is personal and individual as well as corporate. The king plays a key role in worship as well as in ruling the realm. The reintroduction of the Psalter in Jerusalem's worship called for major reinterpretation. There was no king present. Ezra-Nehemiah is full of thanks to the emperor for permission and help in rebuilding and running the temple. But there is no suggestion that Artaxerxes could take the place of David or Solomon in worship. Beyond the expectation that they should pay their taxes (Neh 9:37) and pray for the emperor (Ezra 6:22; 7:27), the temple worshippers owed no other service to the Persian authority. Due to the presence of trusted Persian administrators like Ezra and Nehemiah, there was no longer suspicion that earlier monarchical ideas would breed rebellion. There is little evidence that the psalms were used in Babylon before this time. An obvious exception is Ps 137. But several psalms, like Ps 147:2, do refer to conditions of the exilic period. An entire section is dedicated to pilgrimage to Jerusalem, which becomes a major part of Israel's worship experience in this period. Pss 120–34 all have headings of "a song of ascents" or a pilgrimage song.

Psalms clearly served a liturgical purpose, but the placement of Torah psalms (1 and 119) indicates that "the psalms have become the word of God, which is to be read and meditated on again and again; like the Torah, they manifest God's will and show the right way to those who observe it."[16] The psalms were "the hymn book of the second temple" and also the prayer book of Judaism.

While the psalms met Jewish worship needs, most of them reflect the worldview of an earlier era, that of the First Temple. Through the psalms, the rich religious traditions of Solomon's temple are transmitted into the bloodstream of Judaism. Through the psalms, the ideals of kingship identified with David and Solomon are rehabilitated for Jews from the ash heap of Deuteronomistic History. From here on, Jews sang the songs of David at the same time that they tried to live by the Torah of Moses. One psalm bears the name of Moses (Ps 90) to be cherished alongside Deut 32 and 33. The psalms strive to reconcile Torah and Wisdom (Pss 2 and 119). While they praise strong Davidic leadership in Psalms like 2 and 110, there are many psalms of individual piety that depict struggles with problems from the oppression of enemies to threats to health and life. These portray David as one who was an example of steadfast courage and dependence on God. Modern scholars refer to these as "laments." There are other psalms about the kingship of Yahweh (especially Pss 68 and 93–100). And many psalms give thanks and praise suitable to temple worship to the glorious King of Heaven who has shown his power in salvation for his people, Israel, and in his temple in Zion.

## THE WISE IN JERUSALEM: PROVERBS

If Job and Ecclesiastes demonstrate the limits of Wisdom, Proverbs shows how it can be used positively in Israel. The place of "the wise" in Israel's life, especially related to kings in Jerusalem, is witnessed throughout Scripture. When kings could no longer be their patrons, some continued their style of life and worked to preserve the fruit of their thought. The book of Proverbs is the major repository of wisdom in Scripture.

The book purports to represent a collection tracing its roots to Solomon (Prov 1:1). But it also notes a stage of work from the reign of Hezekiah (Prov 25:1) and contributions from philosophers other than

---

16. Rendtorff, *Old Testament*, 249.

Israelites (Prov 30:1; 31:1). But the book is careful also to exalt the Torah (Prov 1:8; 6:20, 23; 13:14; 28:4, 7, 9; 29:18). Torah and Wisdom are seen as compatible and mutually supportive. While a proverb is a natural medium for the wise, it is certainly not the only one.[17]

The wise are credited in Scripture with writing poetry (the Song of Songs) and a lengthy poetic treatment of a major philosophical and theological theme (Job and Ecclesiastes). While the wise are credited with developing a rational view of the world and a strong moral view of life,[18] they also developed challenges to these dogmatic conclusions (Job and Ecclesiastes). Rather than thinking of the wise as representatives of a single view, we would do well to think of them as Israel's intellectuals.[19] R. N. Whybray observes:

> The wisdom books are distinctive in that they are primarily concerned with man and his world, and in particular with the potentiality and limitations of the individual. "Wisdom" as a human attribute is the ability to discern the best way to achieve the best things in life: success, prosperity, happiness, longevity. But since this ability can come only as a gift from God who must himself be supremely wise, the treatment of wisdom in these books also extends to a wide range of theological and moral topics including the necessity of obedience to the will of God as a prerequisite for the attainment of wisdom, the limitations of human capacity to attain what is essentially a divine prerogative, the folly of assuming that one can attain wisdom through one's own efforts, the manifestation of God's wisdom, in the creation and maintenance of the world, and finally the moral and theological problems raised by the perception of the discrepancy between the actual state of the world and belief in a God who is both supremely wise and supremely righteous.[20]

The wise, with the scribes, were the educators and teachers of royalty and bureaucrats in the monarchy.[21] They emerge again in Second Temple Jerusalem to make major contributions to the writings. The wise

---

17. See the bibliography in Whybray, "Social World of the Wisdom Writers," 247–50.

18. Blenkinsopp, *Wisdom and Law in the Old Testament*.

19. Whybray, *Intellectual Tradition*.

20. Whybray, "Social World of the Wisdom Writers," 227–28.

21. Crenshaw, "Education in Ancient Israel," 601–15; Jamieson-Drake, *Scribes and Schools*.

continued to write books in the following periods, as Ecclesiasticus, the Wisdom of Solomon, and Ben Sirach demonstrate.

Proverbs is a collection of collections marked by superscriptions:

- Prov 10:1—22:16: "Sayings of Solomon."
- Prov 24:23-34: "These also are sayings of the wise."
- Prov 25-29: "These are other proverbs of Solomon that the officials of King Hezekiah of Judah copied."
- Prov 30: "The words of Agur son of Jakeh of Massa (or 'an oracle')"
- Prov 31: "The words of King Lemuel. An oracle that his mother taught."

The literary structure of the book of Proverbs is parallel to that of the book of Psalms, both of which were originally written in four "books," to which a fifth "book" was subsequently added to complete the canonical process. The original four books in the book of Proverbs are:

- Prov 1-9: Wisdom discourses/personification of Lady Wisdom
- Prov 10:1—22:16: Proverbs of Solomon, part 1 (375 proverbs)
- Prov 25-29: Proverbs of Solomon, part 2 (138 proverbs—copied by scribes of Hezekiah)
- Prov 30-31: Words of Agur and Lemuel + Ode to the Virtuous Woman

## THE WISE IN JERUSALEM: FIVE FESTAL SCROLLS

Five small books—Ruth, Song of Songs, Ecclesiastes, Lamentations, and Esther—continue the wisdom themes. Three of them are related to either David or Solomon. Ruth ends with a genealogy ending with David. Song of Songs and Ecclesiastes are both related to Solomon in their headings. Each exemplifies ideals of wisdom and of the period. Ruth demonstrates faithfulness to God and family in all its characters. Song of Songs sings the power and beauty of love (see Song 8:6–7). Lamentations raises high the duty to remember disasters, reflect on them, and lament them before God. Esther is the model of one who risks everything for the good of community and family. All of these praise the providence of God who preserves his people and protects individuals who keep the law and fear him. (Dan 1–6 tells of others in the Diaspora who were obedient to the requirements of Law and experienced the special care of God in their lonely lives of faith.)

The number five is used several times in Scripture. The five parts of the Torah make up the Pentateuch. The Psalms are divided into five books. Others relate to the number four. The Latter Prophets are made up of four books in which the last contains twelve smaller units. The books of the Writings, which are enveloped by Chronicles and Ezra-Nehemiah, are Job, Psalms, Proverbs, and the five scrolls. (Daniel falls outside this number.)

## Ruth

The first of the five scrolls relates to David. It tells the story of the marriage of Boaz and the birth of Obed. The ten-generation genealogy (compare the genealogies of Adam to Noah, Gen 5, and of Shem to Abraham, Gen 11:10–26) at the end of the book begins with Perez the son of Judah and leads to David. Compare the same list of twelve generations from Israel (Jacob) to David in 1 Chr 2.[22]

The social setting of the book is an Israelite village. Village culture provides the structure for agrarian life in the Near East and through much of the world even to this day. Village life in Palestine or Mesopotamia or Egypt in the fifth century would have been very similar to that before the monarchy. The book of Ruth describes this life more fully than does any other book.

Ruth is a story in which persons who had lost everything and appeared to be beyond hope find redemption, new life, and fulfillment. Naomi and Ruth have lost husbands, are childless, and have no status in the village. Boaz is a bachelor. Without marriage and children, he cannot be a link in the genealogical chain of his family. The story brings them together, and the continuity of the chain of life is restored. The meaning for exiles is obvious.

The story tells of rewards for faith and faithfulness on the parts of all its characters. The providence and provision of God for his people in their bereavement is central to the story. Elimelech, his wife Naomi, and their two sons are driven from their village, Bethlehem, by a famine. They go to Moab where Elimelech dies. The two sons marry Moabite

22. Bush, *Ruth, Esther*, 87.

women and subsequently die, leaving three women widowed. One daughter decides to stay in Moab with her people. The second, Ruth, insists on returning with her mother-in-law to Bethlehem.

In Bethlehem, they live the life of the poor and bereaved, gathering bits of grain behind the reapers. Naomi conspires to have Ruth meet Boaz, a relative of her late husband who is not married. Boaz falls in love with Ruth and arranges to exercise the rights of levirate marriage (Deut 25:5). By this marriage, Naomi's status and privilege in the village are restored. Their child, Obed, becomes the grandfather of David.

### Ecclesiastes, the Village Wise Man

Ecclesiastes[23] builds on the tradition of Solomon "son of David" as a wise man in his own right (1 Kgs 4:29–39). More than just a collector of poems, Solomon in Ecclesiastes is pictured as a philosopher who meditates on the meaning of life. The preacher exhorts his readers to "fear God" (Eccl 3:14; 7:18; 8:12–13; 12:13). He extols the enjoyment of life (Eccl 2:24; 3:12–13, 22; 8:15). Apparently Solomon is seen as a model. The Song of Songs expands on this picture of Solomon.

The preacher builds to the basic presuppositions of wisdom.[24] He accepts the "omnipotence" of God (Eccl 3:14). But humans "do not understand the action of God and cannot know the divine plan."[25] Nevertheless, God is to be feared, for he is in heaven, humankind on earth (Eccl 5:1). A sense of resignation pervades the book. It is more like Job's reaction to the divine speeches (Job 38–41) than the rest of that book.

At the end, Ecclesiastes makes his peace with Torah: "Fear God, and keep his commandments; for that is the whole duty of man" (Eccl 12:13 RSV). The reintroduction of Davidic and Solomonic elements into the Judaism of the period is not intended as a challenge to the authority of Torah.

The organization of Ecclesiastes, based on Rendtorff, is as follows:[26]

- 1:1 Title
- 1:2–11 Poem about vain toil

---

23. Murphy, *Ecclesiastes*.
24. Rendtorff, *Old Testament*, 266.
25. Ibid.
26. Following Rendtorff, *Old Testament*, 265.

- 1:12—6:9 Critical investigation of human life: "All is vanity and a striving after wind"
- 7:1—8:17 Consequences: Man cannot discover what it is good for him to do
- 9:1—11:6 Consequences: Man does not know what will come
- 11:7—12:8 Poem on youth and old age
- 12:9-14 Epilogue

### Song of Songs, the Village Wedding

A beautiful collection of love songs is recognized as Solomon's song.[27] The setting is apparently that of a village wedding, but the lover addresses "the daughters of Jerusalem" at key places in the cycle. She tells of her love for a village youth, but she refers also to King Solomon and his glory.

The book is classified among the "wisdom books." Song 8:6-7 contains "reflective sayings" about love that fit the context of wisdom ("Love is as strong as death").

### Lamentations

Exilic Jews in Palestine, and perhaps also in Mesopotamia, observed regular times of mourning for Jerusalem. Zech 7 tells of a group who came from Bethel (516 BCE) to learn from authorities in Jerusalem whether they should continue to observe these times. The prophet told them that it was no longer necessary. But it is unlikely that this put a stop to the practice. The book of Lamentations was recited in Judaism on such occasions. It recounts the destruction of Jerusalem in 587 BCE and all the terrible consequences that followed.

There are five songs. They adapt elements from communal laments (Lam 5) and from laments for the dead to apply to memorials of the tragic event.

Jewish tradition ascribed the laments to Jeremiah (*b. B. Bat.* 15a), but they were likely written by different individuals during the exile. Rendtorff asserts that "Lamentations is evidence of a reaction to the catastrophe of 586 with the resources of, and against the background of,

---

27. Garrett in Garrett and House, *Song of Songs/Lamentations*.

the religious tradition."[28] Compare Ps 137 for a similar mourning song that has a background in the Diaspora.[29]

### Esther (Purim) in the Diaspora

This intriguing story of life in the eastern Diaspora[30] belongs to the story of an Israelite (Jew) in the court of a great king as well as stories of Joseph, Moses, and Daniel. It shows how God cares for his own in an alien environment and how by God's help a Jew may be superior to nobles and kings in such an environment.

The antagonists in the story are Mordecai and Haman. Mordecai is "the son of Jair, son of Shimei, son of Kish, a Benjaminite" (Esth 2:5 RSV). The reference is a reminder of Saul, Israel's first king, who was also a Benjaminite, the son of Kish (1 Sam 9:1). Haman, the would-be persecutor of the Jews is called the son of an Agagite (Esth 3:1). Saul fought against King Agag, of the Amalekites and got into trouble with Samuel for keeping him alive (1 Sam 15). That account recalls earlier accounts of troubles with the Amalekites (Exod 17:14, 16; Deut 25:17-19; 1 Sam 15:2-3).

So the story of Mordecai and Haman has echoes of an ancient enmity. The story becomes the basis for a Jewish festival celebrating the victory of Jews over their persecutors, Purim, which is celebrated to this day (Esth 9:26-28) with dramatic reenactments of the story of Esther.

The excellent narrative art of the book is recognized by all. The setting is Susa, the Persian capital. Ahasuerus is usually thought to be Xerxes I, who ruled from 485 to 464 BCE. In the story, he has recently dismissed his queen for insubordination, which necessitates a search through the empire for a suitable replacement. The finalists in that contest are brought to the palace and prepared to be presented to the king. He is to choose one to be his queen (Esth 1:1—2:4).

Mordecai is a member of the Persian government bureaucracy, a Benjaminite (perhaps of the line of Saul since his father was named Kish). Kish had been one of those who were deported to Babylon in 598 BCE (Esth 2:5-6).

---

28. Rendtorff, *Old Testament*, 269.
29. House in Garrett and House, *Song of Songs/Lamentations*.
30. Bush, *Ruth, Esther*.

Mordecai persuades his cousin and adopted daughter, Hadassah, also called Esther, to enter the contest (Esth 2:7). She becomes one of the contestants, a favorite of those who have prepared the girls for presentation to the king. She wins the contest and the king's heart and thus becomes queen (Esth 2:8–18). However, she has not told anyone that she is from a Jewish family.

Mordecai keeps contact with her. On one occasion he is able through Esther to warn the king of a conspiracy to assassinate him (Esth 2:19–23). There is no indication that Mordecai was a Jew who scrupulously kept all the law. But he, like the other Jews in high places that the Bible describes, bowed to no man or symbol of state, although they were often more loyal and trustworthy than any others in the court. Joseph, Moses, and Daniel show these high characteristics along with loyalty to their kin. What Nehemiah did about keeping the law while he was cupbearer to Artaxerxes is not recorded. He was zealous for the Sabbath when he was governor of Jerusalem (Neh 13:15–22). These are attributes praised by the wise.

When Haman's career prospers, it becomes clear that he hates the Jews, and Mordecai particularly. Haman conspires to get a royal decree authorizing him to kill the Jews, and he particularly anticipates with pleasure hanging Mordecai in the court of the palace. Mordecai gets word to Esther of the plot. She with great courage informs the king of the order and reveals that this puts her own person in danger. The king makes a counter decree that authorizes the Jews to rise up against their enemies in a preemptive strike.

The Jews do protest in Susa and throughout the empire. Haman and his sons are hanged on the gallows intended for Mordecai, and thousands of the enemies of the Jews are slaughtered across the empire. The model for the militant Jew down to modern Zionism is established.

The account of this event (the book of Esther) is made the basis for a festival called Purim that was celebrated in Judaism everywhere. Rendtorff says, "Its central concern is the survival of the Jewish minority at a time of rising hostility to Judaism (3:8f)."[31] There is no direct reference to God in the book and no hint of concern for Jerusalem. The Septuagint compensated for these by adding a dream of Mordecai (Esth 11:2–12), expanding his discovery of the plot against the king (Esth 12:1–6); a record of the edict of Haman (Esth 13:1–7); prayers

31. Rendtorff, *Old Testament*, 272.

of Mordecai (Esth 13:8-18) and Esther (Esth 14:1-19); narrative of Esther's unsummoned appearance before the king (Esth 15:4-19); the full edict dictated by Mordecai to counteract that given to Haman (Esth 16:1-24); the interpretation of Mordecai's dream (Esth 10:4-13); and a note at the end that tells how it was brought to the Jewish community in Egypt (Esth 11:1).

### Daniel (Diaspora)

The book of Daniel[32] is composed of six stories and four dream-visions, all of which are related to Daniel. The first stories (Dan 1-6) are clearly set in the Diaspora and show Daniel interacting with persons of the Babylonian and early Persian era. The messages of the chapters are fitting for the Jews of the exilic and postexilic periods.

Daniel is a pious wise man, blessed of God with gifts of administration and of dream interpretation (cf. Joseph). He rises to high positions in the bureaucracy of Babylon and of Persia.

These stories alone give no reason to put the date of their composition later than the Persian period. They, like Esther and Nehemiah, document the place of Jews in high places in these empires. Like Esther, these stories have no relevance to Jerusalem. Unlike Esther, they speak of God repeatedly. They also document the role of the wise for the Diaspora.

The dream-visions of Dan 7-12 reveal the inner life of Daniel with no relation to other persons. These are his own dreams, not interpretations of the dreams of others. They are relevant to events and needs of the Hellenistic age; indeed, one of them relates specifically to the Maccabean revolt. They form the first stage of expansion of the Daniel material. Later expansions include Susanna (Dan 13) and Bel and the Dragon (Dan 14). Dan 7-12 appears in the Hebrew book of Daniel. Dan 13-14 is preserved in the Greek version.

To summarize, Dan 1-6 is composed of stories that relate well to the Persian period. They may be placed in the corpus of Scripture that included the Writings in the late Persian period.

32. Commentaries: Collins, *Daniel*; Goldingay, *Daniel*; Montgomery, *Critical and Exegetical Commentary*; Porteous, *Daniel*. Books and Articles: Bickerman, *Four Strange Books*; Collins, *Apocalyptic Vision*; idem, "Court-Tales in Daniel," 218-34; Dressler, "Identification of the Ugaritic Dnil," 152-61; Gammie, "Classification," 191-204; idem, "On the Intention," 282-92; Kitchen, "Aramaic of Daniel," 31-79; Meadowcraft, "Literary Critical Comparison," 195-99; O. Plöger, *Theocracy and Eschatology*; Rowley, "Unity of the Book of Daniel," 249-80.

The first stage of expansion for Daniel includes the dream-visions of Dan 7–12. These visions reflect the changing world of the second-century Hellenistic period when Rome began to penetrate the East. Seleucid ambitions and their need to raise money to pay Roman tribute led to wars against Egypt that brought instability and violence to Palestine, and Jewish activists found it necessary to take matters into their own hands.

Another stage of growth for the book added the stories of Susanna and Bel and the Dragon. This growth was not taken into the Hebrew Scriptures. It is preserved in the Greek Septuagint.

## 14

# Jewish Literature in the Hellenistic Period (332–164 BCE)

### A CENTURY AND A HALF OF HELLENISTIC RULE

PALESTINE LAY ON THE boundary between Seleucid and Ptolemaic kingdoms, and the two struggled to control the area.[1] Jewish Persian culture continued to be the standard through this period, both in Palestine and in Mesopotamia, resisting the pressure to adopt Hellenistic ways. The Hebrew Bible in three parts became the standard, establishing a text that scribes carefully copied and distributed to synagogues through the centuries. The scribes' work climaxed in the work of the Masoretes in the tenth century CE in Caesarea. The Masoretic text was used by Protestant reformers in the sixteenth century and became the basis for translations into English, German, and many other languages.

However, Hellenistic influence, especially in Egypt, drew many Jews into its sphere of thought. Synagogues grew up for Greek-speaking Jews. In the third century BCE the Jewish Bible was translated into Greek (the Septuagint, LXX).

The cultural conquest of the known world by Alexander's legions and by Hellenist enthusiasts affected Jews as well. Jews eventually mastered Greek and used it for their intellectual development. They translated their Scriptures into Greek, and in Philo produced a major philosopher and writer. Many Jewish writings in that period were in Greek.

---

1. Nickelsburg, *Jewish Literature*; Beckwith, *Old Testament Canon*.

Alexander conquered the east in lightning military actions in the years from 334 to 323 BCE. The conquered territory included Asia Minor, Egypt, and eastward as far as the boundaries of India. At Alexander's death, the continuation of his zeal to spread Hellenism, the Greek language, and its institutions in gymnasium and sports fell on the rulers of the four parts of his empire that survived. The two largest portions in Egypt (Ptolemy) and in Mesopotamia (Seleucus) bracketed Palestine. The struggle for power between these states determined Judaism's fate during the next centuries until Rome assumed control of the region.[2]

Jerusalem and the Jews were not directly involved, although Jews may have had to serve as mercenary draftees from time to time. Samaria was made a Macedonian military center. In the second century, Jews took active part in military activities through the Maccabees and the Hasmonean rulers. This brought them into contact with the Romans, and these wars continued until after 130 CE. But these military activities were not the "total war" that we have come to know in the twentieth century. While soldiers fought and some civilian populations suffered from them, centers of society and civilization prospered despite the unrest.

The first period was under the control of the Ptolemaic dynasty (ca. 302–198 BCE). The second was under the Seleucid kings (198–164 BCE). The Hasmonean rulers regained independence for the Jews (164–67 BCE). Rome assumed control in 67 BCE.

## JUDAISM IN THE HELLENISTIC PERIOD

Alexander the Great burst onto the scene in 330 BCE, quickly demolishing the Persian forces and occupying Asia Minor, Palestine, Egypt, and Mesopotamia and pressing on east to the borders of India. He thought of his military successes as a means of spreading Hellenism, the enlightened philosophy he had learned from his Greek tutor, Aristotle. To this end he founded schools, cities, and theaters wherever he went. He also made the Greek language the language of his empire. Although his empire split into four parts at his death, the unifying forces of Hellenism continued. Palestine was alternately ruled by Seleucid rulers from Babylon or Damascus and Ptolemaic rulers from Egypt from 323 to 164 BCE.

In this period there was undoubtedly heavy Hellenistic influence on Jews. However, the Hebrew Scriptures continued to be the heart of

---

2. Nickelsburg, *Jewish Literature*, 44–69.

synagogue and temple worship. The Persian model continued to dominate that part of the culture that resisted Hellenism.

But an increasing amount of Jewish literature in Greek bears witness to the growing power of that culture and that language. The Greek translation of the Torah that we call the Septuagint was translated in Egypt in the late third century or early second century. The rest of the Hebrew Scriptures were translated during the following period, but there is little information about dates or places.[3]

## JEWS IN EGYPT

After the death of Alexander (323 BCE), Ptolemy, one of his generals, became the king or pharaoh of Egypt. Egypt was the richest and most stable of the four kingdoms that grew out of Alexander's empire. Ptolemy I maintained firm control of Egypt even when his control of Syria Coele (Palestine) fluctuated during the forty years of wars with the other generals. Egypt prospered, and Ptolemy eagerly continued Alexander's mission of Hellenizing the entire culture.[4]

Ptolemy I (Ptolemy Soter, who ruled as pharaoh from 305 to 282 BCE) established a new capital in Alexandria, which Alexander had founded in 331 BCE after conquering Egypt. Ptolemy founded a great library there and a museum. He encouraged poets, scientists, and scholars to settle in the city by subsidizing their work with salaries and free provisions for food and lodging. He himself wrote a history of Alexander the Great. The library flourished under Ptolemy II (Philadelphus, 282-246 BCE). Alexandria became a center for the production of books. Egypt at this time had a monopoly on the production of papyrus. The library may have held as many as 490,000 scrolls and books. Ptolemy II built Alexandria into the cultural capital of the Hellenistic world.

The *Letter to Aristeas* speaks of Ptolemy II's effort to gather books from all the world for this library. In line with this effort, he commissioned the translation of the Hebrew Torah into Greek. This translation may have given Greek-speaking readers access to the Hebrew Torah, but it also served to provide the Torah in Greek to Jewish synagogues in Egypt and elsewhere who had become increasingly unable to understand

---

3. Nickelsburg, *Jewish Literature*.

4. This section is heavily dependent upon the works of Nickelsburg, *Jewish Literature*, 161-85, and Schniedewind, *How the Bible Became a Book*, 198-99.

the readings in Hebrew. Translation of the rest of the Tanak continued in the third century. William Schniedewind writes:

> It is probably not coincidental that the earliest extant Hebrew biblical manuscripts found among the Dead Sea Scrolls date to the mid-third century. That is, the first non-biblical evidence for the earnest study, copying, and translating of biblical literature is precisely in the third century BCE. These manuscripts attest to a lively scribal tradition that developed in the Hellenstic period.[5]

Ptolemy II, according to Aristeas, diplomatically sought permission and support from the high priest in Jerusalem in the translation effort. They put together a team of priest-scribes, skilled in both Hebrew and Greek, for the project. The suggestion that there were seventy of them led to the designation of the version as the Septuagint ("the Seventy").

The creation of the Septuagint involved more than just translation. The order of the Hebrew books within the broad designations of Torah, Prophets, and Writings could vary considerably so long as each was written on a separate scroll. When they were put into a single book and copied on papyrus, that order became fixed, although different manuscripts could vary this order. Copyist of the Greek Bible were no longer bound by the constrictions of the earlier orders. They valued the works of David and Wisdom and inserted them, along with the minor scrolls, before the works of the Latter Prophets, creating the order that is known in Christian Bibles today. They thought of the Former Prophets as historical accounts and placed Chronicles and Ezra-Nehemiah with them. Their organization produced a collection of Torah, History, Poetry, and Prophets. Later, the Christians would exploit the position of the Prophets to relate them directly to the Gospels that follow in the Christian Bible.[6]

---

5. Schniedewind, *How the Bible Became a Book*, 199.
6. Barton, *Oracles of God*, 32.

| Hebrew Scriptures | Greek Septuagint |
|---|---|
| Torah | Pentateuch |
| Former Prophets: | History: |
|     Joshua–2 Kings |     Joshua–2 Kings |
| |     1 & 2 Chronicles |
| |     Ezra-Nehemiah |
| Latter Prophets: | Poetry: |
|     Isaiah, Jeremiah, Ezekiel, Twelve Prophets |     Job, Psalms, Proverbs, Song of Songs |
| Writings: | Prophets: |
|     Psalms, Proverbs, Job, Festal Scrolls, 1 & 2 Chronicles, Ezra-Nehemiah |     Isaiah, Jeremiah, Ezekiel, Twelve Prophets |

The Septuagint translators created a form of "translation Greek" that preserved a relation to Hebrew language and thought, even if it frustrated classical Greek scholars. Christian writers imitated some Septuagint tradition and language in writing New Testament literature.

There were Jewish military communities in Egypt on the island of Elephantine in the fifth century BCE, as the collection of correspondence on papyri shows. There is an early Aramaic fragment of the *Story of Ahikar*.

The translation of the Hebrew Bible into Greek (the Septuagint) in the third to second century BCE attracted a series of other books, which we call the Apocrypha and the Pseudepigrapha, and incorporated them for Christian use, although they were of Jewish origin. These works were all written in Greek and reflect Hellenistic influences.

- *2 Enoch*
- *Sibylline Oracles*, book 3
- Aristeas to Philocrates
- 3 Maccabees
- Additions to Esther
- Wisdom of Solomon
- *Testament of Abraham*

- *Testament of Job*
- *Joseph and Aseneth*
- *3 Baruch (Greek Apocalypse)*

## JEWS IN BABYLON

Perhaps the books of *Enoch* were composed while the Jews lived in Babylon,[7] but Nickelsburg thinks of them as being written in Palestine.[8] The Additions to Daniel were narratives with an Eastern setting following the traditions set by Daniel and Esther. Later the great Babylonian Talmud was produced there.

## JEWS IN PALESTINE

For some twenty-one years after the death of Alexander (321 BCE), Coele-Syria (Palestine) was fought over by the armies of Ptolemy, satrap of Egypt, and of Antigonus, satrap of parts of Asia Minor. With the death of Antigonus in 302 BCE, Ptolemy gained full control of Palestine, an arrangement that continued for a hundred years until 198 BCE.

Ptolemy had a rather benign way of Hellenizing the country. He supervised the construction of about thirty cities in areas other than Judah. They were built on the Mediterranean coast, in Samaria, and in Galilee. In Transjordan they became the first of the cities that would be called the Decapolis (ten cities). Nickelsburg says,

> These cities adopted the political structure of the Greek city. They had an official enrollment of Greek "citizens." Some people assumed Greek names. Greek educational institutions were established. Temples, theaters, and other fine buildings were constructed.[9]

This period was a peaceful and prosperous time. Wisdom was a category of thought and writing that fit well alongside Hellenization. Ecclesiasticus (or Wisdom of Jesus the Son of Sirach), as well as *1 Enoch* 1–36 and 72–82, was probably written in this period.

But this all changed in the following century. Antiochus III, the Seleucid king of Syria, defeated Ptolemy V in 198 BCE and assumed

---

7. Raphael, *Road from Babylon*, 29–30.
8. Nickelsburg, *Jewish Literature*, 46.
9. Ibid.

control of Palestine. He began his rule with friendly measures for the Jews. He allowed them to live "according to their ancestral laws." He recognized the Torah as the official constitution of the state. And he made the high priest the one who would govern.

But in 190 Antiochus was defeated at Magnesia in Asia Minor by the armies of the Roman general Scipio Africanus. Antiochus had to pay the Romans a large amount of money, which put his country into a difficult economic position. He died three years later to be succeeded by his son, Seleucus IV. The need for money may have been the reason that Seleucus's agent Heliodorus tried to take the money deposited in Jerusalem's temple (2 Macc 3; Dan 11:20). Seleucus IV was succeeded in 175 BCE by his brother, Antiochus IV (Epiphanes), who since 189 had been held hostage in Rome. We know the events of this period in detail because of two remarkable books of history written in this time, 1 and 2 Maccabees, and because of the reports in Dan 11.

Antiochus Epiphanes began his reign by making a generous offer of the status of Antiochene citizenship to inhabitants of his empire who would assume the Greek way of life. This offer simply sharpened the division within Judaism between those who became Greek in manner and custom and those who held onto their Hebrew way of life according to Torah.

Jewish Hellenists were led by a priest named Jason (Greek for Joshua), the brother of Onias, the high priest. Jason offered Antiochus a large amount of money for the privilege of establishing a community of Antiochenes in Jerusalem. The offer was accepted, and Jason was made high priest. He founded Greek educational institutions, *gymnasia* and *ephebeia*, to prepare the new citizens for their new roles. To do this, they had to turn against important parts of Torah.

After three years, Jason was succeeded by Menelaus, who bought the position by offering the satrap a large amount of money, which led to Jason's flight to Ammon. Between 170 and 167 BCE, matters came to a head. While Antiochus was on a military campaign to Egypt, it was rumored that he had died. Jason mounted an attack on Jerusalem, but pious (orthodox) Jews in the city took up arms against both Menelaus and Jason.

When Antiochus returned from Egypt, he attacked the city, killed much of the population, and sold the rest into slavery. He plundered the temple but left Menelaus as high priest. After two years and more unrest among pious Jews, he sent an expedition under Apollonius against the city on the Sabbath. Another massacre followed.

Antiochus, convinced that religion was the basis for the unrest in Palestine, issued an edict against the practice of Judaism. Circumcision and the celebration of festivals, including the Sabbath, were forbidden. All copies of Torah were to be destroyed. Idols were installed in the temple, and worshippers had to eat swine's meat. Failure to obey was punishable by death. This was the final act that forced Jews to choose between Hellenism and Torah practice. Some became Hellenes, but others fled to the wilderness in order to continue living according to Torah. Some died refusing to defend themselves on the Sabbath.

Resistance to the Seleucid authorities was organized by Mattathias and his five sons, John, Simeon, Judah, Eleazar, and Jonathan, who were priests of the Hasmonean family. They organized the pious and attacked both apostacizing Jews and Seleucid troops. At the death of Mattathias, Judas (Maccabeus) took command in a series of guerrilla attacks and drove the Syrians from Palestine. Three years later the temple was retaken. In December 164 BCE the sanctuary was purified, the lights relit, and worship according to Torah restored.

## HASMONEAN PERIOD (140-37 BCE)

The period after 164 BCE was troubled for the Seleucids. Antiochus IV died in 164 to be succeeded by his son Antiochus V and a regent named Lysias. Under him, the laws against the Jews were rescinded. Jews were free again. Demetrius I, nephew of Seleucus IV, seized power in Antioch in 161. He appointed Alcimus (Heb. *Yakim*) as high priest to replace Menelaus. In the following years, the Hasmoneans John Hyrcanus (134-103 BCE) and Alexander (103-76 BCE) assumed the high priesthood themselves and brought Jewish independence and prosperity to an expanded territory. But soon after, Judah was annexed into the Roman Empire and the Hasmonean era was ended.

Literary activity continued throughout the period. The recent finding of the Dead Sea (or Desert) Scrolls is a witness to it. Judith, Baruch, 1 Maccabees, 2 Maccabees, and the following Qumran scrolls were found there: *Damascus Document, Commentary on Habakkuk, Commentary on Psalms, Commentary on Nahum, Commentary on Isaiah, The Hymn Scroll* (*Hymns of the Teacher* and *Hymns of the Community*), *Martyrdom of Isaiah,* and *1 Enoch* 92-105.

The bitter struggle that pitted orthodox Jews against Hellenizers and their foreign sponsors produced rhetoric that pictured the struggle as God's war against the evil of the last days. The fighters were exhorted to stand firm in the confidence that divine judgment would consume their enemies.

These sermons turned into books. We call them apocalypses. They were written as divine revelations attributed to ancient prophets or wise men. Among them are 4 Maccabees, Daniel 7–12, *Jubilees, Testament of Moses,* and *1 Enoch* 83–90.

15

## The Roman Era Beginning in 67 BCE

ENCROACHMENT OF ROMAN ARMIES into the area effectively marks the end of the Hellenistic kingdoms. Hellenistic Judaism grew in influence and importance leading up to the Roman conquest, and this trend continued after the Romans conquered the area. Jewish intellectuals like Josephus and Philo wrote extensively in Greek. Jews, especially in the Egyptian and Anatolian Diaspora, used the Septuagint in their synagogues.

When Christian witness pressed into these areas, it found its greatest impact in the Hellenist Jewish population. The Christian Gospels and growing collection of Paul's letters were in Greek. Greek-speaking Christians naturally used the Scriptures of the Septuagint with its additional writings (some of which could have been written by either Jewish or Christian authors) and simply added the Christian books to the canon. The only extant copies of the Septuagint come to us through these Christian sources. Other Greek translations of the Hebrew Scriptures began to circulate.

The Septuagint differs from the Tanak (acronym for Torah, Neviim [Prophets], and Ketuvim [Writings]) in a number of ways. The Greek version of Scripture that the Christians used broke up the separation between Mosaic Torah and Davidic and Solomonic wisdom. It treated Genesis through Nehemiah as history. It placed Psalms and Wisdom between the History and Prophets and placed the Prophets last, including Daniel among them. It moved Ruth to the period of Judges and placed Lamentations after Jeremiah. Wisdom is not allowed to stand alone, and Torah is robbed of its unique status and authority. The Prophets are placed at the end. This worked well for the addition of the Christian books because the prophecies that were interpreted as fulfilled in Christ immediately preceded the Gospels. Matthew follows directly on Malachi.

## THE HERODIAN PERIOD, 37 BCE–44 CE

Judea in the Roman period continued to be the scene of intrigues and violence reflecting, as in Antioch, the violence and intrigue in Rome itself. The period includes the time of John the Baptist and of Jesus. Jewish resistance to oppression is recorded in the writings of Josephus and of Philo. The spirit of the times is reflected in the literature "of messianic hope, apocalyptic cataclysm and the exhortations of courage and resistance"[1] interpreting biblical stories and tradition. We know these compositions today because they were written in Greek and were preserved by Christian leaders, although they originated in Jewish circles. They are examples of haggadah, scriptural interpretation of narrative:

- *Apocalypse of Moses*
- *Book of Biblical Antiquities* (Pseudo-Philo)
- *Genesis Apocryphon* from Qumran
- *Joseph and Aseneth*
- *Life of Adam and Eve*
- *Testament of Abraham*
- *Testament of Job*
- *Testaments of the Three Patriarchs*
- *Testaments of the Twelve Patriarchs*

The situation in Palestine brought things to a head in the second half of the first century CE. The events were parallel to the threats of 164 BCE, to which the Hasmoneans responded, and to the events of the sixth century BCE, when Babylon destroyed the temple. "Chaos and revolt brought on the devastation of Judea and the destruction of Jerusalem."[2] The temple was leveled and would not be rebuilt.

At Jamnia (Javneh) on the coast, Rabbi Yohanan ben Zakkai called together a group of scholars and students to "begin the process of crys-

---

1. Nickelsburg, *Jewish Literature*, 203.
2. Ibid., 277.

tallizing the interpretation of the Torah which was their heritage. This ... led to new definition and interpretation"[3] that would be followed by generations of rabbis. "The literary deposits of their activities are to be found in the bulky collections that we know as Mishnah, Tosefta, the Palestinian and Babylonian Talmuds, and the rabbinic commentaries."[4]

Apocalyptic writings responded to the crisis, exploring the "why?" and the "whither?"[5]

- *2 Baruch*
- *3 Baruch*
- *4 Ezra*
- *Apocalypse of Abraham*
- Gospel of Matthew

## THE SECOND REVOLT AGAINST ROME

The Roman emperor Trajan's closing years, 115–117 CE, were marked by Jewish unrest and opposition in several places across the Roman Empire, especially in the western Mediterranean area. Egypt, Cyrene, Cyprus, and Mesopotamia were the scenes of massive riots and numerous casualties. The specific reason for the unrest is not known.

Trajan's successor, Hadrian, provoked the Jews in Palestine in the latter half of his reign when he traveled through the area founding new cities, building new buildings. Games and cults were promoted—all the marks of aggressive Hellenization. The ruins of Jerusalem were refounded as a Roman city in 130 CE, named Aelia Capitolina using Hadrian's family name, Aelius. In 132 CE a massive Jewish revolt took shape.

Another cause of the rebellion may have been Hadrian's ban of circumcision anywhere in the empire. This struck the Jews particularly hard in that it banned the sign of the covenant, which was central to their religious practice.

The leader of the rebellion in Palestine was Simon bar Kosibah. Some in Israel called him a prince of Israel. Some sources call him *bar Kokhba*, "son of the star," with a hint of the messianic Scripture in

---

3. Ibid., 280.
4. Ibid.
5. Ibid., 289.

Balaam's prophecy in Num 24:17. Others called him *bar Koziba*, "son of the lie," implying that he was a pretender or deceiver. The war spread through Judea, guerrilla-style. The Jews hid out in caves and strongholds, ambushing Roman formations whenever they could. This lasted some three years, finally coming to an end at Beth Ter just southwest of Jerusalem. The war left all of Judea desolate.

Hadrian responded to the rebellion by denying Jews access to Jerusalem. He continued to rebuild the city as a Roman colony with pagan temples included. The ban on circumcision was finally lifted by Hadrian's successor in 138 CE. But Jews were not allowed to enter Jerusalem again until the fourth century, and then only once a year to mourn the loss of the city and the temple.

Despite these losses, the rabbis and their scribes continued the work of preserving the Scriptures, writing new works that passed on to their new generations the religion of Israel. Writings associated with this period are the *Paraleipomena of Jeremiah* ("Things Omitted from Jeremiah"), *Psalms of Solomon*, *Testament of Moses*, *1 Enoch* 37–71, and *4 Maccabees*.

## THE CORPUS BY 300 CE

The Hebrew Scriptures were complete in three parts: Torah, Prophets, and Writings. The Septuagint existed in a revised order and came to include Christian Scripture and additional Greek Jewish books.

## 16

## The Development of the Christian Canon

CHRISTIANITY CAME INTO EXISTENCE at the very point where scribal priestly culture dominated Jewish life and where Hellenism had taken a firm hold on much of the world, including many Jews, though we have no reason to think that Jesus spoke Greek.

After the resurrection, the apostles and others who were witness to the resurrection and to Jesus' being taken up into heaven began to gather themselves and to formulate their witness, as the book of Acts tells it. Peter's sermon on Pentecost is a model of what they were saying (Acts 2:14–46).

The preaching of the apostles in the newly forming churches was a witness to the crucifixion, the resurrection, and the continuing work of the Spirit. By the time Mark began to write the first Gospel, a great portion of the new churches were to be found among Greek-speaking churches founded in Hellenist synagogues that were open to the Christian witness. He put that witness in as the culmination of his written Gospel (Mark 14–16). His model was followed in each of the canonical Gospels (Matt 26–28, Luke 22–24, and John 12–21).

Mark prefaced this account of the crucifixion with an account of the life of Christ from his baptism at the beginning of his ministry on (Mark 1–13). Mark was clear that Jesus is the Christ (Messiah) and the Son of God. Each of the other Gospels followed suit, expanding on the period covered. Matthew and Luke told of his birth. John of his preexistence, even to the time of creation.

All the Gospels were written in Greek. The early church took over the Septuagint translation of the Jewish Tanak. The Gospels built on them.

Even before the Gospels appeared, letters from the apostles, including Paul, were being written and sent out and preserved. They, too, were in Greek. The language of the letters, as also the Gospels, reflects the Greek translation of the Septuagint. They are witnesses to the spread of the church among Hellenist Jews. The contents of the letters reflected what the apostles were saying and preaching among these congregations. So the writings reflected the oral teaching and preaching, just as the Gospels reflected the oral witness of the apostles in the churches. But the writing had the tremendous advantage of being able to be passed on with a precision that oral transmission could, at best, approximate. The church, like Judaism, became a people of the book. Judaism's book was in Hebrew. Christianity's book was in Greek. Hellenism had prepared the way by establishing a culture of Greek thinking and living throughout the known world. Christianity's Greek Scriptures made rapid expansion possible.

## TRANSLATIONS (VERSIONS) IN OTHER LANGUAGES

The world of early Christianity was one of diverse cultures and languages (Acts 2:5–10). It is no wonder that it was necessary to translate the Scriptures into many languages.[1] Many Jews did not understand Hebrew. And many Christians did not understand Greek.

This need is already recognized in Ezra's reading of the Torah to the people (Neh 8:7–8) when the Levites stood beside Ezra "translating it" for the people who understood only Aramaic. Aramaic translations of the Hebrew Scriptures were called Targums. Fragments of the Targum of Job and the Targum of Leviticus have been found at Qumran.

Nigosian tells us that Targums are "marked by a tendency to paraphrase, interpret, smooth out obscurities, correct, and occasionally add comments."[2] Four forms of Aramaic Targum are basic:

- Palestinian Targum (including Neofiti I)
- Pseudo-Jonathan (Jerusalem I) Targum
- Babylonian Targum (Onkelos for the Torah; Jonathan for the prophetic books)
- Samaritan Targum

---

1. See Nigosian, *From Ancient Writings to Sacred Texts*, 18.
2. Ibid., 18.

The Septuagint (LXX) was the first Greek translation of Scripture, but others followed. Aquila, a Greek who became a Jew and studied under Rabbi Akiba, wrote a very literal translation of the Hebrew Bible about 126 CE. It does not include other books, as the Septuagint does. The work was used in Hellenistic synagogues at least to the sixth century.

Symmachus, an Ebionite and a Christian, also became a Jew. In about 170 CE he wrote a Greek translation that tried to combine literal forms with good Greek idioms.

Theodotion's work was apparently a revision near the late second century CE of an existing Greek text with the help of an existing Hebrew text. His translation of Job is one-sixth longer than the Septuagint, and his Daniel shows significant differences from the Septuagint.

The Samaritan Torah was also translated into Greek, but we do not know anything about the translator or the time period of the translation.

Origen (186–253 CE) was a Christian scholar living in Alexandria. He and his colleagues produced a massive work called the *Hexapla* to aid in comparing the various Greek versions. He placed the Septuagint and other Greek versions in parallel columns. The first column contained the Hebrew text, the second a transliterated text of the Hebrew in Greek letters, and subsequent columns the versions of Aquila, Symmachus, the Septuagint, and Theodotion. This was done between 230 and 240 CE. He marked the texts to show additions and omissions. He probably emended the Septuagint column. For some books, he added three other translations, known as fifth, sixth, and seventh columns. This enormous work was composed of 6,000 folio sheets in fifty volumes. A second work of four columns only for the Greek versions followed. No copy of either of these works has survived. Some copies of the Septuagint column called the Hexaplaric recension have come down in fragments or secondary references. A Syriac translation of Origin's Septuagint column was made by Bishop Paul of Tella in 616–617 CE.

Lucian, a Christian from Antioch in Syria, was responsible for an eclectic Greek text based on others existing at his time.

The official translation of the Bible into Latin (the Vulgate) was done on instructions from the pope by Jerome in the fourth century. He translated the Greek text of the Septuagint, but also consulted Hebrew texts for his translation.

## GNOSTIC WRITINGS

The second century CE witnessed a burst of literary activity among Christians. The apostolic fathers in centers like Alexandria and Rome were prolific writers articulating the growth of Christian thought in a Hellenistic environment. Some thinkers and writers moved out in various directions.

Marcion in his writings was exploring the idea of a Christian faith and canon without Old Testament foundations: *Antitheses* (contradictions between the Old Testament diety and the New Testament God), *Gospel of the Lord, To the Galatians.*

Others were exploring the ideas of Gnosticism, which was an applied form of Platonism, as a matrix for Christian thought. This was particularly true in Egypt. A major figure in this movement was Valentinus (ca. 100–ca. 150 CE). Born and educated in Egypt, he established a school in Rome, and even entertained ideas of becoming pope. Failing in that attempt, he moved away from mainstream Christians leaders, earning attacks from Tertullian (*Adversus Valentinianos* I–IV) and Irenaeus, who accused him of attempting to align Christianity with Platonism (Gnosticism). Valentinus is reported to have written *Gospel of Truth* and *On the Three Natures*. Pseudo-Anthinus quotes Valentinus as teaching that God is three "hypostes" (hidden spiritual realities).

Until 1945, the gnostic books were only known by references in writers of the period. But in 1945, thirteen ancient codices containing over fifty texts were discovered in a place called Nag Hammadi in Egypt. By 1970 these had been carefully examined, translated from their Coptic original language, and published (*The Nag Hammadi Library*). They are gnostic texts that allow an understanding of third-century gnostics that was impossible until that time. The works include at least six kinds of writings:[3]

- "Writings of creative and redemptive mythology, including Gnostic alternative versions of creation and salvation": *Apocryphon of John, Hypostasis of the Archons, On the Origin of the World, Apocalypse of Adam,* and *Paraphrase of Shem.*
- "Observations and commentaries on diverse Gnostic themes,

---

3. See the Nag Hammadi texts at the Gnostic Society Library online: <www.gnosis.org/naghamm/nhl.html>. The following subdivisions are those provided by the Gnostic Society Library.

such as the nature of reality, the nature of the soul, the relationship of the soul to the world": *Gospel of Truth, Treatise on the Resurrection, Tripartite Tractate, Eugnostos the Blessed, Second Treatise of the Great Seth, Teachings of Silvanus,* and *Testimony of Truth.*

- "Liturgical and initiatory texts": *Discourse on the Eighth and Ninth, Prayer of Thanksgiving, A Valentinian Exposition, Three Steles of Seth, Prayer of the Apostle Paul,* and *Gospel of Philip.*

- "Writings dealing primarily with the feminine deific and spiritual principle, particularly with the Divine Sophia": *Thunder, Perfect Mind, Thought of Norea, Sophia of Jesus Christ,* and *Exegesis on the Soul.*

- "Writings pertaining to the lives and experiences of some of the apostles": *Apocalypse of Peter, Letter of Peter to Philip, Acts of Peter and the Twelve Apostles, (First) Apocalypse of James, (Second) Apocalypse of James,* and *Apocalypse of Paul.*

- "Scriptures which contain sayings of Jesus as well as descriptions of incidents in His life": *Dialogue of the Savior, Book of Thomas the Contender, Apocryphon of James, Gospel of Philip* [see also above], and *Gospel of Thomas.*[4]

## THE BIBLE AMONG CHRISTIANS

Once the Roman Empire became Christian under Constantine, the empire sponsored the publication of the Greek canon. There remain three fourth- or fifth-century manuscripts of the complete Christian canon extant: Sinaiticus, now in the British Museum; Alexandrinus, also in the British Museum; and Vaticanus, in the Vatican Library in Rome.

The Torah has always had for Jews a higher authority than the Prophets or the Writings. Some Jews (Sadducees) and Samaritans have recognized only the Torah as authoritative Scripture. Some Christians also elevate part of their canon over others. Their liturgies use readings from any part of Scripture, but they read only from the Gospels for the homily at mass. They thus elevate the Gospels as Jews have elevated the Torah. Protestants have generally put all Scripture on a level basis, but some have insisted that only the teachings of Jesus (the Gospels) have

---

4. For texts see Robinson, *Nag Hammadi Library.*

absolute authority and that all Scripture must be interpreted in accordance with the New Testament.

One consequence of elevating Gospels or New Testament above the Old Testament was a tendency to ignore and even forget the Hebrew text of the latter. In the middle ages, very few Christian scholars could read Latin or, in Western Europe, even Greek. In 1453, Constantinople fell to the Turks, and for classical scholarship, at least, this apparent catastrophe produced an unexpected gain. Greek exiles fleeing to Italy brought Greek manuscripts with them, and Pope Nicholas V, a true bibliophile, eagerly gathered them up and had them transcribed. Upon his death in 1455, he left behind a vast library of five thousand tomes. Meanwhile, many exiled scholars had begun to teach at European universities.

As their knowledge spread, Greek was reintroduced into the curriculum at the university of Paris in 1458; a new Greek grammar was published in 1476; a Greek lexicon in 1480; and from 1492, Greek studies became a fixture at Oxford under William Grocyb and Thomas Linacre, who had both studied in Florence with Greek tutors to the Medecis.

Meanwhile, Hebrew learning had also taken root. The first Hebrew grammar appeared in 1503 and the first Hebrew lexicon in 1506. Part of the Old Testament or Hebrew Scriptures had already been printed in 1477, and the entire text, with vowel signs and accents, in Soncino, Italy, in February 1488. A fully annotated edition (on which subsequent Hebrew Bibles would be based) was prepared by Jacob Ben Chayyim and published in 1525.

Regius (royal) professorships in Hebrew were founded at Oxford and Cambridge, and similar positions were created at the universities of Paris, Wittenberg and Louvain.

As universities were established in Europe in the fifteenth and sixteenth centuries using the knowledge of Latin and Greek as requisites for admission, theological faculties added Hebrew to the list of requirements. Printed Hebrew Bibles (the Old Testament) were available for study, as were Greek New Testaments. This made it possible for translations into various languages to go behind the Latin Vulgate to its source texts. The use of Hebrew raised the question of the extent of the Old Testament canon, which was shorter in the Hebrew that it was in the Greek Septuagint or the Latin Vulgate.

An English translation was produced by John Wycliffe in the fourteenth century in spite of strong objections by Roman church authorities. Luther, in the sixteenth century, translated the Hebrew and Greek Scriptures into German, limiting the Old Testament to the books of the Hebrew canon, and using the order of the familiar Vulgate. See appendix B for the different shapes of the canon that resulted. The rest of the books in the Vulgate were called Apocrypha. King James of England in 1611 authorized a committee to produce a version that would take the place of the numerous varying translations. This Authorized Version became the standard text for English-speaking peoples until a variety of new translations blossomed in the twentieth century.

Translations into other languages were made. In the twentieth century the Wycliffe translators and other Bible societies set out to put the Scriptures into every language used by humanity. Now there are translations in over 1,500 languages.

# Appendix A

# Words for "Writing" in the Hebrew Bible

## NAMED SCROLLS

The following are named scrolls, many of which use the words ספר *sefer*, "scroll," כתב *katav*, "write," or דבר *diver*, "word," in their designation.

Gen 2:4: The generations of the heavens and the earth
(תולדות השמים והארץ)

Gen 5:1: The *scroll* of the generations of Adam (ספר תולדת אדם)

Gen 6:9: The generations of Noah (תולדת נח)

Gen 10:1: The generations of the sons of Noah (תולדת בני־נח)

Gen 11:10: The generations of Shem (תולדת שם)

Gen 11:27: The generations of Terah (תולדת תרח)

Gen 25:12: The generations of Ishmael (תלדת ישמעאל)

Gen 25:19: The generations of Isaac (תולתד יצחק)

Gen 36:1: The generations of Esau (תלדות עשו)

Gen 37:2 (46:8–25): The generations of Jacob (תלדות יעקב)

Exod 24:3: Moses recited to the people all the words of Yahweh
(משה יספר לעם את כל דברי יהוה)

Exod 24:4: And then Moses wrote down all the words of Yahweh
(ויכתב משה כל דברי יהוה)

## APPENDIX A

Exod 24:7: And he took the book of the covenant and read (it) in the hearing of the people (ויקח ספר הברית ויקרא באזני העם)

Deut 1:1: These are the speeches that Moses spoke to all Israel
(אלה הדברים אשר דבר משה אל־כל־ישראל)

Deut 4:44: This is the Torah that Moses placed before the Israelites
(וזאת התורה אשר־שם משה לפני בני ישראל)

Deut 28:61; 31:26; Josh 1:8: Written in the scroll of this Torah
(כתוב בספר התורה הזאת)

Deut 29:20; 30:10: The covenant written in the scroll of this Torah
(הברית הכתבה בספר התורה הזאת)

Josh 8:31: Written in the scroll of the Torah of Moses
(כתוב בספר התורת משה)

Josh 24:26: The scroll of the Torah of God (ספר תורת אלהים)

2 Kgs 14:6; 22:8,11; Neh 8:8: The scroll of the Torah (ספר התורה)

2 Kgs 23:2; 23:21: The scroll of the covenant (ספר הברית)

2 Kgs 23:25: The Torah of Moses (תורת משה)

2 Chr 25:4; 35:12; Ezra 6:18; Neh 13:1: The scroll of Moses (ספר משה)

Num 21:14: It says in the scroll of the wars of Yahweh
(יאמר בספר מלחמות יהוה)

Josh 10:13; 2 Sam 1:18: It is written in the scroll of Jashar
(כתובה על ספר הישר)

Josh 24:26: Joshua wrote these words in the scroll of the Torah of God
(ויכתב יהושע את הדברים האלה בספר תורת אלהים)

1 Kgs 11:41: Written in the scroll of the words of Solomon
(כתבים על ספר דברי שלמה)[1]

2 Kgs 23:28: Written in the scroll of the words (or deeds) of the days of the kings of Judah
(כתובים על ספר דברי הימים למלכי יהודה)

2 Chr 12:15 The words of Rehoboam in the words of Shemiah the prophet and of Iddo the visionary.

---

1. Note how these are cited: "Are not these written (said) in the scroll of . . . ?"

- 2 Chr 13:22: The rest of the words (acts) of Abijah, his ways and his words, (are) written in the *midrash* of the prophet Iddo.
- 2 Chr 20:34: The acts of judgment by Jehoshaphat . . . written in the words of Jehu son of Hanani, which are inserted on the scroll of the kings of Judah.
- 2 Chr 24:27: Written in the *midrash* of the scroll of the kings (כתבים על מדרש ספר המלכים)
- 2 Chr 25:26: The rest of the words (events) of Amaziah son of Joash king of Judah . . . written on the scroll of the of the kings of Judah and Israel.
- 2 Chr 26:22: The rest of the words (events) of Uzziah Isaiah son of Amoz the prophet wrote.
- 2 Chr 27:7: The rest of the words of Jotham . . . written on the scroll of the kings of Israel and Judah.
- 2 Chr 28:26: The rest his (Ahaz's) words (events) . . . behold them written on the scroll of the kings of Judah and Israel.
- 2 Chr 32:32: The rest of the words (events) of Hezekiah and his acts of mercy behold them written in the vision of Isaiah the son of Amoz the prophet on the scroll of the kings of Judah and Israel.
- 2 Chr 33:18–19: The rest of the words of Manasseh and his prayers to his God and the words of the seers spoken to him in the name of Yahweh God of Israel, behold them written on the words of the Kings of Israel. . . . Behold them written in the words of seers.
- 2 Chr 34:14: The scroll of the Torah of Yahweh by the hand of Moses (ספר תורת יהוה ביד משׁה)
- 2 Chr 34:30: The scroll of the covenant found in the house of Yahweh (ספר הברית הנמצא בית יהוה)
- 2 Chr 35:12: Written in the scroll of Moses (כתוב בספר משׁה)
- 2 Chr 35:25: Jeremiah composed a lament concerning Josiah, which all the male and female singers spoke in their laments concerning Josiah to this day, and it became an ordinance for Israel, and behold it written on the Lamentations (הקינות).

2 Chr 35:26: The rest of the words of Josiah and his mercies according to what is written in the Torah of Yahweh . . . behold them written on the scroll of the kings of Israel and Judah.

2 Chr 36:8: The rest of the words of Jehoiakim . . . behold them written on the scroll of the kings of Israel and Judah.

Isa 34:16: The scroll of Yahweh (ספר יהוה)

Nah 1:1: The scroll of the vision of Nahum the Elkoshite
(ספר חזון נחום האלקשי)

Ezra 7:11: Ezra the priest, the scribe, scribe of the words of the commands of Yahweh and his decrees upon Israel
(עזרא הכהן הספר ספר דברי מצות יהוה וחקיו על ישראל)

## TORAH

*Torah* (תורה), meaning "instruction" or "direction," frequently refers to instruction from God and is often used in parallel to other Hebrew words of similar meaning, as in the following examples.

Deut 1:5; 4:8, 44; 17:18; 31:9, 11: "this torah" (התורה הזאת)

Deut 27:26; 31:24: "the words of this torah" (דברי התורה הזאת)

Deut 17:19; 27:3, 8; 28:58; 29:28; 31:12; 32:46: "all the words of this torah" (כל דברי התורה הזאת)

Deut 28:61; 29:20; 30:10; 31:26; Josh 1:8: "the book of this torah" (ספר התורה הזאת)

Deut 8:24; 2 Kgs 22:8 // 2 Chr 34:14: "the scroll of the torah" (ספר התורה)

Josh 8:24; 2 Kgs 23:24: "the words of the torah" (דברי התורה)

Josh 1:7; 22:5; 2 Kgs 17:13, 34, 37; 21:8: "the torah that Moses commanded" (התורה אשר צוך משה)

Josh 8:31, 32; 23:6; 1 Kgs 2:3; 2 Kgs 14:6: "the scroll of the torah of Moses" (ספר תורת משה)

2 Chr 25:4; 2 Kgs 23:25: "the torah in the scroll of Moses" (התורה בספר משה)

2 Kgs 22:11: "the words of the scroll of torah" (דברי ספר התורה) =
2 Chr 34:19: "the words of torah" (דברי התורה)

2 Kgs 10:31: "the torah of Yahweh" (תורת יהוה)

Perhaps also Pss 1:2; 94:12; 1 Chr 22:12; 2 Chr 6:16 = 2 Kgs 8:25. Similar uses are found in the Priestly Code and the entire Pentateuch.

2 Chr 23:18; 30:16; Ezra 3:2; 7:6; Neh 8:1; Dan 9:11, 13; Mal 3:22: "the scroll of the torah of Moses" (ספר תורת משה)

1 Chr 16:40; 2 Chr 12:1; 17:9; 31:3, 4; 34:14; 35:26; Ezra 7:10; Neh 9:3; Pss 19:3; 119:1: "the scroll of the torah of Yahweh" (ספר תורת יהוה)

Neh 8:8, 18; 10:29, 30: "the scroll of the torah of God" (ספר תורת האלהים)

Neh 8:3: "the scroll of torah" (ספר התורה)

Neh 8:9, 13: "the words of torah" (דברי התורה)

2 Chr 14:3; 31:21; 33:8; Ezra 10:3; Neh 8:2, 7, 14; 10:35, 37; 12:44; 13:3: "torah" (התורה)

Ps 119:72: "the torah of your mouth" (תורת פיך)

Neh 9:26, 29, 34; Ps 119:18, 19, 34, 44, 51, 53, 55, 61, 70, 77, 85, 92, 97, 109, 113, 126, 136, 142, 150, 153, 163, 165, 174; Dan 9:11: "your torah" (תורתך)

# Appendix B

# Canons of Scripture (Old Testament)

| Jewish (Hebrew) | Eastern Orthodox (Greek) | Protestant (vernacular: German, English, etc.) |
|---|---|---|
| תרה *Torah+* | Pentateuch | Pentateuch |
| בראשית *Bereshith*, "In the beginning" <br> שמות *Shemoth*, "Names" <br> ויקרא *Wayiqra*, "And he called" <br> במדבר *Bemidbar*, "In the Wilderness" <br> דברים *Devarim*, "Words" | Genesis, "Origin" <br> Exodus, "Going Out" <br> Leviticus, "Levitical" <br> Numbers (refers to census) <br> Deuteronomy, "Second Law" | Genesis <br> Exodus <br> Leviticus <br> Numbers <br> Deuteronomy |

## Canons of Scripture (Old Testament)

| Jewish (Hebrew) | Eastern Orthodox (Greek) | Protestant (vernacular: German, English, etc.) |
|---|---|---|
| נבאים *Nevi'im*, "Prophets" | *History* | *History* |
| Joshua<br>Judges<br>Samuel<br>Kings<br>Isaiah<br>Jeremiah<br>Ezekiel<br>The Twelve Prophets: Hosea, Joel, Amos, Obadiah, Jonah, Micah, Nahum, Habakkuk, Zephaniah, Haggai, Zechariah, Malachi | Joshua<br>Judges<br>Ruth<br>1 Samuel<br>2 Samuel<br>1 Kings<br>2 Kings<br>1 Chronicles<br>2 Chronicles<br>Ezra<br>Nehemiah<br>Tobit*<br>Judith*<br>Esther (with additions)*<br>1 Maccabees*<br>2 Maccabees*<br>3 Maccabees[d]<br>4 Maccabees[d] | Joshua<br>Judges<br>Ruth<br>1 Samuel<br>2 Samuel<br>1 Kings<br>2 Kings<br>1 Chronicles<br>2 Chronicles<br>Ezra<br>Nehemiah<br>Esther |
| כתבים *Ketuvim*, "Writings" | *Poetry and Wisdom* | *Poetry and Wisdom* |
| תהלים *Tehillim*, "Psalms"<br>איוב *Iyyob*, "Job"<br>משלי *Mishle*, "Proverbs"<br>Five Festival Scrolls: Ruth, Song of Songs, קהלת *Qoheleth* "Preacher" (Ecclesiastes), איכה *Ekah* "How" (Lamentations), Esther<br>Daniel<br>Ezra-Nehemiah<br>Chronicles | Job<br>Psalms<br>Proverbs<br>Ecclesiastes<br>Song of Songs<br>Wisdom of Solomon*<br>Ecclesiasticus (Wisdom of Ben Sirach)* | Job<br>Psalms<br>Proverbs<br>Ecclesiastes<br>Song of Solomon |

## APPENDIX B

| Jewish (Hebrew) | Eastern Orthodox (Greek) | Protestant (vernacular: German, English, etc.) |
|---|---|---|
| | *Prophets* | *Prophets* |
| When the Scrolls are counted separately the total number is 24. | Isaiah<br>Jeremiah<br>Lamentations<br>Baruch and Letter of Jeremiah* (a)<br>Ezekiel<br>Daniel* (includes Prayer of Azariah, Song of the Three Young Men, Susanna, Bel and the Dragon)<br>Hosea<br>Joel<br>Amos<br>Obadiah<br>Jonah<br>Micah<br>Nahum<br>Habakkuk<br>Zephaniah<br>Haggai<br>Zechariah<br>Malachi | Isaiah<br>Jeremiah<br>Lamentations<br>Ezekiel<br>Daniel<br>Hosea<br>Joel<br>Amos<br>Obadiah<br>Jonah<br>Micah<br>Nahum<br>Habakkuk<br>Zephaniah<br>Haggai<br>Zechariah<br>Malachi |

| Jewish (Hebrew) | Eastern Orthodox (Greek) | Protestant (vernacular: German, English, etc.) |
|---|---|---|
| | | *Apocrypha* |
| | | 1 Esdras (b)<br>2 Esdras (c)<br>Tobit<br>Judith<br>Additions to Esther<br>Wisdom of Solomon<br>Ecclesiasticus<br>Baruch<br>Letter of Jeremiah<br>Prayer of Azariah and the Song of Tree Young Men<br>Susanna<br>Bel and the Dragon<br>Prayer of Manasseh (b)<br>1 Maccabees<br>2 Maccabees<br>3 Maccabees<br>4 Maccabees<br>Psalm 151 (b) |
| | New Testament | New Testament |

+ The only Scripture of the Samaritans
* Deuterocanonical for Catholics
(a) Not listed by Eastern Orthodox
(b) Listed as 2 Esdras in Greek/Slavonic
(c) Listed as 3 Esdras in Slavonic
(d) Not listed by Roman Catholics

# Abbreviations

| | |
|---|---|
| *AJSL* | *American Journal of Semitic Languages and Literatures* |
| AnBib | Analecta biblica |
| *AO* | *Der Alte Orient* |
| *BA* | *Biblical Archaeologist* |
| *BASOR* | *Bulletin of the American Schools of Oriental Research* |
| BBB | Bonner biblische Beiträge |
| BHT | Beiträge zur historischen Theologie |
| *Bib* | *Biblica* |
| BKAT | Biblischer Kommentar, Altes Testament. Edited by M. Noth and H. W. Wolff |
| *BR* | *Biblical Research* |
| BWANT | Beiträge zur Wissenschaft vom Alten und Neuen Testament |
| *EvT* | *Evangelische Theologie* |
| FRLANT | Forschungen zur Religion und Literatur des Alten und Neuen Testaments |
| HDR | Harvard Dissertations in Religion |
| *HTR* | *Harvard Theological Review* |
| *HUCA* | *Hebrew Union College Annual* |
| IB | *Interpreter's Bible*. Edited by G. A. Buttrick et al. 12 vols. New York: Abingdon-Cokesbury, 1951–57 |
| IDB | *The Interpreter's Dictionary of the Bible*. 4 vols. Edited by George Arthur Buttrick. Nashville: Abingdon, 1962 |
| *JAOS* | *Journal of the American Oriental Society* |
| *JBL* | *Journal of Biblical Literature* |

| | |
|---|---|
| JBR | *Journal of Bible and Religion* |
| JNES | *Journal of Near Eastern Studies* |
| JSOTSup | Journal for the Study of the Old Testament: Supplement Series |
| JSS | *Journal of Semitic Studies* |
| JTS | *Journal of Theological Studies* |
| OTL | Old Testament Library |
| OtSt | Oudtestamentische Studiën |
| PEQ | *Palestine Exploration Quarterly* |
| RB | *Revue biblique* |
| RGG | *Religion in Geschichte und Gegenwart*. Edited by K. Galling. 7 vols. 3rd ed. Tübingen, 1957–1965 |
| SBLDS | Society of Biblical Literature Dissertation Series |
| SBS | Stuttgarter Bibelstudien |
| SBT | Studies in Biblical Theology |
| ST | *Studia theologica* |
| SThU | *Schweizerische Theologische Umschau* |
| TB | Theologische Bücherei: Neudrucke und Berichte aus dem 20. Jahrhundert |
| ThSt | Theologische Studiën |
| TLZ | *Theologische Literaturzeitung* |
| TZ | *Theologische Zeitschrift* |
| VT | *Vetus Testamentum* |
| VTSup | Supplements to Vetus Testamentum |
| ZAW | *Zeitschrift für die alttestamentliche Wissenschaft* |
| ZDMG | *Zeitschrift der deutschen morgenländischen Gesellschaft* |
| ZDPV | *Zeitschrift der deutschen Palästina-Vereins* |
| ZTK | *Zeitschrift für Theologie und Kirche* |

# Bibliography

Aalen, Sverre. *Die Begriffe 'Licht' und 'Finsternis' im Alten Testament im Spätjudentum und im Rabbinismus.* Oslo: Dybwad, 1951.

Achtemeier, Elizabeth Rice. *Nahum-Malachi.* Interpretation. Atlanta: John Knox, 1986.

Ackroyd, Peter R. *Exile and Restoration: A Study of Hebrew Thought of the Sixth Century B.C.* OTL. Philadelphia: Westminster, 1968.

———. *Israel under Babylon and Persia.* London: Oxford University Press, 1970.

———. "The Temple Vessels—A Continuity Theme." In *Studies in the Religion of Ancient Israel,* VTSup 23, 166-81. Leiden: Brill, 1972.

Aharoni, Yohanan, and Michael Avi-Yonah. *The Macmillan Bible Atlas.* Rev. ed. New York: Macmillan, 1977.

Ahlström, Gösta W. *The History of Ancient Palestine.* Minneapolis: Fortress, 1993.

Akenson, Donald H. *Surpassing Wonder: The Invention of the Bible and the Talmuds.* Chicago: University of Chicago Press, 1998.

Albertz, Rainer. *From the Beginnings to the End of the Monarchy.* Vol. 1 of *A History of Israelite Religion in the Old Testament Period.* Translated by John Bowden. OTL. Louisville: Westminster John Knox, 1994.

Albright, William Foxwell. "The Biblical Period." Chap. 1 in *The Jews,* edited by L. Finkelstein. New York: Harper, 1949. Reprinted separately, Oxford: Oxford University Press, 1952.

———. *From the Stone Age to Christianity: Monotheism and the Historical Process.* 2nd ed. with new introduction. Baltimore: Johns Hopkins Press, 1957.

———. *Yahweh and the Gods of Canaan: A Historical Analysis of Two Contrasting Faiths.* London: Athlone, 1968.

Allen, Leslie C. *Ezekiel 1-19.* WBC 28. Waco, TX: Word, 1994.

———. *Ezekiel 20-48.* WBC 29. Waco, TX: Word, 1990.

———. *Psalms 101-151.* Rev. ed. WBC 21. Nashville: Nelson, 2002.

Alt, Albrecht. "God of the Fathers." In *Essays on Old Testament History and Religion,* translated by R. A. Wilson, 1-77. Oxford: Blackwell, 1966. Originally published as *Der Gott der Väter: Ein Beitrag zur Vorgeschichte der israelitischen Religion.* BWANT 3.12. Stuttgart: Kohlhammer, 1929. Reprinted in *Kleine Schriften,* 1:1-78. Tübingen: Mohr (Siebeck), 1962.

———. "Josua." In *Werden und Wesen des Alten Testament,* edited by P. Volz et al., 13-29. BZAW 66. Berlin: Töpelmann, 1936.

———. "Königtum in Israel." In *RGG* 2:1709-12.

———. "The Origins of Israelite Law." In *Essays in Old Testament History and Religion,* translated by R. A. Wilson, 101-71. Oxford: Blackwell, 1966.

———. "Die Wallfahrt von Sichem nach Bethel." In *Kleine Schriften zur Geschichte des Volkes Israel,* 1:79–88. Munich: Beck, 1953.
Andersen, Francis I. *Hosea: A New Translation with Introduction and Commentary.* AB 24. Garden City, NY: Doubleday, 1980.
Andersen, Francis I., and David Noel Freedman. *Amos: A New Translation with Notes and Commentary.* AB 24A. New York: Doubleday, 1989.
Andersen, K. T. "Der Gott meines Vaters." *ST* 16 (1962) 170–88.
Anderson, A. A. *The Book of Psalms.* 2 vols. NCBC. London: Oliphants, 1972.
Anderson, B. W. "The Place of Shechem in the Bible." *BA* 20 (1957) 10–19.
Anderson, R. T. "Samaritans." In *ISBE* 4:303–8.
Auerbach, Elias. "'Am haares." In *Proceedings of the First World Congress of Jewish Studies, 1947,* 362–66. Jerusalem, 1952.
Barton, John. *Oracles of God: Perceptions of Ancient Prophecy in Israel after the Exile.* Oxford: Oxford University Press, 1986.
Baudissin, Wolf Wilhelm, Graf von. *Kyrios, als Gottesname in Judentum und seine Stelle in der Religionsgeschichte.* 4 vols. Giessen: Topelmann, 1929.
Beckwith, Roger T. *The Old Testament Canon of the New Testament Church and Its Background in Early Judaism.* Grand Rapids: Eerdmans, 1985.
Begg, Christopher T. "A Bible Mystery: The Absence of Jeremiah in the Deuteronomistic History." *IBS* 7 (1985) 139–64.
———. "The Non-mention of Amos, Hosea and Micah in the Deuteronomistic History." *BN* 32 (1986) 41–53.
———. "The Non-mention of Zephaniah, Nahum and Habakkuk in the Deuteronomistic History." *BN* 38/39 (1987) 19–25.
Bentzen, Aage. "The Cultic Use of the Story of the Ark in Samuel." *JBL* 67 (1948) 37–53.
Ben Zvi, Ehud. *A Historical-Critical Study of the Book of Obadiah.* BZAW 242. Berlin: De Gruyter, 1996.
Berry, George Ricker. "The Code Found in the Temple." *JBL* 39 (1920) 44–51.
Bickerman, Elias J. "The Edict of Cyrus in Ezra 1." *JBL* 65 (1946) 249–75.
———. *Four Strange Books of the Bible: Jonah, Daniel, Koheleth, Esther.* New York: Schocken, 1967.
———. *From Ezra to the Last of the Maccabees: Foundations of Post-Biblical Judaism.* New York: Schocken, 1962.
———. *The Jews in the Greek Age.* Cambridge: Harvard University Press, 1988.
———. *Studies in Jewish and Christian History.* 3 vols. AGJU. Leiden: Brill, 1976–1986.
Blenkinsopp, Joseph. *The Pentateuch: An Introduction to the First Five Books of the Bible.* New York: Doubleday, 1992.
———. *Prophecy and Canon: A Contribution to the Study of Jewish Origins.* Notre Dame, IN: University of Notre Dame Press, 1977.
———. *Wisdom and Law in the Old Testament: The Ordering of Life in Israel and Early Judaism.* Oxford Bible Series. Oxford: Oxford University Press, 1983.
Blum, Erhard. *Die Komposition der Vätergeschichte.* WMANT 57. Neukirchen-Vluyn: Neukirchener Verlag, 1984.
———. *Studien zur Komposition des Pentateuch.* BZAW 189. Berlin: De Gruyter, 1990.
Bosshard-Nepustil, Erich. *Rezeptionen von Jesaia 1–39 im Zwölfprophetenbuch: Untersuchungen zur literarischen Verbindung von Prophetenbüchern in babylonischer und*

*persischer Zeit*. Freiburg: Universitätsverlag; Göttingen: Vandenhoeck & Ruprecht, 1997.
Botterweck, G. Johannes. "Zur Eigenart der chronistischen Davidgeschichte." *TQ* 136 (1956) 402–35.
Bowman, John. *Samaritan Documents: Relating to the Their History, Religion, and Life*. Pittsburgh: Pickwick, 1977.
———. *The Samaritan Problem: Studies in the Relationships of Samaritanism, Judaism, and Early Christianity*. Translated by Alfred M. Johnson Jr. Pittsburgh: Pickwick, 1975.
Braun, Roddy L. "Solomonic Apologetic in Chronicles." *JBL* 92 (1973) 502–16.
———. "Solomon, the Chosen Temple Builder: The Significance of 1 Chronicles 22, 28, and 29 for the Theology of Chronicles." *JBL* 95 (1976) 581–90.
Brawer, A. H. "'Am haares kipesuto bammiqra." *BethM* 15 (1969–1970) 202–6.
Bright, John. *A History of Israel*. Philadelphia: Westminster, 1959, 1976, 1981.
Budde, Karl. "Das Deuteronomium und die Reform Josias." *ZAW* 44 (1926) 177–224.
Bush, Frederick W. *Ruth, Esther*. WBC 9. Dallas: Word, 1992.
Busink, Th. A. *Der Tempel Salomos*. Vol. 1 of *Der Tempel von Jerusalem, von Salomo bis Herodes*. Leiden: Brill, 1970.
———. *Von Ezechiel bis Middot*. Vol. 2 of *Der Tempel von Jerusalem, von Salomo bis Herodes*. Leiden: Brill, 1970.
Butler, Trent C. *Joshua*. WBC 7. Waco, TX: Word, 1983.
Carlson, Rolf August. *David the Chosen King: A Traditio-Historical Approach to the Second Book of Samuel*. Translated by Eric J. Sharpe and Stanley Rudman. Stockholm: Almqvist & Wiksell, 1964.
Carr, D. M. *Writing on the Tablet of the Heart: Origins of Scripture and Literature*. New York: Oxford University Press, 2005.
Christensen, Duane. L. *Transformation of the War Oracle*. HDR. Missoula: Scholars Press, 1975.
Clements, R. E. "Deuteronomy and the Jerusalem Cult Tradition." *VT* 15 (1965) 300–12.
———. *God and Temple*. Oxford: Blackwell, 1965.
Clines, David J. A. *Job 1–20*. WBC 17. Dallas: Word, 1989.
———. *Job 21–37*. WBC 18A. Nashville: Nelson, 2005.
———. *Job 38–42*. WBC 18B. Nashville: Nelson, forthcoming.
Cody, Aelred. *A History of the Old Testament Priesthood*. AnBib 35. Rome: Pontifical Biblical Institute, 1969.
Coggins, R. J. *Samaritans and Jews: The Origins of Samaritanism Reconsidered*. Atlanta: John Knox, 1975.
Collins, John Joseph. *The Apocalyptic Vision of the Book of Daniel*. HSM 16. Missoula: Scholars Press, 1977.
———. "The Court-Tales in Daniel and the Development of Apocalyptic." *JBL* 94 (1975) 218–34.
———. *Daniel: A Commentary on the Book of Daniel*. Hermeneia. Minneapolis: Fortress, 1993.
Cook, Stanley A. "The Semites." In *The Cambridge Ancient History*, edited by J. B. Bury et al., 2nd ed., 1:181–237. Cambridge: Cambridge University Press, 1928.
Corney, R. W. "Zadok the Priest." In *IDB* 4:928–29.
Coulmas, Florian. *The Writing Systems of the World*. Oxford: Blackwell, 1989.

Craigie, Peter C. *Psalms 1-50*. 2nd ed. with supplement by Marvin E. Tate. WBC 19. Nashville: Nelson, 2004.
Craigie, Peter C., Page H. Kelley, and Joel F. Drinkard, Jr. *Jeremiah 1-25*. WBC 26. Waco, TX: Word, 1985.
Crawford, Sidnie White. *Rewriting Scripture in Second Temple Times*. Studies in the Dead Sea Scrolls and Related Literature. Grand Rapids: Eerdmans, 2008.
Crenshaw, J. L. "Education in Ancient Israel." *JBL* 104 (1985) 601-15.
———. "YHWH Ṣ$^e$ba'ôt Š$^e$mô: A Form-critical Analysis." *ZAW* 81 (1969) 156-75.
Crim, Keith R. *The Royal Psalms*. Richmond: Knox, 1962.
Cross, Frank Moore, Jr. "Aspects of Samaritan and Jewish History in Late Persian and Hellenistic Times." *HTR* 59 (1966) 201-11.
———. "Jahweh and the God of the Patriarchs." *HTR* 55 (1962) 225-59.
———. "A Reconstruction of the Judean Restoration." *JBL* 94 (1975) 4-18.
Crown, Alan David. *A Bibliography of the Samaritans*. Metuchen, NJ: Scarecrow; Philadelphia: American Theological Library Association, 1984.
Daiches, Samuel. "The Meaning of עם הארץ in the Old Testament." *JTS* 30 (1929) 245-49.
Davies, G. Henton. "The Ark of the Covenant." In *IDB* 1:222-26.
Davies, Graham I. *Hosea: Based on the Revised Standard Version*. NCB. Grand Rapids: Eerdmans, 1992.
Davies, Philip R. *In Search of 'Ancient Israel.'* JSOTSup 148. Sheffield: JSOT Press, 1992.
Davies, W. D., and Louis Finkelstein, editors. *The Cambridge History of Judaism*. Vol. 1, *Introduction: The Persian Period*. Cambridge: Cambridge University Press, 1984.
Dietrich, Walter. "Josia und das Gesetzbuch (2 Reg 22)." *VT* 27 (1977) 13-35.
———. *Prophetie und Geschichte: Eine redaktionsgeschichtliche Untersuchung zum deuteronomistischen Geschichtswerk*. FRLANT 108. Göttingen: Vandenhoeck & Ruprecht, 1972.
Dillard, Raymond B. *2 Chronicles*. WBC 15. Waco, TX: Word, 1987.
Diringer, David. "Semitic Languages." In *Twentieth Century Encyclopedia of Religious Knowledge*, edited by A. Loetscher, 2:1014-15. Grand Rapids: Baker, 1955.
Dressler, Harold H. P. "The Identification of the Ugaritic Dnil with the Daniel of Ezekiel." *VT* 29 (1979) 152-61.
Driver, Godfrey Rolles. *Semitic Writing from Pictograph to Alphabet*. Edited by S. A. Hopkins. Rev. ed. London: Oxford University Press, 1976.
Dus, Jan. "Der Brauch der Ladewanderung im alten Israel." *TZ* 17 (1961) 1-16.
Eichrodt, Walter. "Der neue Tempel in der Heilshoffnung Hesekiels." In *Das Ferne und nahe Wort: Festschrift Leonhard Rost*, edited by Fritz Maass, BZAW 105, 37-48. Berlin: Töpelmann, 1967.
———. "Religionsgeschichte Israels." In *Historia Mundi*. Vol. 2. Bern, 1953.
Eissfeldt, Otto. "Gottesnamen und Gottesvorstellungen bei den Semiten." *ZDMG* 83 (1929) 35. Reprinted in *Kleine Schriften*, 1:204. Tübingen: Mohr (Siebeck), 1962.
———. "Jahwe Zebaoth." In *Miscellanea academica Berlinensia*, 128-50. Berlin, 1950.
———. "Lade und Gesetztafeln." *TZ* 16 (1960) 281-84.
———. *The Old Testament: An Introduction*. Translated by Peter Ackroyd from 3rd German edition. New York: Harper and Row, 1965. Originally published as *Einleitung in das Alte Testament unter Einschluss der Apokryphen und Pseudeprigraphen: Entstehungsgeschichte des Alten Testatments*. Tübingen: Mohr, 1934.

Elliger, K. "Die großen Tempelkristeien im Verfassungsentwurf des Ezechiel (42, 1ff)." In *Geschichte und Altes Testament,* edited by William Foxwell Albright et al., BHT 16, 79–103. Tübingen: Mohr, 1953.
Engnell, Ivan. *Studies in Divine Kingship in the Ancient Near East.* Uppsala: Almqvist & Wiksells, 1943.
Finley, Thomas J. *Joel, Amos, Obadiah.* WEC. Chicago: Moody Press, 1990.
Fohrer, Georg. *Geschichte der israelitischen Religion.* Berlin: De Gruyter, 1969.
———. "Der Vertrag zwischen König und Volk in Israel." *ZAW* 71 (1959) 1–22.
Fredriksson, Henning. *Jahwe als Krieger: Studien zum alttestamentlichen Gottesbild.* Lund: Gleerup, 1945.
Freed, Alexander. "The Code Spoken of in 2 Kings 22-23." *JBL* 40 (1921) 76–80.
Freedman, David Noel. "Deuteronomic History." In *IDBSup,* 226–28.
Fried, Lisbeth S. *The Priest and the Great King: Temple-Palace Relations in the Persian Empire.* Winona Lake, IN: Eisenbrauns, 2004.
Friedman, Richard Elliott. *The Exile and Biblical Narrative: The Formation of the Deuteronomistic and Priestly Works.* HSM 22. Chico, CA: Scholars Press, 1981.
Galling, Kurt. *ZDPV* 36 (1945) 34–43.
———. "Das Königtum im Deuteronomium." *TLZ* 76 (1951) 133–38.
———. *Studien zur Geschichte Israels im persischen Zeitalter.* Tübingen: Mohr, 1964.
Gammie, John G. "The Classification, Stages of Growth, and Changing Intentions in the Book of Daniel." *JBL* 95 (1976) 191–204.
———. "On the Intention and Sources of Daniel I–IV." *VT* 31 (1981) 282–92.
Garrett, Duane, and Paul R. House. *Song of Songs/Lamentations.* WBC 23B. Nashville: Nelson, 2007.
Gelston, A. "The Foundations of the Second Temple." *VT* 16 (1966) 232–35.
Gemser, Berend. "God in Genesis." In *Studies on the Book of Genesis,* OtSt 12, 1–21. Leiden: Brill, 1958.
Gerbrandt, Gerald Eddie. *Kingship according to the Deuteronomistic History.* SBLDS 87. Atlanta: Scholars Press, 1986.
Gese, Hartmut. "Die Entstehung der Büchereinteilung des Psalters." In *Wort, Lied, und Gottesspruch: Festschrift für Joseph Ziegler,* 2:657–64. Würzburg: Echter, 1972. Also published in *Von Sinai zum Zion: Alttestamentliche Beiträge zur biblischen Theologie,* BEvT 64, 159–67. Munich: Kaiser, 1974.
———. *Der Verfassungsentwurf des Ezechiel (Kap. 40–48) traditionsgeschichtlich Untersucht.* BHT 25. Tübingen: Mohr (Siebeck), 1957.
Gibson, J. C. L. "Light from Mari." *JSS* 7 (1962) 44–62.
Gieselmann, Bernd. "Die sogenannte josianische Reform in der gegenwärtigen Forschung." *ZAW* 106 (1994) 223–42.
Gillischewski, Eva. "Der Ausdruck עַם הָאָרֶץ im AT." *ZAW* 40 (1922) 137–42.
Goldingay, John E. *Daniel.* WBC 30. Dallas: Word, 1989.
Gordon, C. H. "The Patriarchal Narratives." *JNES* 13 (1954) 56–59.
Gottwald, Norman K. *A Light to the Nations: An Introduction to the Old Testament.* New York: Harper, 1959.
Graham, William A. *Beyond the Written Word: Oral Aspects of Scripture in the History of Religion.* Cambridge: Cambridge University Press, 1987.
Granild, S. "Einige Voraussetzungen des Gesetzbuches in 2 Kön. 22:8." *DTT* 19 (1956) 199–210.

Greenberg, Moshe. "Another Look at Rachel's Theft of the Teraphim." *JBL* 81 (1962) 239–48.
Greenberg, Moshe, and A'haron Oppenheimer. "Am ha-arez." In *EncJud* 2:833–36.
Gressman, Hugo. "Josia und das Deuteronomium." *ZAW* 42 (1924) 313–37.
Gunkel, Hermann. *Die Psalmen.* 6th ed. Göttingen: Vandenhoeck & Ruprecht, 1986.
Gunneweg, Antonius H. J. *Leviten und Priester: Hauptlinen der Traditionsbildung und Geschichte des israelitisch-jüdischen Kultpersonals.* FRLANT 89. Göttingen: Vandenhoeck & Ruprecht, 1965.
Habel, Norman C. *The Book of Job: A Commentary.* OTL. Philadelphia: Westminster, 1985.
Haldar, Alfred. *Associations of Cult Prophets among the Ancient Semites*, Uppsala: Almqvist & Wiksells, 1945.
Halpern, Baruch. *The First Historians: The Hebrew Bible and History.* San Francisco: Harper and Row, 1988.
Hammersgaimb, E. "Semiten." In *RGG* 5:1694–96.
Haran, Menahem. *Temples and Temple-Service in Ancient Israel: An Inquiry into the Character of Cult Phenomena and the Historical Setting of the Priestly School.* Oxford; New York: Clarendon, 1978.
Harrelson, Walter J. "The City of Shechem: Its History and Importance." Thesis, Union Theological Seminary, New York, 1953.
———. *From Fertility Cult to Worship.* Garden City, NY: Doubleday, 1969.
———. "The Religion of Israel." In *A Companion to the Bible*, edited by H. H. Rowley, 2nd ed., 335–38. Edinburgh: T. & T. Clark, 1963.
Hartley, John D. *The Book of Job.* NICOT. Grand Rapids: Eerdmans, 1988.
Hayes, John H. *Amos, the Eighth-Century Prophet: The Man and His Preaching.* Nashville: Abingdon, 1988.
———. "The Tradition of Zion's Inviolability." *JBL* 83 (1963) 419–26.
Hayes, John H., and J. Maxwell Miller, editors. *Israelite and Judaean History.* OTL. Philadelphia: Westminster, 1977.
Henninger, Joseph. *Über Lebensraum und Lebensformen der Frühsemiten.* Köln: Westdeutscher Verlag, 1968.
Herrman, Siegfried. "Die konstruktive Restauration: Das Deuteronomium als Mitte biblischer Theologie." In *Probleme biblischer Theologie: Gerhard von Rad zum 70. Geburstag*, edited by Hans Walter Wolff, 155–70. Munich: Kaiser, 1971.
Hillers, Delbert R. *Micah: A Commentary on the Book of the Prophet Micah.* Edited by Paul D. Hanson with Loren Fisher. Hermeneia. Philadelphia: Fortress, 1984.
Hobbs, T. R. *2 Kings.* WBC 13. Waco, TX: Word, 1985.
Hoffmann, Hans-Detlef. *Reform und Reformen: Untersuchungen zu einem Grundthema der deuteronomistischen Geschichtsschreibung.* ATANT 66. Zürich: Theologischer Verlag, 1980.
Hoftijzer, J. *Die Verheissungen an die drei Erzväter.* Leiden: Brill, 1956.
Hogland, Kenneth G. *Achaemenid Imperial Administration in Syria-Palestine and the Missions of Ezra and Nehemiah.* SBLDS 125. Atlanta: Scholars Press, 1992.
Hooke, S. H. "The Early Background of Hebrew Religion." In *A Companion to the Bible*, edited by T. W. Manson. New York: Scribner's, 1947.
House, Paul R. *The Unity of the Twelve.* JSOTSup 97. Sheffield: Almond, 1990.
Hulst, A. R. "גוי/עם 'am/gôy people." In *TLOT* 2:896–919.

Humbert, Paul. *La "terouʿa": Analyse d'un rite biblique.* Neuchâtel: Universitéd Neuchâtel, 1946.
Hyatt, J. Philip. "Yahweh as the God of My Father." *VT* 5 (1965) 130–35.
Ihromi, T. O. "Der Königmutter und der ʿamm haʿarez im Reich Juda." *VT* 24 (1974) 421–29.
Im, Tae-Soo. *Das Davidbild in den Chronikbüchern: David als Idealbild des theokratischen Messianismus für den Chronisten.* Frankfurt am Main; New York: Lang, 1985.
Irwin, W. A. "Samuel and the Rise of the Monarchy." *AJSL* 58 (1941) 113–34.
Ishida, Tomoo. "'The People of the Land' and the Political Crises in Judah." *AJBI* 1 (1975) 23–38.
Jacobsen, Thorkild. *The Treasures of Darkness: A History of Mesopotamian Religion.* New Haven, CT: Yale University Press, 1976.
Jamieson-Drake, David W. *Scribes and Schools in Monarchic Judah: A Socio-Archeological Approach.* JSOTSup 109; SWBA 9. Sheffield: Almond, 1991.
Janssen, Enno. *Juda in der Exilszeit: Ein Beitrag zur Frage der Entstehungdes Judentums.* FRLANT NS 51. Göttingen: Vandenhoeck & Ruprecht, 1956.
Janzen, J. Gerald. *Job.* IBC. Atlanta: John Knox, 1985.
―――. "The Place of the Book of Job in the History of Israel's Religion." In *Ancient Israelite Religion: Essays in Honor of Frank Moore Cross.* Edited by Patrick D. Miller Jr. et al., 528–37. Philadelphia: Fortress, 1987.
Japhet, Sara. *I & II Chronicles: A Commentary.* OTL. Louisville: Westminster John Knox, 1993.
Jeremias, Jörg. *The Book of Amos: A Commentary.* Translated by Douglas W. Stott. OTL. Louisville: Westminster John Knox, 1998.
Jirku, Anton. "Die Mimation in den nordsemitischen Sprachen und einige Bezeichnungen der altisraelitischen Mantik." *Bib* 34 (1953) 78–80.
Johnson, Aubrey R. *The Cultic Prophet in Ancient Israel.* 2nd ed. Cardiff: University of Wales Press, 1962.
―――. *Sacral Kingship in Ancient Israel.* 2nd ed. Cardiff: University of Wales Press, 1967.
Johnson, R. F. "Moses." In *IDB* 3:441.
Judge, H. G. "Aaron, Zadok, and Abiathar." *JTS* 7 (1956) 70–74.
Kalami, Isaac. "Die Abfassungszeit der Chronik—Forschungsstand und Perspektiven." *ZAW* 105 (1993) 223–33.
Kapelrud, Arvid Schou. *Israel: From the Earliest Times to the Birth of Christ.* Translated by J. M. Moe. Oxford: Blackwell, 1965.
―――. "Nochmals Jahwä Mālāk." *VT* 13 (1963) 229–31.
Keller, Carl A. "Über einige alttestamentliche Heiligtumslegenden: I und II." *ZAW* 67 (1955) 141–68; 68 (1956) 85–97.
Keown, Gerald L., Pamela J. Scalise, and Thomas G. Smothers. *Jeremiah 26–52.* WBC 27. Waco, TX: Word, 1986.
Kilian, Rudolf. *Die vorpriesterlichen Abrahamüberlieferungen: Literarkritisch und traditionsgeschichtlich untersucht.* BBB 24. Bonn: Hanstein, 1966.
Kippenberg, Hans G. *Garizim und Synagoge: Traditionsgeschichtliche Untersuchungen zur samaritan Religion der aramäischen Periode.* RVV 30. Berlin: De Gruyter, 1971.
Kitchen, K. A. "The Aramaic of Daniel." In D. J. Wiseman et al., *Notes on Some Problems in the Book of Daniel,* 31–79. London: Tyndale, 1965.

Kjaer, Hans. "Shiloh: A Summary Report of the Second Danish Expedition, 1929." *PEQ* 63 (1931) 71–88.

Knight, Douglas A. *Rediscovering the Traditions of Israel: The Development of the Traditio-historical Research of the Old Testament, with Special Consideration of Scandinavian Contributions*. SBLDS9. Missoula: Society of Biblical Literature for the Form Criticism Seminar, 1973.

Koch, Klaus. "Ezra and the Origins of Judaism." *JSS* 19 (1974) 173–97.

———. "Tempeleinlassliturgien und Dekaloge." In *Studien zur Theologie alttestamentlicher Überlieferungen*, edited by Rolf Rendtorff and Klaus Koch, 45–60. Neukirchen-Vluyn: Neukirchener Verlag, 1961.

Köhler, Ludwig. "Die Hebräische Rechtsgemeinde." Rector's address, University of Zürich, April 29, 1931. Reprinted in *Hebrew Man*. London: SCM Press, 1956.

Kraus, Hans-Joachim. "Gilgal, ein Beitrag zur Kultusgeschichte Israels." *VT* 1 (1951) 181–91.

———. *Die Königsherrschaft Gottes im Alten Testament: Untersuchungen zu den Liedern von Jahwes Thronbesteigung*. BHT 13. Tübingen: Mohr, 1951.

———. *Psalmen*. 2 vols. BKAT 15:1–2. Neukirchen-Vluyn: Neukirchener Verlag. 1960.

———. *Worship in Israel: A Cultic History of the Old Testament*. Translated by Geoffrey Buswell. Richmond: John Knox, 1966.

Kuhrt, Amélie. "The Cyrus Cylinder and Achaemenid Imperial Policy." *JSOT* 25 (1983) 83–97.

Kutsch, Ernst. "Erwägungen zur Geschichte der Passahfeier und des Massotfestes." *ZTK* 55 (1958) 1–35.

———. "Zelt." In *RGG* 6:1893–94.

———. "Zur Geschichte des Passah-Massot-Festes im Alten Testament." *EvT* 18 (1958) 47–67.

Kutscher, Edward Yechezkel. *A History of the Hebrew Language*. Jerusalem: Magnes, 1982.

Laato, Antti. *Josiah and David Redivivus: The Historical Josiah and the Messianic Expectations of Exilic and Postexilic Times*. ConBOT 33. Stockholm: Almqvist & Wiksell, 1992.

Labuschagne, C. J. "Teraphim: A New Proposal for Its Etymology." *VT* 16 (1966) 115–17.

Leiman, Shnayer Z. *The Canonization of Hebrew Scripture: The Talmudic and Mishnaic Evidence*. Transactions—The Connecticut Academy of Arts and Sciences 47. Hamden, CT: Archon, 1976.

Leslie, Elmer A. *Old Testament Religion in Light of Its Canaanite Background*. New York: Abingdon, 1936.

Levenson, Jon Douglas. *Sinai and Zion: An Entry into the Jewish Bible*. New Voices in Biblical Studies. Minneapolis: Winston, 1985.

———. *Theology of the Program of Restoration of Ezekiel 40–48*. HSM 10. Missoula: Scholars Press for Harvard Semitic Museum, 1976.

Liagre Böhl, Francisco Mario Theodoro de. "Die Zeitalter Abrahams." In *Opera Minora*, 26–49. Groningen: Wolters, 1953. Originally published in *AO* 29 (1930).

Lind, Millard C. *Yahweh Is a Warrior: The Theology of Warfare in Ancient Israel*. Scottdale, PA: Herald, 1980.

Lipiński, Edward. "עַם." In *TDOT* 11:163–78.

Lohfink, Norbert. "Die Bundesurkunde des Königs Josias." *Bib* 44 (1963) 261-88, 461-98.

———. "The Cult Reform of Josiah of Judah: 2 Kings 22-23 as a Source for the History of Israelite Religion." In *Ancient Israelite Religion: Essays in Honor of Frank Moore Cross*, edited by Patrick D. Miller Jr. et al., 459-76. Philadelphia: Fortress, 1987.

———. "Die Gattung der 'Historischen Kurzgeschichte' in den letzten Jahren von Juda und in der Zeit des Babylonischen Exils." *ZAW* 90 (1978) 319-47.

———. "Zur neueren Diskussion über 2 Kön 22-23." In *Das Deuteronomium: Entstehung, Gestalt und Botschaft*, edited by Norbert Lohfink, BETL 68, 24-48. Louvain: Peeters/University Press, 1985.

Longman, Tremper III, and Daniel G. Reid. *God Is a Warrior*. Grand Rapids: Zondervan, 1995.

Maag, Victor. "Der Hirte Israels." *SThU* 28 (1958) 2-28.

———. "Jahwäs Heerscharen." *SThU* 20 *(Festschrift Ludwig Köhler)* (1950) 27-51.

———. "Malkût JHWH." In *Congress Volume: Oxford 1959*, VTSup 7, 127-53. Leiden: Brill, 1960.

MacDonald, John. *Theology of the Samaritans*. NTL. London: SCM Press, 1964.

Macintosh, A. A. *A Critical and Exegetical Commentary on Hosea*. ICC. Edinburgh: T. & T. Clark, 1997.

Mackay, C. "Der Hirte Israels." *SThU* 28 (1958) 1-28.

———. "Why Study Ezekiel 40-48?" *EvQ* 37 (1965) 155-67.

May, H. G. "The God of My Father—A Study of Patriarchal Religion." *JBR* 9 (1941) 155-58, 199-200.

———. "The Patriarchal Idea of God." *JBL* 60 (1941) 113-28.

McCarthy, Dennis J. *Old Testament Covenant: A Survey of Current Opinions*. Richmond: John Knox, 1972.

———. *Treaty and Covenant: A Study in Form in the Ancient Oriental Documents and in the Old Testament*. AnBib 21. Rome: Pontifical Biblical Institute, 1963.

McConville, J. Gordon. *Grace in the End: A Study in Deuteronomic Theology*. Grand Rapids: Zondervan, 1993.

———. *Law and Theology in Deuteronomy*. JSOTSup 33. Sheffield: JSOT Press, 1984.

McEvenue, Sean E. "The Political Structure in Judah from Cyrus to Nehemiah." *CBQ* 43 (1981) 353-64.

McKenzie, John L. "The 'People of the Land' in the Old Testament." In *Acts of the 24th International Congress of Orientalists, Munich 1957*, 206-8. Wiesbaden,1959.

Meadowcraft, Tim. "A Literary Critical Comparison of the Masoretic Text and Septuagint of Daniel 2-7." [Summary of an Edinburgh dissertation.] *TynBul* 45 (1994) 195-99.

Mendelsohn, Isaac. "Samuel's Denunciation of Kingship in the Light of the Akkadian Documents from Ugarit." *BASOR* 143 (1956) 17-22.

Mettinger, Tryggve N. D. *The Dethronement of Sabaoth: Studies in the Shem and Kabod Theologies*. Translated by Frederick H. Cryer. ConBOT 18. Lund: Gleerup, 1982.

Meyer, Rudolf. "Der 'Am ha-'Ares: Ein Beitrag zur Religionssoziologie Palästinas im ersten und zweiten nachchristlichen Jahrhundert." *Jud* 3 (1947) 169-99.

Meyers, Carol L., and Eric M. Meyers. *Haggai, Zechariah 1-8: A New Translation with Introduction and Commentary*. AB 25B. Garden City, NY: Doubleday, 1987.

———. *Zechariah 9-14: A New Translation with Introduction and Commentary*. AB 25C. New York: Doubleday, 1993.

Meyers, Eric M. "The Persian Period and the Judean Restoration: From Zerubbabel to Nehemiah." In *Ancient Israelite Religion: Essays in Honor of Frank Moore Cross*, edited by Patrick D. Miller Jr. et al., 509–21. Philadelphia: Fortress, 1987.

Miller, Patrick D. Jr., Paul D. Hanson, and S. Dean McBride, editors. *Ancient Israelite Religion: Essays in Honor of Frank Moore Cross*. Philadelphia: Fortress Press, 1987.

Möhlenbrink, Kurt. *Der Tempel Salomos: Eine Untersuchung seiner Stellung in der Sakralarchitektur des alten Orients*. BWANT 59. Stuttgart: Kohlhammer, 1932.

Montgomery, James A. *A Critical and Exegetical Commentary on the Book of Daniel*. New York: Scribner, 1927.

———. *The Samaritans: The Earliest Jewish Sect, Their History, Theology, and Literature*. 1907. Reprint, New York: Ktav, 1968.

Morgenstern, Julian. "Amos Studies I." *HUCA* 11 (1963) 19–40.

———. "Jerusalem—485 B.C." *HUCA* 27 (1956) 101–79; 28 (1957) 15–47; 30 (1960) 1–29.

Moscati, Sabatino. *Ancient Semitic Civilizations*. London: Elek, 1957.

———. *The Semites in Ancient History*. Cardiff: University of Wales Press, 1959.

Moscati, Sabatino, editor. *An Introduction to the Comparative Grammar of Semitic Languages: Phonology and Morphology*. Wiesbaden: Harrassowitz, 1965.

Mowinckel, Sigmund. *He That Cometh*. Translated by G. W. Anderson. New York: Abingdon, 1954.

———. *Psalmenstudien*. 2 vols. Oslo: Dybwad, 1923. Reprint, Amsterdam: Schippers, 1961.

———. *The Psalms in Israel's Worship*. Translated by D. R. Ap-Thomas. 2 vols. Oxford: Blackwell, 1968.

———. *Religion und Kultus*. Göttingen: Vandenhoeck und Ruprecht, 1953.

———. *Zum israelitischen Neujahr und zur Deutung der Thronbesteigungspsalmen*. Oslo: Dybwad, 1952.

Muilenburg, James. "The Form and Structure of the Covenantal Formulations." *VT* 9 (1959) 347–65.

———. "The Site of Ancient Gilgal." *BASOR* 140 (1955) 11–27.

Murphy, Roland. *Ecclesiastes*. WBC 23A. Dallas: Word, 1992.

Myers, Jacob Martin. *The World of the Restoration*. Englewood Cliffs, NJ: Prentice-Hall, 1968.

Na'aman, Nadav. "The Kingdom of Judah under Josiah." *Tel Aviv* 18 (1991) 3–71.

Nelson, Richard D. *Double Redaction of the Deuteronomistic History*. JSOTSup 18. Sheffield: JSOT Press, 1981.

Neugebauer, Otto. "Jews and Judaism under Iranian Rule: Bibliographical Reflections." *HR* 8 (1968) 159–77.

Newman, Murray Lee. *The People of the Covenant: A Study of Israel from Moses to the Monarchy*. Nashville: Abingdon, 1962.

———. "The Sinai Covenant Traditions in the Cult of Israel." Diss., Union Theological Seminary, New York, 1960.

Nicholson, Ernest W. "The Meaning of the Expression עַם הָאָרֶץ in the Old Testament." *JSS* 10 (1965) 59–66.

Nickelsburg, George W. E. *Jewish Literature between the Bible and the Mishnah: A Historical and Literary Introduction*. Philadelphia: Fortress, 1981.

Nielsen, Eduard. "The Burial of the Foreign Gods." *ST* 8 (1954) 103–22.

———. *Shechem: A Traditio-Historical Investigation*. 2nd rev. ed. Copenhagen: Gad,1959.

———. "Some Reflections on the History of the Ark." In *Congress Volume: Oxford 1959*, VTSup 7, 61–74. Leiden: Brill, 1960.

Nigosian, S. A. *From Ancient Writings to Sacred Texts: The Old Testament and the Apocrypha*. Baltimore: Johns Hopkins University Press, 2004.

Noglaski, James. *Literary Precursors to the Book of the Twelve*. BZAW 217. Berlin: De Gruyter, 1993.

———. *Redactional Processes in the Book of the Twelve*. BZAW 218. Berlin: De Gruyter, 1993.

Noth, Martin. "Das Amt des Richters Israels." In *Festschrift, Alfred Bertholet*, edited by Walter Baumgartner, 404–17. Tübingen: Mohr, 1950.

———. *The Deuteronomistic History*. Translated by J. Doull et al. JSOTSup 15. Sheffield: University of Sheffield, Department of Biblical Studies, 1981. Originally published in German as *Überlieferungsgeschichtliche Studien*, 2nd ed., 1–110. Tübingen: Niemeyer, 1957.

———. *The History of Israel*. Translated by Stanley Godman. New York: Harper, 1958.

———. "Jerusalem and the Israelite Tradition." In *The Laws in the Pentateuch, and Other Studies*. Translated by D. R. Ap-Thomas, 132–44. Philadelphia: Fortress, 1967.

———. *Überlieferungsgeschichte des Pentateuch*. 2nd ed. Stuttgart: Kohlhammer, 1948.

———. *Überlieferungsgeschichtliche Studien: Die sammelnden und bearbeiten Geschichtswerke im Alten Testament*. 2nd ed. Tübingen: Niemeyer, 1957.

———. "Die Vergegenwärtigung des Alten Testaments in der Verkündigung." In *Probleme alttestamentlicher Hermeneutik: Aufsätze zum Verstehen des Alten Testaments*, edited by Claus Westerman, TB 11. Munich: Kaiser, 1960. Translated as "The 'Representation' of the Old Testament in Proclamation," in *Essays on Old Testament Hermeneutics*, edited by James Luther Mays, 2nd ed., 76–88. Richmond: John Knox, 1964.

O'Brien, Mark A. *The Deuteronomistic History Hypothesis: A Reassessment*. OBO 92. Göttingen: Vandenhoeck & Ruprecht, 1989.

Oesterley, W. O. E. "Early Hebrew Festival Rituals." In *Myth and Ritual*, edited by S. H. Hooke, 111–46. London: Oxford University Press, 1933.

Olmstead, A. T. *History of the Persian Empire*. Chicago: University of Chicago Press, 1948.

Oppenheimer, A'haron. *The 'am ha-aretz: A Study in the Social History of the Jewish People in the Hellenistic-Roman Period*. ALGHJ 8. Leiden: Brill, 1977.

Otto, Eckart. *Das Mazzotfest in Gilgal*. BWANT 107. Stuttgart: Kohlhammer, 1975.

Ouellette, Jean. "Le vestibule du Temple de Salomon était-il un *bit hilani*?" *RB* 76 (1969) 365–78.

Owens, John Joseph, John D. W. Watts, and Marvin E. Tate. "Job." In *The Broadman Bible Commentary*, edited by Clifton J. Allen et al., 4:22–152. Nashville: Broadman, 1969–1972.

Patterson, Richard Duane. *Nahum, Habakkuk, Zephaniah*. WEC. Chicago: Moody Press, 1991.

Paul, Shalom M. *Amos: A Commentary on the Book of Amos*. Edited by Frank Moore Cross. Hermeneia. Minneapolis: Fortress, 1991.

Peckham, Brian. *The Composition of the Deuteronomic History*. HSM 35. Atlanta: Scholars Press, 1985.

———. *History and Prophecy: The Development of Late Judean Literary Traditions*. New York: Doubleday, 1993.
Pedersen, Johannes. *Israel III–IV*. Copenhagen: Branner, 1940.
Perlitt, Lothar. *Bundestheologie im Alten Testament*. WMANT 36. Neukirchen-Vluyn: Neukirchener Verlag, 1969.
Person, Raymond F. Jr. "II Kings 24:18—25:30 and Jeremiah 52: A Text-Critical Case Study in the Redaction History of the Deuteronomistic History." *ZAW* 105 (1994) 174–204.
Petersen, David L. *Haggai and Zechariah 1–8: A Commentary*. OTL. Philadelphia: Westminster, 1984.
Pfeiffer, Charles F. *The Patriarchal Age*. Grand Rapids: Baker, 1961.
Plöger, Josef G. *Literarkritische, formgeschichtliche und stilkritische Untersuchungen zum Deuteronomium*. BBB 26. Bonn: Hanstein, 1967.
Plöger, Otto. *Theocracy and Eschatology*. Translated by S. Rudman. Oxford: Blackwell, 1968.
Polzin, Robert. *Moses and the Deuteronomist: Deuteronomy, Joshua, Judges*. Bloomington: Indiana University Press, 1993. Originally published as part 1 in *A Literary Study of the Deuteronomic History*. New York: Seabury, 1980.
———. *Samuel and the Deuteronomist: 1 Samuel*. Bloomington: Indiana University Press, 1993. Originally published as part 2 in *A Literary Study of the Deuteronomic History*. San Francisco: Harper & Row, 1989.
Pomykala, K. E. *The Davidic Dynasty Tradition in Early Judaism: Its History and Significance for Messianism*. Early Judaism and Its Literature 7. Atlanta: Scholars Press, 1995.
Pope, M. H. "'Am Ha'arez." In *IDB* 1:106–7.
Porteous, Norman. *Daniel, A Commentary*. OTL. Philadelphia: Westminster, 1965.
Porter, J. R. "The Interpretation of 2 Samuel VI and Psalm CXXXII." *JTS* 5 (1954) 161–73.
Provan, Iain W. *Hezekiah and the Books of Kings: A Contribution to the Debate about the Composition of the Deuteronomistic History*. BZAW 172. Berlin: De Gruyter, 1988.
Purvis, James D. *The Samaritan Pentateuch and the Origin of the Samaritan Sect*. HSM 2. Cambridge: Harvard University Press, 1968.
Rad, Gerhard von. *Deuteronomium-Studien*. FRLANT 40. Göttingen: Vandenhoeck & Ruprecht, 1947.
———. *Das Formgeschichtliche Problem des Hexateuchs*. BWANT 4. Stuttgart: Kohlhammer, 1938.
———. *Das Gottesvolk im Deuteronomium*. BWANT 47. Stuttgart: Kohlhammer, 1929.
———. *Holy War in Ancient Israel*. 1958. Reprint, Grand Rapids: Eerdmans, 1991.
———. *Moses*. New York: Association Press, 1960.
———. *Old Testament Theology*. Translated by D. M. G. Stalker. 2 vols. New York: Harper; Edinburgh: Oliver & Boyd, 1962–65.
———. *The Problem of the Hexateuch and Other Essays*. Translated by E. W. Trueman Dicken. Edinburgh: Oliver & Boyd, 1966. Originally published as *Das Formgeschichtliche Problem des Hexateuchs*. BWANT 4.26. Stuttgart: Kohlhammer, 1938. Reprinted in *Gesammelte Studien zum Alten Testament*, vol. 1, TB 8. Munich: Kaiser, 1958.

———. *Studies in Deuteronomy*. Translated by David Stalker. SBT 9. Chicago: Regnery, 1953. Originally published as *Deuteronomium-Studien*. Göttingen: Vandenhoeck & Ruprecht, 1947.

Radjawane, Arnold Nicolaas. "Das deuteronomistische Geschichtswerk: Ein Forschungsbericht." *TRev* 38 (1973-74) 177-216.

Rainey, Anson F. "The Satrapy 'Beyond the River.'" *AJBA* 1 (1969) 51-78.

Raphael, Chaim. *The Road from Babylon: The Story of Sephardi and Oriental Jews*. New York: Harper & Row, 1985.

Renckens, Henry. "Enthronement Festival or Covenant Renewal?" *BR* 7 (1962) 45-48.

———. *The Religion of Israel*. Translated by N. B. Smith. New York: Sheed and Ward, 1966.

Rendtorff, Rolf. *The Old Testament: An Introduction*. Philadelphia: Fortress, 1986.

———. "The Paradigm Is Changing: Hopes and Fears." *BibInt* 1 (1993) 34-53.

Ringgren, Helmer. *Israelite Religion*. Translated by David E. Green. Philadelphia: Fortress, 1966.

Roberts, J. J. M. "The Davidic Origin of the Zion Tradition." *JBL* 92 (1973) 329-44.

———. *Nahum, Habakkuk, and Zephaniah: A Commentary*. OTL. Louisville: Westminster John Knox, 1991.

Robertson, O. Palmer. *The Books of Nahum, Habakkuk, and Zephaniah*. NICOT. Grand Rapids: Eerdmans, 1990.

Robinson, James M., general editor. *The Nag Hammadi Library in English*. 4th rev. ed. Leiden: Brill, 1996.

Rose, Martin. *Der Ausschliesslichkeitsanspruch Jahwes: Deuteronomische Schultheologie und die Volksfrömmigkeit in der späten Königszeit*. BWANT 106. Stuttgart: Kohlhammer, 1975.

———. *Deuteronomist und Jahwist: Untersuchungen zu den Berührungspunkten beider Literaturwerke*. Zurich: Theologischer Verlag, 1981.

Rost, Leonhard. "Die Gottesverehrung der Patriarchen im Lichte der Pentateuchquellen." In *Congress Volume: Oxford 1959*, 346-59. VTSup 7. Leiden: Brill, 1960.

———. *Das kleine Credo und andere Studien zum Alten Testament*. Heidelberg: Quelle & Meyer, 1964.

———. *Die Überlieferung von der Thronnachfolge Davids*. BWANT 3. Stuttgart: Kohlhammer, 1926.

Rowley, H. H. *The Biblical Doctrine of Election*. London: Lutterworth, 1950.

———. "Israel, the History of." In *IDB* 2:754-57.

———. "Melchizedek and Zadok." In *Festschrift, Alfred Bertholet*, edited by Walter Baumgartner, 461-72. Tübingen: Mohr, 1950.

———. "Nehemiah's Mission and Its Background." *BJRL* 37 (1955) 528-51.

———. "Recent Discoveries and the Patriarchal Age." In *Servant of the Lord, and Other Essays on the Old Testament*, rev. ed., 269-305. Oxford: Blackwell, 1965. Originally published in *BJRL* 32 (1949-50) 44-79.

———. "Sanballat and the Samaritan Temple." *BJRL* 38 (1955) 166-98.

———. "The Unity of the Book of Daniel." In *The Servant of the Lord, and Other Essays on the Old Testament*, 2nd, rev. ed., 249-80. Oxford: Blackwell, 1965.

———. *Worship in Ancient Israel*. London: SPCK, 1967.

———. "Zadok and Nehushtan." *JBL* 58 (1939) 113-41.

Rudolph, W. "Die Einheitlichkeit der Erzählung vom Sturtz der Atalja (2 Kön 11)." In *Festschrift, Alfred Bertholet,* edited by Walter Baumgartner, 473–78. Tübingen: Mohr, 1950.

Rylaarsdam, J. C. "Booths, Feast of." In *IDB* 1:455–58.

———. "Weeks, Feast of." In *IDB* 4:827–28.

Safire, William. *The First Dissident: The Book of Job in Today's Politics.* New York: Random House, 1992.

Saur, Markus. *Die Königspsalmen: Studien zur Entstehung und Theologie.* BZAW 340. Berlin: De Gruyter, 2004.

Schäfer-Lichtenberger, Christa. "Der הארץ עם—eine Anti-Jerusalem-Gruppierung?" In *Stadt und Eidgenossenschaft im Alten Testament,* BZAW 156, 391–94. Berlin: De Gruyter, 1983.

Schaff, Philip. *History of the Christian Church.* 8 vols. Peabody, MA: Hendrickson, 1996.

Schmidt, Martin. *Prophet und Tempel: Eine Studie zum Problem der Gottesnähe im Alten Testament.* Zollikon-Zürich: Evangelischer, 1948.

Schmidt, Werner H. *Alttestamentlicher Glaube und seine Umwelt.* Neukirchen-Vluyn: Neukirchener Verlag, 1968.

Schniedewind, William M. *How the Bible Became a Book: The Textualization of Ancient Israel.* New York: Cambridge University Press, 2004.

Scroggie, W. Graham. *Psalms.* Rev. ed. 3 vols. London: Pickering & Ingles, 1949.

Seebass, Horst. "Die Vorgeschichte der Königserhebung Sauls." *ZAW* 79 (1967) 155–71.

Slouch, N. "Representative Government among the Hebrews and Phoenicians." *JQR* 4 (1913–1914) 303–10.

Smend, Rudolf. *Elemente alttestamentlichen Geschichtsdenekens.* ThSt 95. Zurich: EVZ, 1968.

———. "Das Gesetz und die Völker: Ein Beitrag zur deuteronomistischen Redaktionsgeschichte." In *Probleme biblischer Theologie: Gerhard von Rad zum 70. Geburtstag,* edited by Hans Walter Wolff, 494–509. Munich: Kaiser, 1971.

Smith, George Adam. *The Early Poetry of Israel in Its Physical and Social Origins.* London: British Academy of Oxford University Press, 1912.

Smith, Morton. "II Isaiah and the Persians." *JAOS* 83 (1963) 415–20.

———. *Palestinian Parties and Politics that Shaped the Old Testament.* Lectures on the History of Religions NS 9. New York: Columbia University Press, 1971.

Smith, Ralph L. *Micah-Malachi.* WBC 32. Waco, TX: Word, 1984.

Smith, W. Robertson. *Lectures on the Religion of the Semites: The Fundamental Institutions.* With notes by Stanley A. Cook. 3rd ed. New York: Macmillan, 1927.

Snaith, Norman Henry. *The Jewish New Year Festival: Its Origins and Development.* London: SPCK, 1947.

Soden, W. von. "Semiten." In *RGG* 5:1690–93.

Soggin, J. Alberto. "Der judäische 'am-ha'ares und das Königtum in Juda." *VT* 13 (1963) 187–95.

———. *Das Königtum in Israel: Ursprünge, Spannungen, Entwicklung.* BZAW 104. Berlin: Töpelmann, 1967.

Steinmann, Jean. *David: roi d'Israel.* Témoins de Dieu 11. Paris: Cerf, 1947.

Stern, Ephraim. *Material Culture of the Land of the Bible in the Persian Period, 538–332 B.C.* Warminster: Aris & Philips, 1982.

———. "The Province of Yehud: The Vision and the Reality." In *Jerusalem Cathedra*, edited by Lee I. Levine, 1:9–21. Detroit: Wayne State University Press, 1981.
Steuernagel, Carl. *Jahwe und der Vätergötter.* Stuttgart: Kohlhammer, 1935. Also published in *Festschrift Georg Beer*, 62–71. Stuttgart, 1935.
Stinespring, W. F. "Temple, Jerusalem." In *IDB* 4:534–60.
Stuart, Douglas K. *Hosea-Jonah.* WBC 31. Waco, TX: Word, 1987.
Sulzberger, Mayer. *The am ha-aretz, the Ancient Hebrew Parliament: A Chapter in the Constitutional History of Ancient Israel.* 2nd ed. Philadelphia: Greenstone, 1910.
Sundberg, Albert C. *The Old Testament of the Early Church.* Cambridge: Harvard University Press,1964.
Sweeney, Marvin A. *The Twelve Prophets.* Edited by David W. Cotter et al. 2 vols. Berit Olam. Collegeville, MN: Liturgical, 2000.
Tadmor, Hayim. "'The People' and the Kingship in Ancient Israel: The Role of Political Institutions in the Biblical Period." *Cahiers d'histoire mondiale* 11 (1968) 46–68.
Talmon, Shemaryahu. "The Emergence of Jewish Sectarianism in the Early Second Temple Period." In *King, Cult, and Calendar in Ancient Israel*, 165–201. Jerusalem: Magnes, 1986.
———. "The Judean 'am ha'ares in Historical Perspective." In *Proceedings of the Fourth World Congress of Jewish Studies, 1965,* 1:71–76. Jerusalem, 1967.
Tate, Marvin E. *Psalms 41–100.* WBC 20. Dallas: Word, 1990.
———. "Yahweh Reigns as King (Pss. 96:1—99:9)." In *Psalms 51–100,* 504–31. WBC 20. Dallas: Word, 1990.
Terrien, Samuel L. *The Elusive Presence: Toward a New Biblical Theology.* San Francisco: Harper & Row, 1978.
———. "The Yahweh Speeches and Job's Responses." *RevExp* 68 (1971) 497–509.
Thomas, D. Winton. "The Sixth Century B.C.: A Creative Epoch in the History of Israel." *JSS* 6 (1961) 33–46.
Tombs, L. E. "Ideas of War." In *IDB* 4:797–98.
Tuell, Steven Shawn. "The Nature of Persian Involvement in the Religious Institutions of Subject Peoples." In *The Law of the Temple in Ezekiel 40–48,* HSM 49, 78–102. Atlanta: Scholars Press, 1992.
Van Seters, John van. "The Problem of Childlessness in Near Eastern Law and the Patriarchs of Israel." *JBL* 87 (1968) 401–8.
Vaux, Roland de. *Ancient Israel: Its Life and Institutions.* Translated by John McHugh. New York: McGraw-Hill, 1961.
———. "Decrees of Cyrus and Darius on the Rebuilding of the Temple." In *Bible and the Ancient Near East,* translated by Damian McHugh, 63–96. Garden City, NY: Doubleday, 1971. Originally published in *RB* 46 (1937) 29–57.
———. *Die Patriarchenerzählungen und die Geschichte.* SBS 2. Stuttgart: Katholisches Bibelwerk,1964.
———. "Les patriarches hébreux et les déconvertes modernes." *RB* 53 1946) 321–48; 55 (1948) 321–47; 56 (1949) 5–36.
———. "Le sens de l'expression 'peuple du pays' dans l'Ancien Testament et le rôle politique du people en Israël." *RA* 58 (1964) 167–72.
Veijola, Timo. *Die ewige Dynastie: David und die Entstehung seiner Dynastie nach der deuteronomistischen Darstellung.* Helsinki: Suomalainen Tiedeakatemia, 1975.

———. *Das Königtum in der Beurteilung der deuteronomistischen Historiographie: Eine redaktionsgeschichtliche Untersuchung.* AASF 198. Helsinki: Suomalainen Tiedeakatemia, 1977.
Verhoef, Pieter A. *The Books of Haggai and Malachi.* NICOT. Grand Rapids: Eerdmans, 1987.
Vogt, Hubertus C. M. *Studien zur nachexilischen Gemeinde in Esra-Nehemia.* Werl: Dietrich-Coelde, 1966.
Vriezen, Th. C. *De Godsdienst van Israël.* Arnhem: De Haan, 1963.
Wallis, Gerhard. *Geschichte und Überlieferung: Gedanken über alttestamentliche Darstellungen der Frühgeschichte Israels und der Anfänge seines Königtums.* Stuttgart: Calwer, 1968.
———. "Jüdische Bürger in Bäbylonien während der Achämeniden-Zeit." *Persica* 9 (1980) 129–88.
Wambacq, B. N. *L'epethète divine Jahvé Sebaôt: Étude philologique, historique et éxégétique.* Paris: Desclée, de Brouwer, 1947.
Watts, John D. W. *Basic Patterns in Old Testament Religion.* 2nd ed. South Pasadena: Jameson, 1978.
———. "Deuteronomic Theology." *RevExp* 74 (1977) 321–36.
———. "Deuteronomy." In *The Broadman Bible Commentary,* vol. 2. Nashville: Broadman, 1970.
———. *Isaiah 1–33.* Rev. ed. WBC 24. Nashville: Nelson, 2005.
———. *Isaiah 34–66.* Rev. ed. WBC 25 Nashville: Nelson, 2005.
———. *Obadiah: A Critical Exegetical Commentary.* Grand Rapids: Eerdmans, 1969. Reprint, Winona Lake, IN: Alpha, 1981.
———. *Vision and Prophecy in Amos.* Expanded anniversary edition. Macon, GA: Mercer University Press, 1997.
———. "Yahweh Malak Psalms." *TZ* 21 (1965) 341–48. Reprinted in *Basic Patterns in Old Testament Religion,* 2nd ed., 150–58. South Pasadena: Jameson, 1978.
Weeks, Noel. *Admonition and Curse: The Ancient Near Eastern Treaty/Covenant Form as a Problem in Inter-cultural Relationships.* JSOTSup 407. London: T. & T. Clark, 2004.
Weinberg, Joel P. "Der 'am ha-ares des 6.-4. Jh. v.u.Z." *Klio* 56 (1974) 325–35.
———. "Demographische Notizen zur Geschichte der nachexilischen Gemeinde in Juda." *Klio* 54 (1972) 45–59.
Weinfeld, Moshe. *Deuteronomy and the Deuteronomic School.* Oxford: Clarendon Press, 1972.
Weippert, Helga. "Das deuteronomistische Geschichtswerk: Sein Ziel und Ende in der neueren Forschung." *TRu* 50 (1985) 213–49.
Weiser, Artur. "Die Darstellung der Theophanie in den Psalmen und im Festkult." In *Festschrift, Alfred Bertholet,* edited by Walter Baumgartner, 513–31. Tübingen: Mohr, 1950.
———. *Glaube und Geschichte im Alten Testament.* BWANT 4.4. Stuttgart: Kohlhammer, 1931.
———. *The Psalms: A Commentary.* Translated by Herbert Hartwell. Philadelphia: Westminster, 1962.
Weitzman, Steven. "Why Did the Qumran Community Write in Hebrew?" *JAOS* 119 (1999) 35–45.

Wellhausen, Julius. *Prolegomena to the History of Israel*. Translated by J. Sutherland Black and Allan Menzies. 1885. Reprint, Atlanta: Scholars Press, 1994.

Westerholm, Stephen. "The Significance of the Temple." In *ISBE* 4:767-68.

———. "Temple." In *ISBE* 4:759-76.

Westermann, Claus. *Die Geschichtsbücher des Alten Testaments: Gab es ein deuteronomistisches Geschichtswerk?* Gütersloh: Kaiser, 1994.

———. *Das Loben Gottes in den Psalmen*. 4th ed. Göttingen: Vandenhoeck & Ruprecht, 1968.

Whitley, Charles Francis. *The Exilic Age*. Philadelphia: Westminster, 1957.

Whybray, R. N. *The Intellectual Tradition in the Old Testament*. BZAW 135. Berlin: De Gruyter, 1974.

———. Review of *Das Königtum in der Beurteilung*, by Timo Veijola. *JTS* 31 (1980) 121-23.

———. "The Social World of the Wisdom Writers." In *The World of Ancient Israel*, edited by R. E. Clements, 247-50. Cambridge: Cambridge University Press, 1989.

———. *The Succession Narrative: A Study of II Samuel 9-20; I Kings 1 and 2*. SBT 9, 2nd ser. Naperville, IL: Allenson, 1968.

Widengren, Geo. *Sakrales Königtum im Alten Testament und im Judentum: Franz Delitzsch-Vorlesungen 1952*. Stuttgart: Kohlhammer, 1955.

Wiesehoufer, Josef. *Der Aufstand Gaumātas und die Anfänge Dareios' I*. Bonn: Habelt, 1978.

Wildberger, Hans. *Jahwes Eigentumsvolk: Eine Studie zur Traditionsgeschichte und Theologie des Erwählungsgedankens*. ATANT 37 Zürich: Zwingli, 1960.

Williamson, Hugh G. M. "The Accession of Solomon in the Books of Chronicles." *VT* 26 (1976) 351-61.

———. "The Concept of Israel in Transition." In *The World of Ancient Israel*, edited by R. E. Clements, 141-62. Cambridge: Cambridge University Press, 1989.

———. *Ezra, Nehemiah*. WBC 16. Waco, TX: Word, 1985.

———. "Nehemiah's Wall Revisited." *PEQ* 116 (1984) 81-88.

Wolf, C. Umhau. "Semite." In *IDB* 4:269.

———. "Traces of Primitive Democracy in Ancient Israel." *JNES* 6 (1947) 98-108.

Wolff, Hans Walter. *Hosea: A Commentary on the Book of the Prophet Hosea*. Translated by Gary Stansell. Edited by Paul D. Hanson. Hermeneia. Philadelphia: Fortress, 1974.

———. *Joel and Amos: A Commentary on the Books of the Prophets Joel and Amos*. Translated by Waldemar Janzen et al. Edited by S. Dean McBride Jr. Hermeneia. Philadelphia: Fortress, 1977.

———."Das Kerygma des deuteronomistische Geschichtswerks." *ZAW* 73 (1961) 171-86. Reprinted in *Gesammelte Studien zum Alten Testament*, 2nd ed., TB 22, 308-24. Munich: Kaiser, 1973.

———. "The Kerygma of the Deuteronomic Historical Work." In *The Vitality of Old Testament Traditions*, by Walter Brueggemann and Hans Walter Wolff, 83-100. Atlanta: John Knox, 1975. Translated from "Das Kerygma des deuteronomistische Geschichtswerks." *ZAW* 73 (1961) 171-86.

———. *Micah: A Commentary*. Translated by Gary Stansell. Minneapolis: Augsburg, 1990.

———. *Obadiah and Jonah: A Commentary*. Minneapolis: Augsburg, 1986.

Wright, George Ernest. *Biblical Archaeology*. Philadelphia: Westminster, 1957.

———. "The Book of Deuteronomy." In *IB* 2:315–16.
———. *God Who Acts: Biblical Theology as Recital*. London: SCM Press, 1952.
———. "The Present State of Biblical Archaeology." In *The Study of the Bible Today and Tomorrow*, edited by Harold R. Willoughby. Chicago: University of Chicago Press, 1947.
———. "The Samaritans at Shechem." *HTR* 55 (1962) 357–66.
Würthwein, Ernst. *Der 'amm ha'arez im Alten Testament*. BWANT 4. Stuttgart: Kohlhammer, 1936.
Yamauchi, Edwin M. *Persia and the Bible*. Grand Rapids: Baker, 1990.
Yee, Gale A. *Composition and Tradition in the Book of Hosea: A Redaction-Critical Investigation*. SBLDS 102. Atlanta: Scholars Press, 1987.
Zadok, Ran. *The Jews in Babylonia during the Chaldean and Achaemenian Periods according to the Babylonian Sources*. Haifa: University of Haifa, 1979.

www.ingramcontent.com/pod-product-compliance
Lightning Source LLC
Chambersburg PA
CBHW052058230426
43662CB00036B/1350